GCSE

Information Communication Technology

Complete Revision and Practice

Contents

Section One — What is a Computer?

Section Two — The Parts of a Computer System

Section Three — Using a Computer System

Section Four — Systems Analysis

Section Five — Text and Image Processing Software

Section Six — Spreadsheets and Databases

Contents

Section Seven — Measurement, Control and Simulation

Section Eight — The Internet

Section Nine — Computers in the Real World

Section Ten — Computers and Society

INject Printers

Dot per inch (dpi)

Published by Coordination Group Publications Ltd

Editors:
Simon Little, Chrissy Williams.

Contributors:
Martin Chester, Charley Darbishire, Rachel Goodwin, Colin Harber-Stuart, Simon Little, Iain Nash, Andy Park, Glenn Rogers, Ian Sanderson, Emma Singleton, Claire Thompson, Richard Vickery, Sharon Watson, Helen Woodgate.

With thanks to Kimberley Turner for the proofreading.

Please note that AQA questions from pre-2003 papers are from legacy syllabuses and not from the current specification.
CGP has carefully selected the questions contained in the paper to cover subject areas which are still relevant to the current specification. As such the exam provides a good test of your knowledge of the syllabus areas you need to understand to get a good grade in the real thing.

ISBN 1 84146 376 0
Website: www.cgpbooks.co.uk
Printed by Elanders Hindson, Newcastle upon Tyne.
Clipart source: CorelDRAW and VECTOR

Data and Computer Systems

This section will run through the basics for you. A computer is simply a machine that processes data. Make sure you know what data is and what a computer does with it.

Data has No Meaning

Data is information that has no meaning.

If someone walks up to you and gives you a piece of paper with 120987 written on it, the number could mean absolutely anything. It could be their birthday, or how much money you owe them. Data only becomes information when you know the context of the data.

Information = Data + Meaning

1) **Computers are machines that process data. They're stupid — they don't understand the data they process.**

2) **If you get a computer to process data that's incorrect, the results will be meaningless.**

   E.g. If you program a computer to work out the total cost of buying fifty pizzas at £2.99 each, but you type in £29.9 by mistake, you'll get the wrong answer.

   This is called Garbage In, Garbage Out (GIGO).

3) **Some people call this 'computer error'. They're wrong — it's human error. Computers hardly ever make mistakes. They just do what they're programmed to do.**

Data is stored in Bytes

Computers run on electricity — try using a computer without it. They consist of a number of electric circuits, and each circuit can be in one of only two states — on or off.

1) **Computers use a binary code (i.e. they use only 2 digits) to represent data. A circuit that's switched on represents the digit 1, and a circuit that's switched off represents the digit 0.**

   (Morse code works in a similar way — it's either a dot or a dash.)

2) **Each character from the keyboard is given an 8-bit (i.e. 1 byte) ASCII code (pronounced ASSKEY). For example the letter D is represented by 01000100 and the number 6 by 00110110.**

Bit	Each individual 1 or 0 is called a bit — short for binary digit.
Byte	8 bits is called a byte.
Kilobyte	1 kilobyte (1 Kb, or simply 1 K) is about a thousand bytes. To be exact, 1 Kb = 2^{10} = 1024 bytes.
Megabyte	1 megabyte (1 Mb) is about a million bytes. To be exact, 1 Mb = 2^{20} = 1 048 576 bytes.
Gigabyte	1 gigabyte (1 Gb) is about a thousand million bytes. To be exact, 1 Gb = 2^{30} = 1 073 741 824 bytes.

A standard floppy disk can hold 1.44 megabytes of data.

Make sure you have these basics sorted before moving on

It's quite important to understand that data and information are two different things. Make sure you've understood what data actually is, and that it always needs some sort of context in order to make sense. Remember — Information = Data + Meaning.

Data and Computer Systems

It's vital to know about the 3 parts of a computer system. A computer system is an integrated system of hardware and software that enables data to be input, then processed and the results communicated to the user.

"Hardware" is just the physical parts of a computer system, e.g. mouse, hard disk.

"Software" is a general term for any programs that a computer runs.

(A) **Data** is entered at the **Input** Stage

1) Information is converted into data before it's entered into the computer.
2) This might mean having to convert information into a code.

   E.g. the date 26th September 1964 might be converted into 260964.
3) In Microsoft's Excel program this date is given the code 23646.

   This is because it's 23646 days from January 1st, 1900.
4) The data that's been entered should be validated (checked) to make sure it's the right type.

   E.g. a percentage should be between 0 and 100.
5) The data should also be verified — checked that it was entered correctly.
   E.g. if the examination mark was 67% then 67 should have been entered.

(B) The Computer then **Processes** the Data

See page 18 for more stuff about CPUs.

1) Processing involves turning the input data into something else.
2) For example, a set of examination results could be put into a computer which then calculates the average score.

Processing is carried out using the computer's Central Processing Unit (CPU).

(C) The Results are then **Shown** at the **Output** stage

1) Output is when the computer communicates the results of the data processing to the user.
2) The two most common ways are a screen display and printed paper.
3) At this point the data becomes information again.
4) The information obtained at the output stage might then be used as feedback to input more data. This turns the system into a cycle.

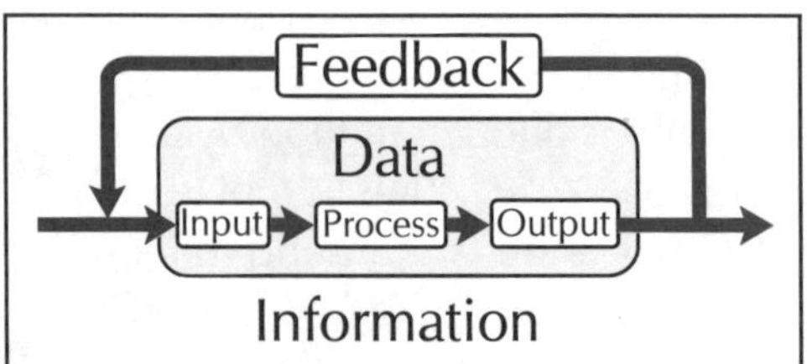

Remember "Input, Process, Output" and you won't go wrong

Study the diagram, memorise it, then write it out and explain what happens at each stage. That way, when you read the rest of the book, you can try to work out which stage of the cycle is being explained. This diagram is really what ICT is all about, so make sure you know it.

Data and Computer Systems

Using a Computer System has lots of **Benefits**

The government stores information about all the cars registered in the UK on a large computer database. It could also store the same information in a manual paper-based system. There are six main advantages to using a computerised system.

BENEFITS of a computerised system	PROBLEMS of a paper-based system
1) It takes up a lot less space — there's no need for grey filing cabinets.	1) It takes up a lot of space — that means lots of grey filing cabinets.
2) Searching for records is very quick.	2) Searching for records can take a long time.
3) More than one person at a time can access the same data from their network PC.	3) Only one person can access the data at a time.
4) The data stays within the computer's memory — it won't get lost or misfiled.	4) The data might get misfiled or even lost.
5) Fewer staff are needed to look after the computer system.	5) Need to employ clerical staff to look after the filing system.
6) Reports can be generated very quickly — often by an automated processing routine.	6) Reports can be written — but only after looking at each relevant record and transferring information by hand. Time-consuming and chances of human error.

Using a Computer System also has lots of **Problems**

There are four main problems with using a Computerised System:

1) Setting up a computer system is very expensive. Big systems in large organisations such as the NHS can cost millions of pounds.
2) Computer systems need people to maintain and use them. Training costs can be high — and the money is wasted if the person leaves.
3) Computer systems are not perfect — if there's a system failure or a power cut, then important data might get corrupted or lost.
4) It can be easy to copy files and so remove confidential information from the system. The system needs to be kept secure from unauthorised users and hackers.

Most people think that the benefits outweigh the problems — just about every organisation today uses computers.

Computer Systems have problems as well as benefits

This page should be quite easy to learn — there isn't any complicated technical jargon on it, just a few simple lists to memorise. The information here will definitely be in the exam in one form or another, so you'd better be sure to learn it all.

Data and Computer Systems

There are three main types of computer. You need to know what the differences between them are.

Mainframes are the **Biggest**

1) Mainframes are powerful — they can perform hundreds of millions of instructions per second (MIPS).
2) They're very large, and generate a lot of heat — so they need big air-conditioned rooms.
3) They're very expensive — typically costing around £3-4 million.
4) They're used to run large computer systems and networks in banks, insurance companies and e-commerce firms on the Internet.

Minicomputers are in the **Middle**

1) Minicomputers are less powerful than mainframes but more powerful than microcomputers.
2) As a result they cost less than mainframes — but still require a special operating environment.
3) They are typically used to run medium-sized systems in small businesses.

The term "mini-computer" isn't used much any more — a "mini" these days is basically a large server.

Microcomputers are the **Most Common**

Since you're studying ICT you probably use a microcomputer quite a bit. They're often found in the home now too, and are usually called personal computers, or PCs.

1) Microcomputers were designed to stand alone, but are now often linked together in a network.
2) They are far less powerful than mainframes but can cope better with the demands made by individual users. They typically cost around £1000.
3) PCs can be either desktops or laptops (also called notebooks).
4) Desktops often have more facilities than laptops. Laptops have the advantage that they can be used anywhere because they can run on battery power. But laptops use an LCD monitor and this can easily be damaged, especially when exposed to strong sunlight. They're also more expensive, and can be lost.

Computers are Everywhere

1) Personal Digital Assistants (PDAs) such as electronic organisers can be used instead of a diary. They can also contain some standard software, such as spreadsheets and word processors.
2) Mobile phones are increasingly being used as simple computers — for example to send and receive text messages and connect to the Internet.
3) Small microprocessors are also embedded in many consumer products such as cars, microwave ovens, video recorders and DVD players. We don't notice them because they input, process and output data all inside the equipment.

Main, Mini and Micro — learn them all

Everything on this page might seem a little obvious, but make sure you've got it all learnt, as you'll need to know it all. It's a good idea to make a table with these headings: "Type of Computer," "Uses" and "Problems". Then study the page, cover it up and fill in the table.

Quick Questions

This section's not too hard. You just need to make sure you've got all the basics down before you start tackling the rest of it. You probably won't get asked any long questions about these things, but you MUST know what all the different terms mean. Have a go at these questions, and keep doing them until you don't have to look up the answers any more.

Quick Questions

1) What is the difference between data and information?
2) What do the initials "GIGO" stand for?
3) What is "bit" short for?
4) How many bits are there in a byte?
5) How many bytes are there in a kilobyte?
6) How many bytes are there in a megabyte?
7) How many bytes are there in a gigabyte?
8) How many megabytes of data does a standard floppy disk hold?
9) What are the 3 basic stages of a computer system?
10) What do the initials "CPU" stand for?
11) Name 3 benefits of using a computerised system.
12) Name 2 problems with using a paper-based system.
13) Name 4 problems with using a computerised system.
14) What do the initials "MIPS" stand for?
15) What do the initials "PDA" stand for?
16) Which of these is the most powerful: mainframe, minicomputer or microcomputer?
17) Which of these is the most common: mainframe, minicomputer or microcomputer?

Make sure you can sail through all these technical terms

Once you've got all of this information stored away, it'll make the rest of the course much easier. Make sure you go over it enough so that all these terms and abbreviations are rolling off your tongue. This is probably the most boring bit, but it's well worth learning properly.

Networks

A network is two or more computers connected together. Computers on a network can communicate with each other. The Internet is also a type of network — but that's covered later on in the book (Section 8). A computer needs a network interface card to connect to a network.

LANs are small, local Networks

LANs (Local Area Networks) are the networks that you see in most offices and schools. They usually need the following hardware in order to operate:

1) **A Network File Server is a dedicated computer that runs the software needed by the network and stores the files that users have created.**
2) **Terminals are individual workstations that give access to the network. Using a terminal gives access to the network's software and files.**
3) **If a group of terminals share use of a printer then the system needs a Print Server. If two or more documents are sent to the printer at the same time the print server will put them into a queue. Users can then carry on with other work whilst waiting for the document to be printed.**
4) **For the network to operate, data needs to be sent to and from all parts of the network. This can be done using wire cables or fibre optic cables, or via radio signals.**

WANs are long range Networks

WAN is short for Wide Area Network. They are used when the computers that need to be connected together are in different places, sometimes different countries.

1) **Like LANs, WANs need servers to operate the network, but users connect up to the network using modems, usually connected to the telephone system. Wireless technology such as microwaves or satellites can also be used — but this is very expensive.**
2) **WANs are used by companies who have employees working away from the firm's main sites. A good example would be oil exploration engineers who work in remote parts of the world. They're also used by firms who have a lot of teleworkers.**

*There are **Advantages** and **Disadvantages** to Using Networks*

Advantages

1) Peripherals such as printers can be shared amongst many different users.
2) Some networks use terminals which are cheaper than stand-along PCs.
3) Software can be shared amongst different users.
4) Communication across the network is cheap and fast.

Disadvantages

1) Cabling can be expensive to install and replace.
2) A fault with the server will prevent the whole network from working.
3) Security measures are needed to restrict access to the network.
4) WANs are vulnerable to hackers and viruses.

Networks aren't all good

LAN and WAN are two different ways to connect computers together. Make sure you know the differences between them, as well as what equipment they need — it's all important.

Networks

Network configurations can seem pretty complicated, but if you give it a bit of thought, the pros and cons of each type should seem fairly obvious.

Star Networks Give Access to a *Central Computer*

1) Star networks are used when a large number of workstations need to be connected to a central computer such as a mainframe.
2) Each workstation is connected directly to the central computer.

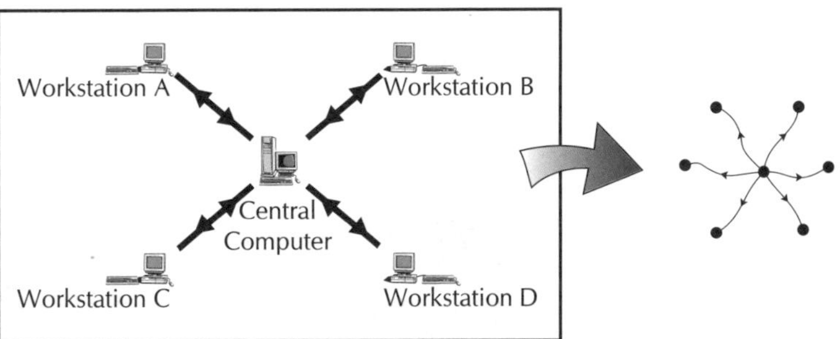

PROS

1) The direct connections mean it's quick.
2) Performance in one part of the network is unaffected by events elsewhere.
3) If a cable fails, it's likely to only affect one workstation.

CONS

1) Failure in the central computer causes the whole network to break down.
2) It uses more cabling, so it is more expensive.

Line Networks are the *Cheapest*

1) In line networks (bus networks) data is sent to and from the file server along a line of cable.
2) All terminals are connected to this central line.

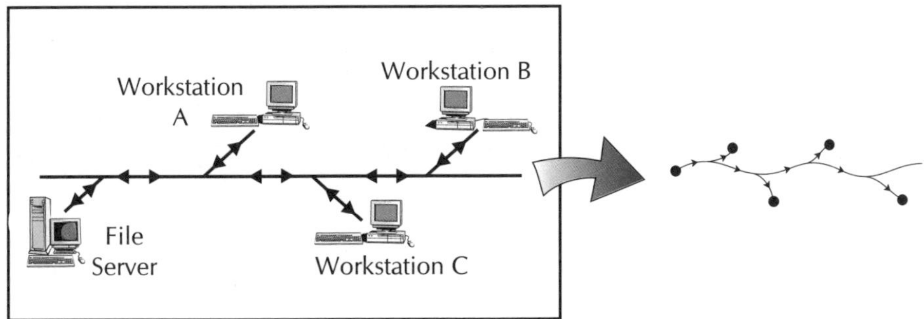

PROS

1) It is cheap because it uses less cabling.

CONS

1) With lots of users the system becomes very slow, as all data goes along a central line.
2) Failure of the central cable will bring the whole network down.

Learn all the pros and cons of different types of networks

This page isn't as bad as it looks. You need to know these common network topologies, and what their advantages and disadvantages are. There's another one on the next page too.

Networks

Ring Networks are Faster than Line Networks

1) Ring networks are a bit like line networks, except that all the equipment is linked in a ring.
2) Data flows around the network in one direction only.

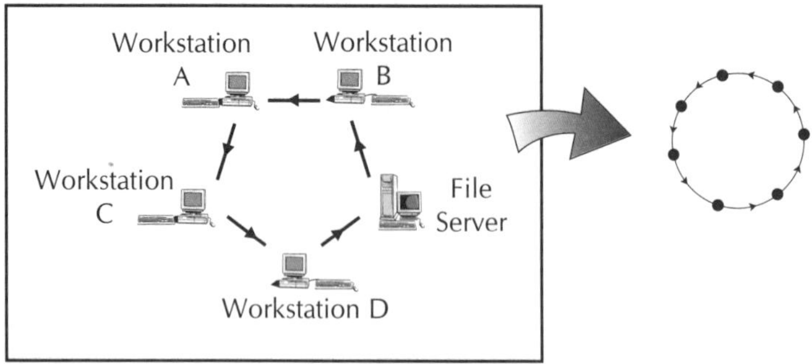

PROS

1) Cheap to expand.
2) Fast — as data flows in one direction only.

CONS

1) With lots of users the system becomes slower, as all the data is sent along a single line.
2) Failure of central cable brings the whole network down.

There are three main types of network security: physical, access and data security.

Physical Security Protects the Hardware

Hardware is expensive — follow these 7 SAD FLAB rules to keep it safe.

1) **Serial numbers** — Keep a record of all serial numbers, and mark the organisation's name and postcode on all equipment — this helps police to identify stolen property.
2) **Alarms** — Computer rooms should be protected by burglar alarms.
3) **Doors** should be locked when the rooms are not in use.
4) **Fire protection** — Use fireproof doors and smoke alarms. Also, automatic gas-flooding systems could be used to put out any fire to prevent water damaging the equipment.
5) **Lock** windows to prevent access.
6) **Avoid** putting computers on the ground floor of buildings, where they can be easily seen from outside.
7) **Blinds** or curtains should be closed at night, and monitors should be switched off, so the computers are less visible.

PROTECT HARDWARE WITH THE 7 SAD FLAB RULES

There's no point in having decent hardware if you don't protect it

Everyone needs to know this information. Especially all the bits about physical security. It may all seem like common sense, but it'll definitely come up in the exam. You need to remember all this information, so that you can show off to the examiner and give as full an answer as possible.

Networks

Access Security Limits a Person's Use of the Network

1) All authorised users should be given user names and create their own passwords. This will limit unauthorised access to the network.
2) Users should change their password frequently.
3) Individual users can be assigned access rights — for example, network managers can be given access to the software that controls how the network is run. Other users can be limited to certain types of applications software such as word processors.

Data Security Prevents Loss of Data

1) Some software and files can be password-protected so that a password is needed to view and amend data.
2) Files can be made read-only, so that they cannot be altered or deleted. Other files may be hidden so that they are not visible to the user.
3) Regular back-ups should be made of the data on the system using suitable backing storage. The main method used to back-up network data is the ancestral method.

Ancestral Method for File Back-up

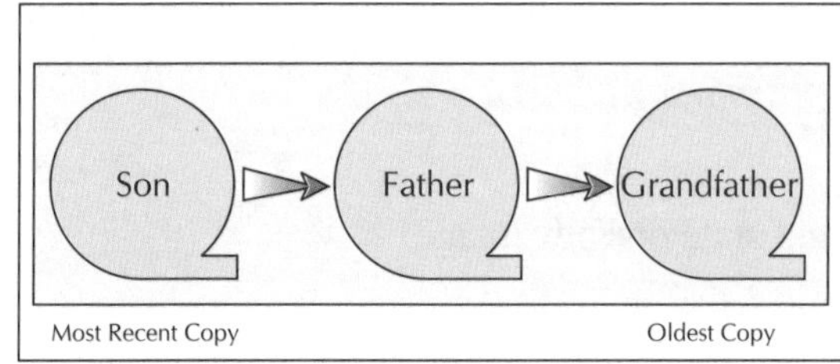

1. The son is the most recent copy of the file. When the next back-up is made, this becomes the father.
2. When the next back-up is made, the father becomes the grandfather. The grandfather file is deleted when a new son is created.
3. If the original file is lost or damaged, there are three back-up files available.

4) Back-up files should be kept secure — ideally in locked fireproof rooms in a different location to the network.
5) Archiving means copying or moving a file somewhere for long-term storage.

Making copies of everything is irritating but essential

We've all learnt this the hard way at one point or another. You really need to back-up all your work. Passwords are vital too — particularly if you break up with someone who still has access to your Inbox. You've been warned...

Warm-Up and Worked Exam Questions

Networks always come up in the exams. Examiners will want to know that you understand the basics of what each different type of network is and what their various advantages and disadvantages are. Have a go at these warm-up questions:

Warm-up Questions

1) Draw a ring network.
2) What is a LAN?
3) What is a WAN?
4) Give 3 physical security measures that can be used to protect hardware.
5) What is a back-up file?
6) What does read-only mean?

Worked Exam Questions

Look at the worked exam questions below. Examiners want you to show that you know what you're talking about. You don't need to write loads — just enough to make your points.

1 Describe the difference between a WAN and a LAN.

A LAN (Local Area Network) is a computer network located on one site, connected by cables. A WAN (Wide Area Network) is a computer network that is spread across a wide geographical area using telecommunications.

You'll get a mark each for a brief description of a WAN and LAN. (You won't get the marks for just saying what WAN and LAN stand for.)

(2 marks)

2 Draw a diagram of a bus/line network and state one advantage and one disadvantage of it.

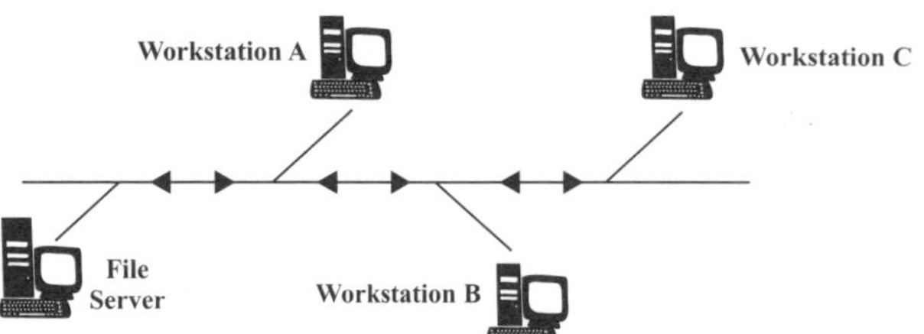

There are 2 marks up for grabs here: 1 mark for drawing the main cable with workstations connected separately, 1 mark for drawing and labelling the file server connected to the main cable.

Advantage: A bus or line network is cheaper as it uses less cabling than a ring or star network. Disadvantage: Can be slow when there are lots of users on the network

...or failure of main cable will bring whole network down.

(4 marks)

Exam Questions

Now have a go at these practice exam questions to make sure you've got the hang of everything.

1 Westforth School wishes to connect their computers using a LAN.
The LAN will be a star network.

(a) Draw a diagram showing the layout of a star network and state one advantage and one disadvantage of it.

If one workstation is down it does not affect the other computer. If server goes down whole system goes down.

(4 marks)

(b) State four things the school could do to protect the hardware from being stolen.

passwords, Locks,

(4 marks)

2 An advertising company has 6 stand-alone computers. The manager decides that the computers should be connected as a LAN. State two advantages of using a LAN.

using lan he can share hardware and software. They can use network leicense which are far more cheap than standalone computers

(2 marks)

3 Townley NHS Trust uses a computer network in all its hospitals to store details on patients. All staff using the system have to enter a username and password.
The data on the system is backed up every night.

(a) Explain the terms username and password.

Username and password is used to make the system secure.

(2 marks)

(b) What is meant by the term backup, and where should backed up files be stored?

The term backup mean creating a copy of original files and it should be placed some where same.

(2 marks)

Revision Summary for Section One

Well that's the first section almost over and done with. Before you move onto section two, here's a final test to check that you've learnt everything. These short questions cover pretty much everything from the section, so they'll help you find out which bits you've forgotten. You need to be able to do them without looking up the answers, so keep going through them until you're word perfect.

1) Explain the difference between data and information.
2) In what way are computers stupid?
3) What do the letters GIGO stand for?
4) How many bits are there in a byte?
5) What are the three stages in the processing of data called?
6) Explain four ways that a computerised information system is better than a paper-based system.
7) Explain two problems with using computerised systems.
8) What are the differences between a mainframe and a PC?
9) What are the differences between a laptop and a desktop computer?
10) Explain two advantages and two disadvantages of using a laptop.
11) What is a PDA?
12) What do the letters LAN and WAN stand for?
13) How could a LAN become part of a WAN?
14) What hardware does a WAN need that a LAN doesn't need?
15) Explain two advantages and two disadvantages of connecting computers in a network.
16) Sketch diagrams of a star network, a ring network and a line network.
17) Which network uses the most cable?
18) Which network should be used if you want as few network failures as possible?
19) Which two networks are the slowest?
20) Explain three measures that can be taken to reduce the risk of damage to hardware.
21) Who should have the right to know your password?
22) What does 'read-only' mean?
23) Draw a diagram to show how the ancestral method of file back-up works.
24) After how many back-ups will a back-up file be destroyed (using the ancestral method)?
25) Where should back-up files be stored?
    a) A secure place in a different building
    b) In a cardboard box under the network manager's desk

Input Devices

An input device is any hardware which is used to enter data into the computer system.

QWERTY *Keyboards are the* **Most Common Input Device**

1) **QWERTY keyboards are the most common type of keyboards. The name comes from the first row of letters on the keyboard.**
2) **Each key is connected to a switch which closes when the key is pressed. This sends a signal to the CPU based on the character's ASCII code.**
3) **QWERTY keyboards are based on the way typewriters were designed.**
4) **A problem is that keying in can be slow unless the user has been trained or knows how to type.**

Concept Keyboards *are Faster but* **More Limited**

1) Concept keyboards are typically found in shops and restaurants. Each switch has a symbol (or word) on it, representing a piece of data (e.g. the price) stored in the computer.
2) For example, if you go to a fast-food restaurant and order a burger, the assistant will press the picture of that burger. The CPU then tells a display panel to show the correct price and sends a message to the kitchen and stock-control.

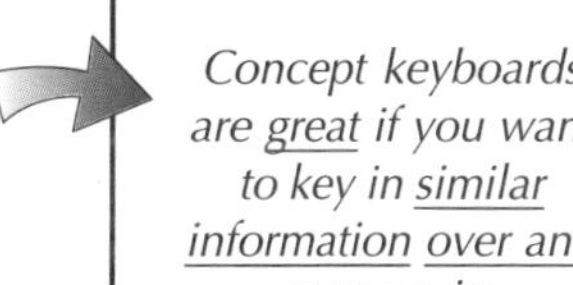

Concept keyboards are great if you want to key in similar information over and over again.

Mice *and the like...*

Most people find using a mouse easy. A mouse has two main parts:

1) There are usually two or three buttons. When the cursor is over an icon, menu item, or the edge of a picture, the mouse buttons can be clicked or double-clicked. This gives the computer a command. The button can also be held down to drag something across the screen.
2) Under the mouse is a ball. The ball rotates when the mouse is moved across a flat surface. Sensors measure the movement of the ball in two directions. From this, the computer can work out the direction and distance the mouse has travelled. This is used to move the cursor on the screen.

   (N.B. optical mice use optical sensors to detect movement instead of balls).

All Input devices are useful for different reasons

All of this section will be fairly straightforward. It's not hard to learn everything you need to know about input devices. Make sure you know the difference between the two types of keyboard. You might need to write about each of their benefits and problems in the exam.

Input Devices

Laptops have Tracker Balls or Touch-sensitive pads

Laptops have tracker balls, or little pimples, or touchy-feely pads:

1) A tracker ball works in the same way as a mouse, but the ball's moved by hand, so it takes up less space. Most people find using them a bit fiddly, and not that accurate or quick.
2) Touch-sensitive pads look like small screens. You move your finger across the pad to move the cursor. They use less space than a mouse, but they're easily damaged and not very reliable.
3) Little pimples work by putting a finger on them, and pushing in a direction, which moves the cursor. They're really really small, not very accurate, and a bit weird.

Graphics Pads make Drawing Easier and More Accurate

1) Graphics tablets are like a pen and paper. They're made of a touch-sensitive membrane (like the piece of paper) and a rigid stylus (like the pen).
2) The user presses on the surface with the stylus, and the membrane registers its position, and displays it on the screen.

A Joystick can Input Movement

1) These are mainly used to play computer games — but they can also be used to move a computer-controlled device such as a robot or a hospital body scanner.
2) The joystick is fixed to a base but can be moved in any direction. Sensors convert the movement into coordinates, which tell the computer how to move the screen display or robot device.

Scanners Convert Images into Digital Data

1) **A scanner works a bit like a fax machine. A picture is passed through the scanner and is converted into digital data — light and dark parts of the picture are given different codes. The computer then builds up a 'map' of the information based on these individual 'bits' of data.**
2) **A problem is that these bitmap files can be very large and so take up a lot of memory. A benefit is that the scanned image can be manipulated and edited easily and quickly.**
3) **Small scanners are often hand-held. Larger flat-bed scanners fit onto a worktop.**

Don't scan this page — read it slowly

You're bound to have used some of these input devices before. That's good, as it should help you remember all the important things about them. Just stick to the basic facts and you should be able to handle any exam questions that ask you about them.

Input Devices

OCR Scanners can Read Text

1) OCR stands for Optical Character Recognition. OCR software takes the scanned digital information and looks for familiar patterns that might make up letters or numbers.
2) Each recognised letter or number is given an ASCII code (see page 1 for more about ASCII). This means that the scanned text can be edited using word-processing software.
3) This makes it quick and easy to enter large blocks of text. But the software is not perfect, so the result needs to be proofread. Also, most OCR software cannot cope with text in columns.

Don't forget MICR for Cheques and OMR for Registers

MICR — Magnetic Ink Character Recognition	OMR — Optical Mark Recognition
MICR is used by banks to process the payment of cheques. At the bottom of cheques are numbers printed with ink containing iron. When the ink is magnetised a scanner can read the numbers and so know which account to take the money from. This is very fast and almost 100% accurate. But the system is very expensive.	OMR is used in some schools to take the daily class register. The teacher fills in different boxes with a pencil if a pupil is present or absent. A scanner detects the carbon in the boxes on the page and inputs the data into the computer system. The system is quick and accurate — but only if the OMR sheet is filled in properly.

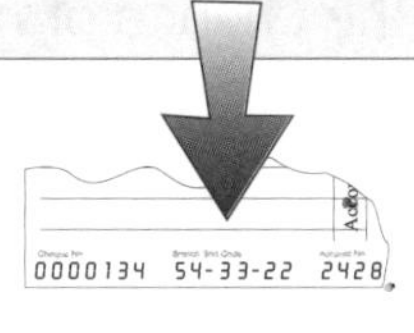

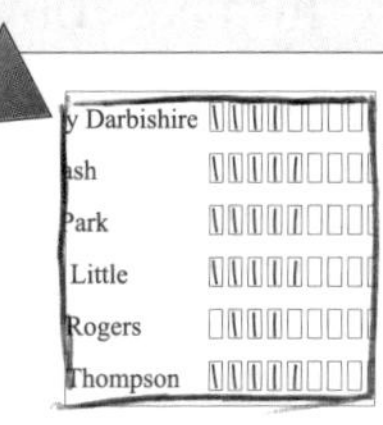

Credit Cards have a Magnetic Stripe on the Back

1) Magnetic stripe cards are made by sealing a short length of magnetic tape into the surface of a plastic card.
2) They carry information so the computer can identify the customer (credit/debit cards) or the number of units available (phone cards).

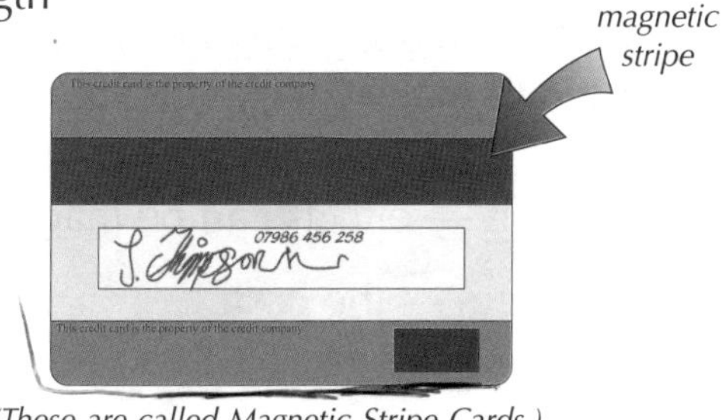

(These are called Magnetic Stripe Cards.)

Be sure to learn what MICR and OMR are

Have a think about these input devices too: 1) Infra-red remote controls (TVs, stereos, etc.) send data to a receiver by infra-red waves. 2) MIDI instruments convert notes played on a MIDI-compatible instrument into data which a computer converts back into notes.

Input Devices

These are the last two pages on input devices. You've got to read them and make sure you know everything they say.

Here are **Seven More** Input Devices

1 **DIGITAL CAMERAS are a bit like scanners. They save an image as a series of dots called pixels. The image can then be uploaded to a computer and edited using photo-editing software.**

Benefits — photographic film is not needed and the image is available for immediate use. It can also be sent via an e-mail attachment to anywhere in the world.

Problem — high-resolution images use lots of memory and currently use a lot of battery power.

2 **LIGHT PENS or LASER SCANNERS are used in supermarkets and libraries. They are used to read a bar code which contains data about the product being scanned.**

Benefits — it makes buying goods faster and reduces the chance of human error.

Problems — the system is expensive and depends upon the data in the bar code and the computer system being accurate.

3 **VIDEO DIGITISERS convert analogue video pictures from a videotape or video camera into digital images which can then be manipulated using imaging software. This is called image grabbing. The technique is used to make special effects in music videos and cinema movies.**

Benefit — effects can be made that are impossible in real life.

Problem — the cost.

Now you can get digital cameras on your mobile phone

Technology is advancing at such a ridiculous speed, that it sometimes feels as though everything will be possible one day. Make sure you remember what new advances you've heard about or seen on the television. Examiners will love some really recent examples.

Input Devices

4 **TOUCH-SENSITIVE SCREENS are a bit like concept keyboards — but instead of pressing a key, you touch the picture or word on the screen. Most use a grid of infra-red beams over the screen to sense where your finger is.** ***(Some use a see-through membrane instead of infra-red beams.)*** **They're used a lot in information centres and quiz machines in pubs.**

Benefits — easy to use and you can have different options each time the screen display changes.

Problems — more expensive than a keyboard, and inaccurate if you've got large or thick fingers.

5 **MICROPHONES are becoming increasingly used as an input device. They are used to input data into voice-recognition systems, which convert sound into text or commands for the computer. They are also used to record sound so it can be stored digitally and sent over the Internet and by e-mail.**

Benefit — you can use dictation instead of having to type.

Problem — the data uses a lot of memory.

6 **SENSORS are hardware that record environmental information and convert it to data. Examples include temperature sensors, light sensors and infra-red sensors used in burglar alarm systems. (Sensors will be covered in Section 7.)**

7 **TOUCH-TONE TELEPHONES have a different tone for each button on the keypad. This sound is transmitted over the phone line and can be used to input commands into the system at the other end of the line. They are used by cinemas to run on-line box offices, by banks to do direct banking, and by a whole load of other businesses in their telephone helplines.**

Learn all the benefits and problems for each input device

That's a lot of input devices to remember. Make sure you know all their details. You could try making a table with headings for device, how it works, benefits and problems. Then fill it in as best you can, and keep trying until you get it absolutely perfect.

The CPU

The Central Processing Unit is the brain of a computer system, where all the input data is processed. You need to know the three main parts of the CPU — and what happens in each one.

The *Control Unit* makes the *System Work*

The Control Unit (CU) coordinates the work of the whole computer system. It has three main jobs:

1) It controls the hardware attached to the system. The CU monitors the hardware to make sure that the commands given to it by the current program are activated.
2) It controls the input and output of data, so all the signals go to the right place at the right time.
3) It controls the flow of data within the CPU.

The *ALU* is where *Data Processing* Happens

ALU stands for Arithmetic and Logic Unit. It's where the computer processes data by either manipulating it or acting upon it. It has two parts:

1) Arithmetic part — does exactly what it sounds like: it does calculations. E.g. a greengrocer's till working out that if 1 kg of turnips costs 30p then 2 kg costs 60p.
2) Logic part — makes decisions, like whether a number is bigger than –5. E.g. the greengrocer's computer will switch the freezer's cooling unit on if the temperature of frozen turnips recorded by a temperature sensor rises above –5 °C.

The *IAS* is where *Active Data* is *Stored*

1) The Immediate Access Store (IAS) holds any data and programs needed by the computer when they're being used. The CPU reads data and programs kept on the backing storage and stores them temporarily in the IAS's memory.
2) It normally takes longer to read from the backing storage than from the IAS. So the IAS makes the access time much shorter.
3) Backing storage and memory are covered on pages 28-31.

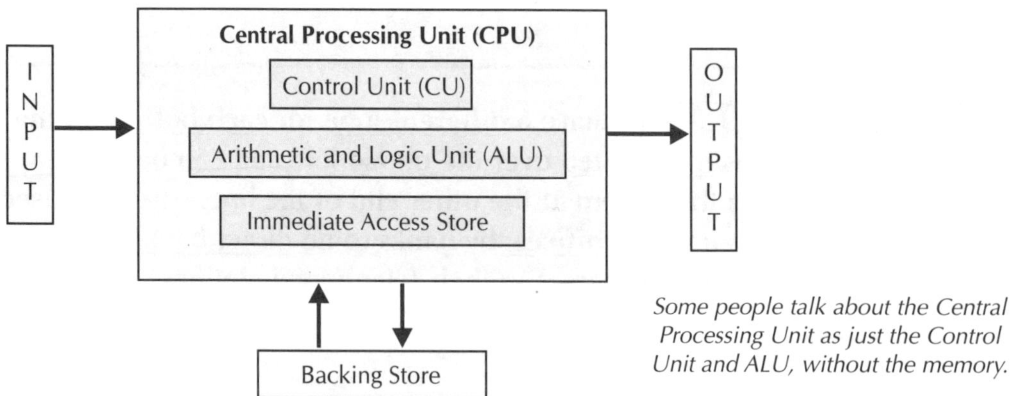

Some people talk about the Central Processing Unit as just the Control Unit and ALU, without the memory.

CPU, CU, ALU and IAS — make sure you know what they all mean

The CPU is pretty technical stuff. Memorise the diagram, and then try drawing it out till you can do it perfectly. Then explain what happens in each part of the CPU. You need to know this.

Warm-Up and Worked Exam Questions

It's time to take a break and find out how much you know. As before, we start with some easy questions to check you've been reading with your eyes open.

Warm-up Questions

1) Where do QWERTY keyboards get their name from?
2) What do the initials "OCR" stand for?
3) What do the initials "OMR" stand for?
4) Name a device that can be used to input sound into a computer system.
5) Name an input device you would use to create a digital image from a picture in a magazine.
6) What does a video digitiser do?

Worked Exam Question

Now time for some practice exam questions. The first one has been kindly done for you. But that doesn't mean you don't have to read it. You should try to answer it yourself and then compare it to how we did it. That's the way you'll learn the most.

1 Fleesam Bank is a large High Street bank. It uses Magnetic Ink Character Recognition (MICR) to transfer information on cheques onto its computer system.

(a) Give two differences between Magnetic Ink Character Recognition (MICR) and Optical Character Recognition (OCR).

i) MICR senses the magnetic ink that is used to print account details at the bottom of the cheque, OCR recognises characters by their shape;

ii) MICR can only read characters that have been printed using magnetic ink, OCR can detect any characters, including hand-written ones.

Another one would be... MICR technology is <u>more expensive</u> than OCR.

(2 marks)

(b) Give two benefits to the bank of using MICR.

i) MICR is much faster than a human transferring the information manually;

ii) MICR results in fewer errors being made.

(2 marks)

...also, fewer human operators are needed, so the bank will save money on wages.

A lot of ICT is about learning advantages and disadvantages like this. They're easy marks to pick up in the exam, so don't throw any away by not learning it.

Exam Questions

1 Chippy's Pizza Shack is a fast food restaurant in Blackpool. Staff use a concept keyboard to enter customer orders onto the computer system.

(a) Describe how a concept keyboard works.

Concept keyboard has icon and picture on them which is when press it do the job. It consist of overlays.

(2 marks)

(b) State one benefit to the restaurant of using a concept keyboard.

faster data input.

(1 mark)

2 Pam Trubshaw is an office assistant at the Harebrayn School, Doncaster. Pat has been asked to take a photograph of the school using a digital camera. The photograph will be used as part of a school newsletter stored on the school's computer system.

Give one benefit and one drawback of using a digital camera to take the photograph.

Digital camera store the image in digital form which mean we do not need to convert it in digital form. However it take lot of space.

(2 marks)

3 John Brown uses a laptop computer when he is working away from his office. John has the choice of using either a mouse or a tracker ball to input data onto the laptop.

(a) State one drawback of using a mouse with a laptop computer.

To work on mouse it need space which can be probrem for laptop

(1 mark)

(b) Describe how a tracker ball works.

tracker ball is some like mouse but has a ball on the top which can be moved by finger.

(2 marks)

(c) Describe the benefits and drawbacks of using a tracker ball as an input device.

take less space. also has no wire. but it can be fiddly and need to learn how it works

(4 marks)

Output Devices

An output device is any hardware used to communicate the result of data processing carried out by the CPU. Make sure you know how each one works and when it is useful.

Dot-Matrix Printers are Cheap but Not Very Cheerful

They are also called impact printers and are the cheapest type of printer — both to buy and to operate. They have two main parts.

1) The **printhead** is a matrix of pins — either 9 or 24 pins, arranged in a vertical line or a block. Each character is formed by using a set pattern of some of the pins.
2) The **ribbon** is a long strip of material with ink on one side. The printhead pins push the ribbon onto the printer paper to print a series of dots. At normal reading distance these dots appear to form characters.

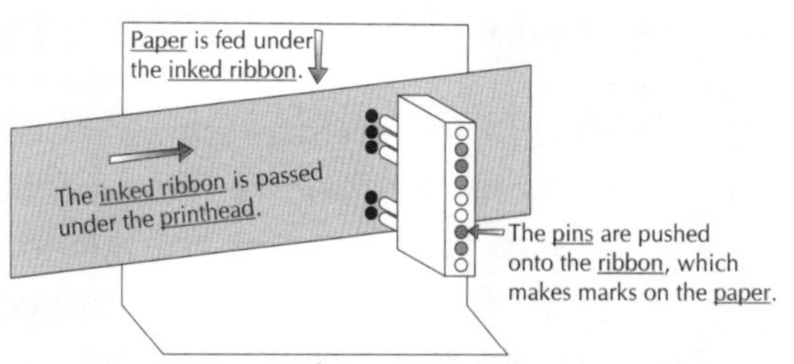

ADVANTAGES	DISADVANTAGES
Cheap to buy and have low operating costs.	Low resolution — print quality is too poor to produce presentation documents.
Can print on continuous stationery or multi-part stationery (e.g. copies of invoices).	Very slow — can be less than 100 characters per minute (cpm).
	Very noisy — can't be used near a phone.

Laser Printers are Great but Expensive

Laser printers are called page printers because the data to be printed is sent to the printer in complete pages — one page at a time. They work in a very similar way to photocopiers. They have four main parts:

1) Electrostatic rotating drum — has a negative electrical charge.
2) Laser — etches onto the drum a mirror-image of the page to be printed. Where the laser hits the drum the negative electrical charge is removed.
3) Toner cartridge — contains ink. When the drum passes over the toner cartridge, the ink is attracted onto the negatively charged areas of the drum. The ink is then transferred onto the printer paper.
4) Fuser unit — heats the paper to fuse the ink onto it.

ADVANTAGES	DISADVANTAGES
Very high resolution — typically 600 dots per inch (dpi) or more. This means they can print high-quality documents.	Expensive to buy — though they're getting cheaper.
Very fast — over 10 pages per minute (ppm).	Lots of complex equipment inside — so expensive to repair.
Laser printers are very quiet.	Can't use continuous or multi-part stationery.

Laser printers — they're brilliant, but they cost a fortune

Printers are used to produce a permanent hard copy of the information on paper. You need to learn the advantages and disadvantages of the main types of printer. One on the next page too.

Output Devices

Knowing about the different types of printers is really important — that's why they get two pages.

Ink-Jet Printers are a Good Compromise

1) These cost less than laser printers and produce better quality printouts than dot-matrix printers. So they're the best compromise between cost and quality for most users.

2) The main component is the printhead. This has lots of tiny nozzles or spouts through which small jets of ink are sprayed onto the paper.

3) There are three different ways of controlling the flow of ink:
   - In some printers the nozzles are controlled by crystals inside the printhead, which change shape when an electrical current is passed through them.
   - In others, the ink is heated so that it expands and pushes through the nozzles onto the paper. Bubble-jet printers work like this.
   - Continuous flow printers squirt ink continuously from the nozzles, then the unused ink is electrically charged and diverted back by charged plates.

4) There are loads more nozzles on an ink-jet than dots on a dot-matrix — so the print resolution is better.

ADVANTAGES OF INK-JET PRINTERS	DISADVANTAGES OF INK-JET PRINTERS
Good resolution — usually 300 to 600 dots per inch (dpi). This means they can print good quality documents (and often in colour). Cheap to buy — the cheapest are well under £100. Small — so ideal for home or office desk use.	Slow(ish) — colour printing often less than 4 ppm. Expensive to run — the cartridges cost more (per page) than laser printer cartridges.

Choose your Printer Wisely

Because of the differences between the printers, they're all suited to different situations.

Use a DOT-MATRIX if you want to print lots of copies of the same text but aren't worried about noise, quality or speed.

Use an INK-JET if you want good quality affordable printing — but not a lot of it.

Use a LASER if you want to print loads of pages of professional quality documents quickly.

Ink-Jets are probably the best for home use

Examiners love to ask you questions about knowing what type of printer is most suitable for a particular use. Learning all about printers will get you easy marks in the exam.

Output Devices

Buffering *and* ***Spooling*** *help make* ***Printing Easier***

Computers process data faster than printers can print it.
There are two ways to prevent hold-ups.

1) A buffer is memory that stores the pages that have not yet been printed. It is found inside the printer. This means the user can do other things while waiting for the printed document.
2) Spooling is when the document to be printed is saved onto the hard disk before being held in a print-queue. This frees up the CPU to continue processing data. Again, this means the user can get on with other tasks without waiting for the printer.

Here are the rest of the main output devices.
You need to know how each one works and when it should be used.

VDUs *give a* ***Visual Display***

Also called a monitor, a Visual Display Unit (VDU) is the most commonly used output device. They're used when visual information is needed but a permanent record isn't. There are two ways that monitors differ from each other — size and resolution.

1) Size — measured in inches across the diagonal. A typical PC monitor has a size of around 17 inches. Laptops have a screen of about 12 inches.

2) Resolution — measured by the number of pixels or dots that make up the image viewed on the screen. The main sizes are high (1024×768 pixels), medium (800×600) and low (640×480). The resolution on most laptops is medium.

Graphics designers and desktop publishers who want to see a whole design or page in great detail should use a large, high-resolution monitor.

The two main types of monitor are:

1) LCDs (used in laptops, and for some desktop PCs — see page 4).
2) Cathode Ray Tubes (CRTs) on PCs. CRTs are the same as the ones in TVs. They can be damaging to the eyes if used for long periods so users need to take precautions (see pages 145-146 on health and safety).

Buffering is in the printer — spooling is on the hard disk

Now you'll never have to be confused by printer error messages again. Well, hopefully not, anyway. Don't get confused between buffering and spooling — remember which is which.

Output Devices

Graph Plotters are Specialised Printers

1) Page (laser) printers are good for most things but they're often not accurate enough for precision drawings such as architects' plans — and they can't print on big enough bits of paper, so graph plotters are used instead.
2) The most common graph plotter is a flat-bed plotter. The paper lies on a flat surface and a plotter arm moves over it from left to right. On the plotter arm is a pen holder which moves up and down. In this way the pen can draw accurate images in any direction.
3) As colour page (laser) printers get cheaper and better, there will be less demand for small graph plotters.

Sound can be Real or Synthesised

1) Since sound can be recorded digitally and stored as data, it can also be processed and output through a speaker. This is how most digital sampling on modern music happens.
2) It is also possible to convert characters in the form of ASCII code into sound through a voice synthesizer — this is called speech synthesis. It is used by people who are visually impaired. It is also used to give out telephone numbers on directory enquiries and confirm customer details on automated telephone payment systems.

The problem with voice synthesizers at the moment is that they don't sound very human. This is because each word is usually pronounced in the same way regardless of the context of the sentence. But, they are slowly getting better...

Large Amounts of Output can be Stored on Microfilm

1) The name of this system is Computer Output on Microfilm — COM. Some people argue this isn't an output device at all — just a different way of storing printed pages.
2) Microfilm is a way of condensing hundreds of pages of information onto a standard roll of 35 mm film. The film is viewed through a microfilm reader — a bit like a personal film projector.
3) This system reduces the storage space required. And film lasts a lot longer than paper.
4) But the system is expensive — and losing a roll of microfilm will lose a lot of valuable information.

Speech synthesizers help people in the community

I know you've heard this before, but you can guarantee that you will be asked about these things somewhere in the exam. Examiners love it when you can cite examples of how technology helps real people in the community. So get learning now.

Output Devices

Signals can Switch On Alarms and Other Equipment

1) All output devices are activated by signals which come originally from the CPU. These signals can be used to switch devices outside the computer on or off.

2) A good example is a burglar alarm system — these can use different output devices, including lights, bells or recording equipment. Or an alarm signal can be sent to the local police station via the telephone network.

3) Most systems will need to have a control interface connecting the computer to the output device. This is because devices often work using a different electrical voltage or processing speed.

Actuators Control Physical Movement

A control interface can also be used to operate actuators — output devices that are able to move and perform simple mechanical tasks. There are three main types of actuator — what makes them different is their source of power.

1. MOTORS are powered by electrical signals from the computer.

   a) Stepper-motors are ones where the signal moves the motor in a series of tiny but accurate steps. Flat-bed scanners are usually powered by stepper-motors.

   b) Servo-motors are ones where the signal enables the motor to move continuously at high speed. These are used to power computer-operated drills.

2. HYDRAULIC ACTUATORS are powered by fluid pressure controlled by the computer. This makes them slow but very powerful, so they're useful for heavy lifting.

3. PNEUMATIC ACTUATORS are like hydraulic ones but are powered by air pressure instead. They're less powerful than hydraulic systems but more responsive, so they're often used to power robots on fast-moving automated production lines.

Learn what the three types of actuator are

Motors, fluid pressure and air pressure — you need to know the technical names for each one. You also need to know what kinds of things they're used for. Examiners love testing you on all sorts of random output devices, so make sure you learn everything on this page.

Warm-Up and Worked Exam Questions

My, my, what a lot of information about printers. Did you learn it all? Let's see...

Warm-up Questions

1) Which of the following printers is usually the most expensive — dot matrix, laser, ink-jet?
2) Which printer will print pictures to a higher quality — a 600 dpi or 1200 dpi?
3) What do the initials VDU stand for?
4) What are the two main types of monitor? How do they differ?
5) What do the initials COM stand for?
6) What is the name given to output devices that can perform simple mechanical tasks?

Time for the fun bit. Don't skip the worked examples below — they're there to help you.

Worked Exam Questions

1 Sally Marshall designs greeting cards on her computer.
She prints the completed designs using her colour ink-jet printer.

(a) Name one other suitable printer that Sally could use.

Colour laser printer

(1 mark)

(b) Give two benefits and two drawbacks of using an ink-jet printer to print the designs.

Benefits: i) Ink-jet printers are cheaper to buy than laser printers; ii) Ink-jet printers can be very small.

Drawbacks: i) Ink-jet printers are more expensive to operate than laser printers (expensive ink cartridges); ii) Ink-jet printers can be slower than laser printers.

(4 marks)

2 (a) Explain what COM is.

COM standards for computer output on microfilm — it is a method of condensing hundreds of pages of information onto standard 35mm films. The film is viewed using a microfilm reader.

(2 marks)

(b) Suggest two drawbacks of using COM.

The equipment is expensive; if a roll of film is lost or damaged, a lot of valuable information would be lost.

(2 marks)

COM used to be a popular storage medium for important information in the olden days... these days, it's not really needed so much...

Exam Questions

1 Joan Grubbins wishes to buy a new printer so she can print her GCSE coursework.
She sees the following advertisement in a newspaper:
"For sale: 1200 dpi, 12 ppm colour laser printer."

(a) What do the initials ppm stand for?

....

(1 mark)

(b) Discuss the advantages and disadvantages of using this printer to print her coursework.

....

....

....

....

(4 marks)

2 John Jones is an architect who uses his computer to design new buildings.
John needs to print large-sized drawings of his designs on single sheets of paper.

Name the output device most suited to printing John's designs.

....

(1 mark)

3 A high street jeweller wants to install a new burglar alarm system.

(a) Name two suitable output devices that could be attached to the burglar alarm system.

....

....

(2 marks)

A control interface might need to be connected between the alarm system and the output devices.

(b) Give one reason why a control interface might be needed.

....

(1 mark)

Storage and Operating Systems

You should remember that the Immediate Access Store (IAS) is where the CPU holds the data that it's processing — it's the computer's memory.

RAM is Temporary Memory

1) RAM is short for Random-Access Memory.
2) RAM stores data as temporary electrical signals. If the electrical power is switched off (e.g. during a power cut or when a laptop battery fails) then all the data that was stored in RAM is lost.
3) That's why it's vital to save your work regularly. Helpfully, a lot of modern software will either save your work automatically every few minutes, or give you a prompt to remind you to save it yourself. The timings for these features can usually be set by the user.
4) Because it is never stored permanently, and can easily be lost, RAM is also known as volatile memory.
5) The amount of RAM a computer has will influence its processing power, speed, and how many programs it can run at the same time. For example, a computer with 256megabytes (Mb) of RAM will be able to run complex programs faster than a similar computer with only 128 Mb of RAM.
6) Lots of people confuse RAM and backing storage on the hard drive — but they're different. The computer stores programs and data that it needs quickly in RAM (if there's room), because it's much quicker to access. But information in RAM needs to be saved on the hard drive before you switch the computer off, otherwise it'll be lost.

ROM is Permanent Memory

1) ROM is short for Read-Only Memory.
2) Data and programs essential for the CPU to start working are put onto the ROM by the manufacturer of the computer system. But no new data or programs can be written to the ROM by the user.
3) ROM is permanent memory, and contains the instructions that enable the operating system to be loaded into the IAS (i.e. the computer's memory) from the backing store (i.e. hard drives etc.). (However, sometimes the computer operating system is stored on ROM.)
4) The amount of ROM in most computers is small compared with the amount of RAM.
5) Because the data stored on ROM is permanent, and won't be lost in a power cut, it's called non-volatile memory.
6) Lots of people also confuse ROM with backing storage on the hard disk — don't be one of them. Luckily backing storage is covered on the next page, and that'll be an end to all this confusion.

RAM — force it into your head

Make sure you understand the difference between ROM and RAM — that's the hard bit. There's one other potential trap that you have to avoid — don't confuse either of these with the hard drive. And don't forget that it's important to save your computer work regularly.

Storage and Operating Systems

A backing store (also known as secondary storage) is any data-storage area outside the CPU. You need to know what the main storage areas are, how they work, and what their main uses are.

Hard Disks are the main Internal Backing Store

1) Hard disks are usually found inside computers. They're rigid circular plates that have been magnetised, and each hard drive usually contains several disks stacked on top of each other.

2) Each disk contains lots of concentric tracks, and these tracks are divided into sectors where the data is stored. Most disks can store data on both sides.

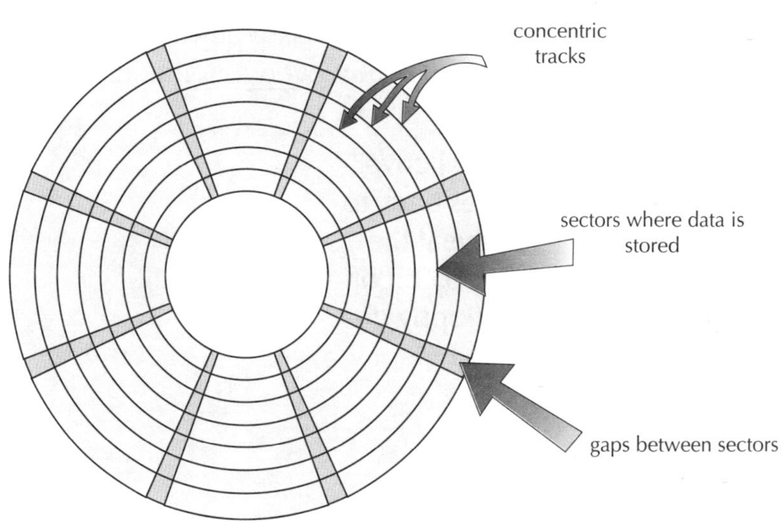

3) The disk rotates at between 5400 and 7200 revolutions per minute (rpm), with read/write heads (one on either side) floating just above the surface of the disk. They're so close that a speck of dust would ruin the hard drive — so the disk drive is kept in a sealed unit.

4) It is possible to connect an external hard drive if additional storage is needed.

5) The main benefit of hard drives is that they have a pretty large capacity — 20 gigabytes or more (1 gigabyte = 1024 megabytes) is now common in a desktop, and 8 gigabytes in a laptop.

6) One potential problem is that the hard drive is usually housed inside the computer, so it's not easy to use it on a different machine (though you can buy removable hard drives). Also, if there's a problem with the hard drive, all of the data stored on it may be lost.

Hard drives have a huge capacity compared to floppy disks

Hard and floppy disks are similar in some ways, but are used for different reasons. Hard drives are much quicker, and can hold far more data, so they're used for most things. But floppy disks can be safely stored away from the computer, and so are useful for backing up important files.

Storage and Operating Systems

Floppy disks are the most common external backing store — most people with home PCs will have used them.

Floppy Disks *are a Common* ***External*** *Backing Store*

1) The most common external backing store is a 3.5-inch floppy disk.

2) A floppy disk is a circular piece of magnetised plastic, but being floppy it can be easily damaged — this is why they have a protective hard plastic sleeve.

3) They work in a pretty similar way to hard disks. The main difference is that the read/write heads access the disk through holes in the protective sleeve.

4) They have a small tab which can be slid down to make the disk read-only. This helps to reduce the chances of data being accidentally overwritten and lost.

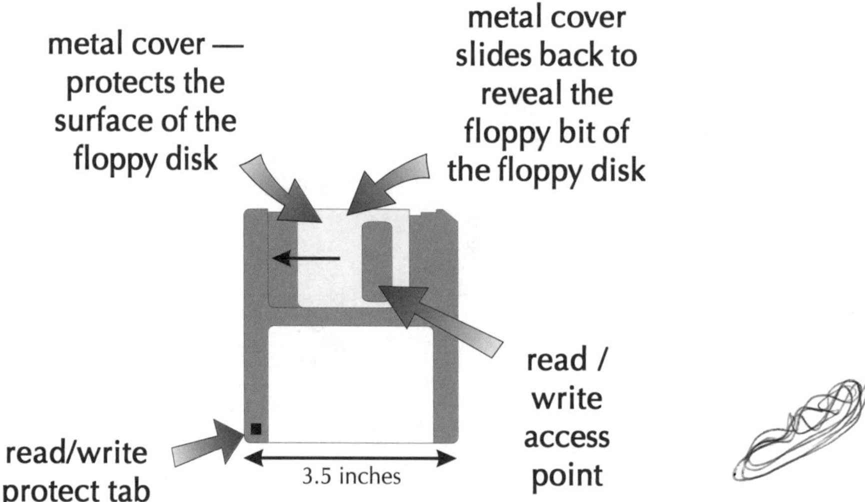

5) Since floppy disks are small and portable, data can be easily transferred between different computers.

6) Unfortunately, the amount of data a floppy disk can hold is quite small — normally only 1.44 megabytes. This can be too small for some big files like bitmap images (i.e. pictures) or movie clips. Accessing data is also very slow.

7) Another problem is that the read/write head actually makes contact with the floppy disk — this reduces the lifespan of a disk, and increases the chances of data corruption. The solution is to make back-up copies of floppy disks.

Data stores are fragile

Data stores are very delicate. They need to be protected from heat, cold, water, magnetic fields, meteor showers and general destruction. Of course, if you've used the ancestral method for backing up your work (see p9), then hopefully you should be okay.

Storage and Operating Systems

There are three more types of backing storage for you to look at.
Once again, make sure you know how each one works and what its uses are.

Magnetic Tape can Back-up Large Amounts of Data

1) Magnetic tape is often used when large amounts of data need to be backed up. The data is written to and read from the tape in the same way as in a video recorder.
2) With magnetic tape, large amounts of data can be stored relatively cheaply. This makes them ideal for backing-up a whole hard drive.
3) However, access time is slow, because the read/write head can't go directly to a particular piece of data. It has to wind through the whole tape. This is called serial or sequential access.

Optical Disks have Fast Access Times

Optical disks include CDs and DVDs. They store digital data as pits (i.e. little indentations) on the surface of a reflective disc. A laser beam is moved across the surface of the disk — and the length of the reflected beam is used to read the data.

There are four main types of optical disk.

1) **CD-ROMs** are the oldest type. They can only be used to read data (as the ROM in the name indicates), but they hold loads more data than a floppy disk — around 650 megabytes. Software is usually sold on CD-ROM.
2) **CD-Rs** are sold as blank CDs, and can have data written onto them, but only once (you need a special kind of CD drive to do it). After that they work in the same way as CD-ROMs. Both CD-ROMs and CD-Rs are known as WORM disks — "Write Once and Read Many times".
3) **CD-RWs** are becoming increasingly popular. RW stands for Read and Write. They are like a CD-R that can have old data deleted and new data written onto the disk.
4) **DVD** stands for Digital Versatile Disk (or Digital Video Disk). They are like CDs but hold much more data — up to 17 gigabytes. As a result they can store whole films digitally. DVD-RAM systems (basically DVDs that can be used to write data to) may eventually replace home video.

A big 'plus' with any kind of optical disk is that direct access to the data is possible — the laser can travel directly to where the data is stored. This means faster access times than with magnetic tape.

ZIP Disks are like Gigantic Floppy Disks

ZIP disks are larger and thicker than normal floppy disks — but work in pretty much the same way. They need their own special ZIP drive, but each disk can hold up to 100 megabytes of data — much more than a floppy disk. They are good for backing up important files.

ZIP disks may soon no longer be used

ZIP disks may become obsolete if CD-RW and writable DVD become more popular.
Make sure you know all the different types of disk and what the benefits are of each one.

Storage and Operating Systems

The Operating System (OS) is the name given to software that enables applications software and the rest of the computer system to work. A computer can't usually be used unless an OS is present. The most popular types of OS are DOS; Windows (e.g. 98, 2000, NT, XP); Mac OS; UNIX and Linux.

*All Operating Systems have **Five Main Tasks**...*

These tasks apply to all computer systems including stand-alone PCs and laptops.

1) To enable applications software to communicate with the system's hardware.

   E.g. clicking on a web address in a document will result in the modem making a connection to the Internet. (Basically, the application tells the OS what it wants, and the OS takes care of it.)

2) To enable the application (e.g. word processor) to operate. Applications are usually designed to run on a particular OS.
3) It manages system resources. For example, it allocates RAM to particular tasks — and in a network, it decides what resources to give to individual users.
4) It monitors the performance of the system, and gives prompts and error messages to the user.

   E.g. it'll tell the user that a floppy disk is full and that a new one needs to be used.

5) It operates utilities, such as print managers and virus-scanning software.

*...and a **Network OS** has **Four Extra Tasks***

An OS that runs a network (called a Multi-user OS) has some extra work to do.

1) It monitors the use of the network by different users. For example, it'll keep a log of who's used the network, for how long and what tasks they performed.
2) It helps to maintain network system security — allows different users to access different parts of the system depending on their access rights (it checks user IDs and passwords against its central register).
3) It manages access time. If people are using a central CPU (e.g. when lots of people connect to a supercomputer), each user needs to be given a share of the CPU's processing time — this is called a time slice.
4) It manages access to shared resources (e.g. printers), and can give some users a higher priority.

The OS is the software that enables applications software to work

Make sure you learn all nine tasks — but it's just as important that you know which ones only apply to networks. Memorise them and write them out until you've got them all right.

Storage and Operating Systems

Operating Systems can be **Multi-tasking**

1) Multi-tasking just means that the operating system can run more than one program at a time. Most systems now are multi-tasking.
2) In fact it's just an illusion caused by the fast processing speed of the CPU. What actually happens is that the CPU divides its time between various tasks — it performs part of a task on one application, followed by part of a task on another application. It then returns to the first application, and so on.
3) Basic systems that aren't multi-tasking are called Single Program Mode Operating Systems.

User Interfaces are how the user communicates with the OS, or other software.
You need to know the three different types, along with their pros and cons.

User Interfaces can be **Command-Driven**

1) A Command-Driven Interface presents the user with a blank screen. The user types in commands (usually abbreviated) which the Operating System then carries out.
2) Once the user has learnt all the commands, the system is quicker to operate than the other two systems, but it can take a long time to learn all the commands you're likely to need.
3) Also, different software will use different commands — so if you want to use different programs, you have to learn different sets of commands.

E.g. One common command-driven operating system is MS-DOS — the command to tell the operating system to display all files is dir.

They can also be **Menu-Driven**

1) Menu-driven systems display a list of commands or options, organised under various headings or menus. The user selects a command by pressing a key on the keyboard corresponding to that option, or by clicking on it with their mouse.
2) This type of user interface means that the user doesn't need to learn lots of commands, but they can be slow and cumbersome to use. It is not always obvious to the user what the logic behind the menu structures is.

A User Interface means HOW you communicate with the OS

There are lots of different types of these to learn. You need to make sure you can write easily about all of them as you're bound to get asked about them in your exam.

Storage and Operating Systems

But Most use a Graphical User Interface (or GUI)

1) These are the most popular type of system — all major modern operating systems use them. A GUI combines a menu-driven interface with icons to represent the main commands.
2) GUIs are also known as WIMPs because they make use of Windows, Icons, Menus and Pointers.

WINDOWS
A window contains information relevant to one particular task — and multi-tasking systems can have many windows 'open' at the same time.

ICONS
These are pictures representing commands — e.g. clicking on the picture of a floppy disk might save the active file.

MENUS
These give the user a list of options — each option corresponds to a possible command.

POINTERS
This is usually an arrow or something similar you can move about the screen using a mouse, touch pad, tracker ball etc.

There are three things to think about when designing a GUI.

1) If you want users of another program to be able to use your software, then your new program should have similar menu options and icons, and they should be positioned on the screen in a similar way, so that new users can learn how to use them without too much trouble.
2) The system should use colour and sound to help the user navigate through the system — but they should be chosen carefully. People who find sound annoying should be able to turn it off.
3) The system should use on-line help (i.e. on-screen help, either built in as part of the program, or available on the Internet) to enable the user to find out how to perform various tasks.

End of the section — better make sure you know it all

Make sure you learn the differences between the three systems, along with their benefits and drawbacks. Keep on hammering away at it until you've learnt everything.

Warm-Up and Worked Exam Questions

It's getting a bit more interesting and complicated now. The last few pages will make much more sense if you think about an actual operating system you've used, like Windows or Linux.

Warm-up Questions

1) What do the initials RAM and ROM stand for?
2) What is the name of the backing storage device found inside a typical desk top personal computer (PC) system?
3) What is the maximum data storage capacity of a 3.5 inch floppy disk?
4) What do the initials CD-RW stand for?
5) Which storage device has the greater capacity: CD or DVD?
6) What does it mean when an operating system is said to be 'multi-tasking'?

That's the easy bit over with — now, the proper hardcore "exam question" stuff...

Worked Exam Question

1 Berkleys Bank uses a command-driven operating system to control its network of computers.

(a) State five tasks performed by an operating system.

i) to enable hardware and software to communicate with each other; ii) to operate applications software; iii) to manage the resources of the computer system; iv) to operate utilities such as virus scanning software; v) to monitor the performance of the system.

(5 marks)

Operating systems have plenty to do...
On page 32, there's an extra <u>four tasks</u> that network operating systems do. You could have used those answers too — make sure you <u>learn them</u> as you could get asked specifically about the <u>network</u> tasks of an OS.

(b) Give two benefits and two drawbacks of using a command-driven operating system.

Benefits: they are quick to operate once the user knows the commands; they need less memory to operate than other operating systems.

Drawbacks: It takes time to learn all the commands — only people who've learn the commands can use it; different operating systems use different commands.

(2 marks)

Command-driven operating systems are the ones you see in lots of films from the 80s, where the computer nerd enters commands and the computer responds to them. Remember — MS DOS is an example of one if you get asked in exam...

Exam Questions

1 Marshall Wallis is planning to buy a new computer to run his computer graphics software. He finds two computers advertised with similar specifications. However, one computer has 64 megabytes of Random Access Memory (RAM), the other has 256 megabytes of RAM.

(a) Explain the purpose of RAM in a computer system.

....

....

(2 marks)

(b) Explain the likely advantages of the computer with the larger RAM capacity.

....

....

....

(2 marks)

2 Jenny Hawkins needs to store back-up copies of the files she has created on her computer system. Some of the files are very large graphics files.

Identify a suitable storage device and explain why it is suitable.

....

....

(2 marks)

3 Milham School is planning to install a new computer network. The network will be run by an operating system with a graphical user interface (GUI).

(a) Explain what is meant by the term 'graphical user interface'.

....

....

(2 marks)

(b) Discuss the benefits and drawbacks of using a graphical user interface to run the operating system.

....

....

....

....

(4 marks)

Revision Summary for Section Two

Section Two is quite important. It gives you all the information you need on what makes up a computer system. Now you've learnt it all, it's time to test yourself with some fiendishly tricky questions — so you can see how much you've really understood. This might all sound a bit scary, but then again, it's better to find out what you don't know now, rather than in the middle of your GCSE exam. That way you can do something about it. So, your basic aim is to get every question right — but don't worry too much if that doesn't happen first time. Just keep going through the questions until you know all the answers.

1) What are the first six letters on a normal keyboard?
2) How are concept keyboards different to the most common keyboards?
3) Describe how a mouse works.
4) Explain one difference between a touch-sensitive pad and a mouse.
5) What type of file is created when an image is put through a scanner? Why is it called this?
6) What do the letters OCR, MICR and OMR stand for? How are they different?
7) List five other input devices — and explain how they work.
8) Meg has been asked to perform the following tasks. For each task, list the input device that she should use:
   a) type text to create a letter,
   b) record a sound message to appear on a web site,
   c) take a photo of herself and e-mail it to a friend.
9) What are the three parts of the CPU called? What does each one do?
10) What would you use a dot-matrix printer for?
    a) printing a glossy full-colour newsletter
    b) printing three copies of a sales invoice
11) How does a laser printer work? Give two advantages and one disadvantage of laser printers compared to dot-matrix printers.
12) What is the difference between an ink-jet and a bubble-jet printer? Why are ink-jets the most popular printers for home and office use?
13) What is the difference between buffering and spooling? Why is each one useful?
14) What are two main ways that VDUs differ from each other?
15) How does speech synthesis work? What are its drawbacks?
16) What are the three different types of actuator called? How do they differ from each other?
17) What is the difference between ROM and RAM?
18) Explain four differences between hard and floppy disks.
19) What does WORM mean? Give the name of two types of WORM disks.
20) Which is quicker — serial or direct access? Why?
21) Explain four tasks performed by an operating system.
22) Which operating system was introduced in 1998?
    a) Windows 95
    b) Windows 98
    c) Grecian 2000

Data Capture

Data capture is the way that information is first gathered and put on a computer system. It's the input part of the 'input — process — output' cycle.

Data Capture *turns* ***Information*** *into* ***Data***

Data capture is sometimes called data collection. It is a two-part process.

1) The information has to be obtained. Information has to be recorded, and then converted into a form suitable for use with the computer system.
2) The data has to be entered onto the computer using an input device.

First *you have to* ***Catch*** *your* ***Rabbit...***

1) Manual methods of obtaining the data include data-capture forms and questionnaires. These are paper-based forms that need someone to write down information in a preset way. This information is then input into the computer exactly as it appears on the form.

   Questionnaires usually need a human operator to key in the results by hand. However some data-capture forms require the operator to enter information in code format — the information is then input automatically using an OMR device (Optical Mark Recognition — see page 15).

   Examples include computerised school registers and multiple-choice answer sheets.

2) Automatic data capture — means collecting information from sensors, bar-code readers and scanners.

   E.g. a temperature sensor records the temperature, and stores this data until it's downloaded onto a computer for processing.

3) Turnaround document — this is a semi-automatic system. E.g. electricity meter reading forms. The computer system prints a form showing the customer details, with a space to record the meter reading. The reading is written on by hand and the form returned to the electricity company. The new data is then added to the customer record on the computer.

Each Method *has its* ***Advantages***

AUTOMATIC DATA CAPTURE SYSTEMS	MANUAL DATA CAPTURE SYSTEMS
Faster and more accurate than manual systems. Humans don't have to be present — so it's useful in dangerous/ inaccessible places (e.g. nuclear reactors).	Sometimes necessary — information such as personal details can only be obtained using a manual data capture form. Cheaper — less hardware and software needed, so the system will be less expensive.

Data capture systems can be automatic or manual

Concentrate on learning one example for each of manual, automatic and semi-automatic data capture. Then make sure you can explain why that particular method is good.

Data Capture

Data capture forms are still the most common way of obtaining new data. You need to know why it's important that they're well designed — and how to design them well yourself.

Data Capture Forms need **Careful Design**

Badly designed data capture forms cause problems. If the person filling the form in doesn't do it properly, the rejection rate can be very high. Follow these rules for a well-designed form:

KEEP IT SIMPLE...

1) Keep the layout simple and uncluttered. Leave enough space to write answers, and don't put answer boxes too close together — or information can get put in the wrong box by mistake.
2) Instructions on how to complete the form should be written in simple language. It should be obvious to the user what to do. Examples of correctly completed boxes can help.
3) The appearance should be interesting. Using different font styles and sizes will help — so long as the form remains simple and uncluttered.

KEEP IT USEFUL...

1) Keep the amount of information requested to a minimum. There's no point requesting information already stored by the computer — or asking for information which won't be used.
2) If possible, get people to record information in a form suitable to enter onto the computer as data. **E.g. people should be asked to give their date of birth in the form dd/mm/yyyy.**

KEEP IT ACCURATE...

1) The content of the form should be checked for accuracy and completeness before it is printed.
2) Most importantly — the form should be pre-tested with a small sample of respondents to make sure it provides accurate information. If necessary the form should be amended and re-tested.

Vampires R Us — Customer Details Form

Vampires R Us PLC
The Old Caves
Bytingham
Cumbria

Please fill in this form and let us have it back.

Telephone number.........

Name and Address:
....
....
....

When would you like to get bitten?
....
....

This is a badly designed form. The layout is muddled and the instructions are very vague.

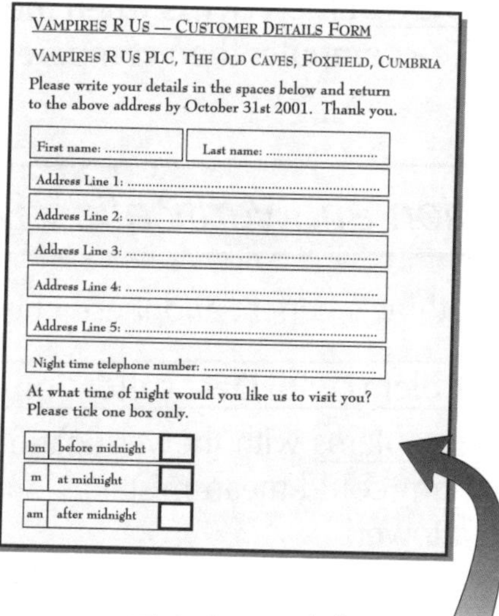

VAMPIRES R US — CUSTOMER DETAILS FORM

VAMPIRES R US PLC, THE OLD CAVES, FOXFIELD, CUMBRIA

Please write your details in the spaces below and return to the above address by October 31st 2001. Thank you.

First name: .... | Last name: ....

Address Line 1: ....

Address Line 2: ....

Address Line 3: ....

Address Line 4: ....

Address Line 5: ....

Night time telephone number: ....

At what time of night would you like us to visit you?
Please tick one box only.

bm	before midnight	☐
m	at midnight	☐
am	after midnight	☐

This is much better.

Getting forms right is an easy way to get marks in an exam

Make sure you can make a list of characteristics of a good form and know how to apply them. Try to actually draw up a form, then come back to this page and check what you missed out.

Data Capture

Here are the two main methods of making sure that the data entered is accurate...

Data Validation Checks the Data is of the Correct Type

Data validation checks that the data is of the right type. For example, a percentage should be between 0 and 100. Validation can be performed automatically by the computer whilst the data is being entered. There are four main validation techniques:

1) RANGE CHECK: This checks that the data is within a specified range.
   For example, a person's month of birth should be a number between 1 and 12.
2) PRESENCE CHECK: This makes sure that important information has actually been entered.
   For example, a customer record might have to contain their postcode, so the software won't allow the postcode field to be left empty.
3) CHECK DIGIT: This checks that numerical data has been entered accurately. The check digit of a number is determined by a formula that uses all the previous digits. So if the number's been entered incorrectly, the check digit will be wrong. A good example is the ISBN number on a book — the last digit is a check digit.
4) DATA TYPE CHECK: This checks that text hasn't been put where numbers are needed, for example. The main benefit of data validation is that it's automatic — so it's quick and easy to spot errors.

Data Verification Ensures the Data is Accurate

Data Verification is different — it means making sure the data which has been input is the same as the original data. There are two main verification techniques:

1) **PROOFREADING is when a person reads the data that has been entered onto the system and compares it with the original. Any incorrectly entered data will be edited.**
2) **DOUBLE-ENTRY is when the data is entered twice by two different people. The computer then compares the two versions. Any errors found are then corrected.**

Validation and Verification Both have their Problems

Sadly, nothing's perfect and these checks are no exception — they both have their problems.

Problems with Data Validation

1) Any problems with the verification program could mean mistakes are allowed.
2) It only makes sure that the data is the right type — not that it is accurate.

Problems with Data Verification

1) Double-entry is time consuming — and so it can be very expensive.
2) Proofreading is also time consuming — and doesn't eliminate human error.

Learn the difference between Validation and Verification

Validation, verification — two fun new ways to say 'checking'. The main thing here is to know the differences between them and the pros and cons of each method.

Warm-Up and Worked Exam Questions

For most people, data capture isn't a topic that is likely to get the pulse racing. But the fact remains — there's a lot of data floating about out there and if you want to use it, you've got to catch it first. So have a go at these questions to see if you've learnt it.

Warm-up Questions

1) Give one example of a manual data capture method.
2) State one benefit of an automatic data capture system.
3) Write down the date December 25th 2004 using the format dd/mm/yy.
4) Write down the name of the validation method that can check if a month between 1 and 12 has been entered.
5) Write down the name of the validation check that can make sure a person has entered a valid credit card number.
6) State one method of data verification.

Time for another worked exam question followed by more lovely exam questions for you to do. The worked questions are there to show you how it's supposed to be done, so make the most of them.

Worked Exam Question

1 Berkleys Bank uses data verification and data validation to help ensure that the data entered onto its computer system is accurate.

(a) Give one difference between data validation and data verification.

Data validation checks that the data that is entered is of the correct type, data verification checks that the data entered is the same as the original data.

It's really important that you understand the difference. You don't want to answer a question on data validation by talking about verification methods.

(1 mark)

(b) Identify and explain two data verification methods and two data validation methods.

Data validation methods: i) range check: checks the data is within a specified range; ii) presence check: checks that data has been entered. Data verification methods: i) proof-reading: the data is read to make sure there are no errors; ii) double-entry: the data is entered twice and compared for differences.

Make sure you also know about check digits and data type checks too — you could be asked about them.

(4 marks)

Exam Questions

1 An electricity company employs people to read customers' electricity meters in their homes. The meter reader enters information onto a card which is returned to the company's offices. The information is then entered onto the computer system.

(a) State one benefit and one drawback of this method of data capture.

....

(2 marks)

(b) Describe how an automatic data capture system might work.

....

....

(3 marks)

2 Joan Morgan is a librarian at Foxfield Central Library. Joan wants to design a form to collect personal information about new customers joining the library.

(a) Give three items of data that the form should ask customers to provide.

....

(3 marks)

(b) Advise Joan about two things she should take into account when designing the form.

....

....

....

(4 marks)

3 A teacher enters test results for her class onto a spreadsheet. The test was marked out of 60. The spreadsheet will calculate the percentage scored by each pupil.

(a) Identify two suitable data validation methods that the teacher could use.

....

(2 marks)

(b) Explain one reason why data validation will not guarantee that the correct test scores are entered onto the spreadsheet.

....

(2 marks)

(c) Explain how the teacher could use data verification to check the accuracy of the data.

....

....

(2 marks)

Using A Computer System

Learn how an OS stores information, and how it keeps track of where it's put it all...

Data is Stored in *Files* and *Directories*

1) A file (or data file) is a block of data that's been organised in some way, and is stored under one name — e.g. a picture file, or a letter written on a word processor.
2) The file may have an extension (an extra bit after the name), which tells the OS what type of file it is, and which program to use to open the file.

   E.g. in Windows all Microsoft Word files have the extension **.doc**
3) A directory is a file, but also a kind of index or database containing information about other files. A directory tells the OS where on a disk the files are, how big each file is, when it was created, and so on.

The information in the directory can be reorganised using preferences set by the user — e.g. the user could reorganise files into date order.

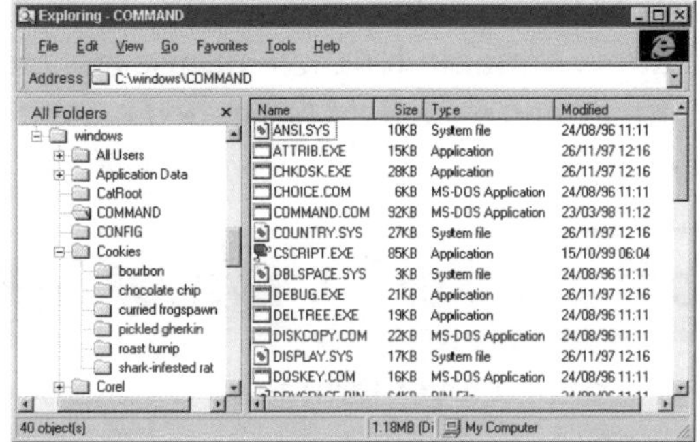

4) With some operating systems, the data in the directory is represented by a picture like this one. In this type of OS, the directories are called folders (see Section 6 for more about databases).

Data Files are Organised into *Fields and Records*

Data files (like your word-processed letter, for example) have to be organised in some way before they're stored. And they're usually organised in the form of records and fields.

1) A data file is an organised collection of data.
2) The data file can be divided into records.
3) Information in each record is organised into categories called fields.
4) So a record is one complete unit of data, and will contain an item of data in each field.

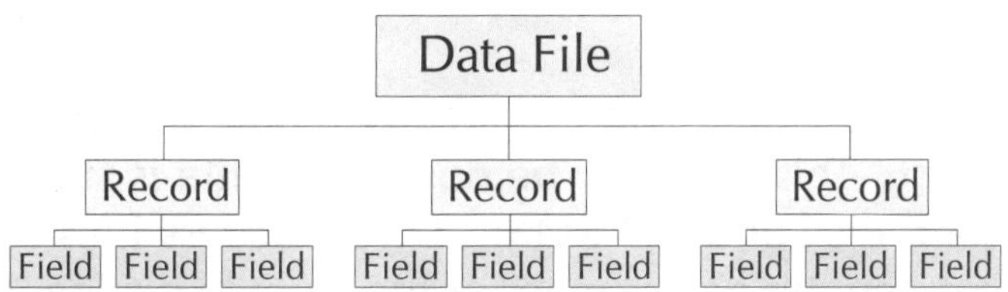

Organising your file structure properly is irritating but very helpful

The information covered on this page should be easy to learn if you've spent any time with a computer. If not, now is the time to have a play. Then you just need to remember that data is stored in data files, and that data files are stored on the hard drive as fields and records.

Using A Computer System

Fields can be **Fixed Length** or **Variable Length**

1) The length of a field is the number of characters (i.e. numbers, letters or symbols) that it contains. The longer the field, the more memory space it uses.
2) A fixed-length field has a specified number of characters.

   E.g. the field 'Surname' might be 20 characters long. The data file will then allow exactly 20 characters for each surname — whether they're needed or not.
3) The benefit of fixed-length fields is speed — the computer knows how many characters to count from the start of any record before it'll reach the field it's looking for. This takes much less processing time. But as each field uses up all its characters (whether they're needed or not) the file uses a lot of memory.
4) A variable-length field is only as long as it needs to be.

   E.g. a variable-length field containing 'Boris' will take up five characters, but one with 'Bob' just three. Variable-length fields use less memory, but the computer needs to be told when each field has ended — so it needs more processing time.

Access can be **Serial**, **Direct** or **Sequential**

Data access is just the clever term for the way the computer finds and reads the data that it needs to process.

1) **SERIAL ACCESS is when records are stored 'one after the other' in the order they were created — rather than in any kind of sensible order.**

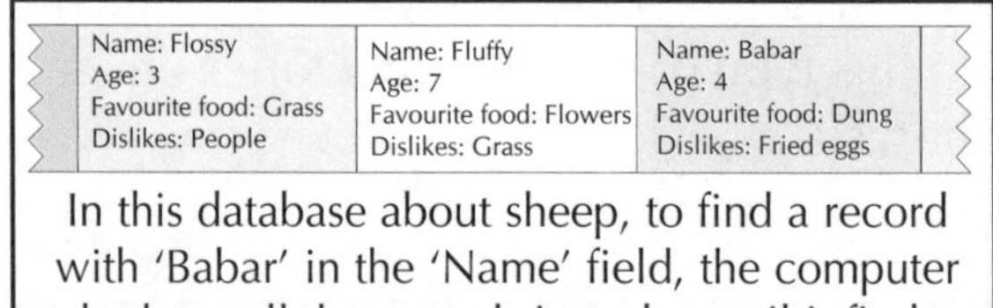

In this database about sheep, to find a record with 'Babar' in the 'Name' field, the computer looks at all the records in order until it finds the right one.

2) **SEQUENTIAL ACCESS is when records are stored one after the other (like serial access) — but they're sorted into a sensible order (and this order can be chosen by the user).**

   Serial or sequential access is used with files on magnetic tape, as tape files can only be read by being played from start to finish.

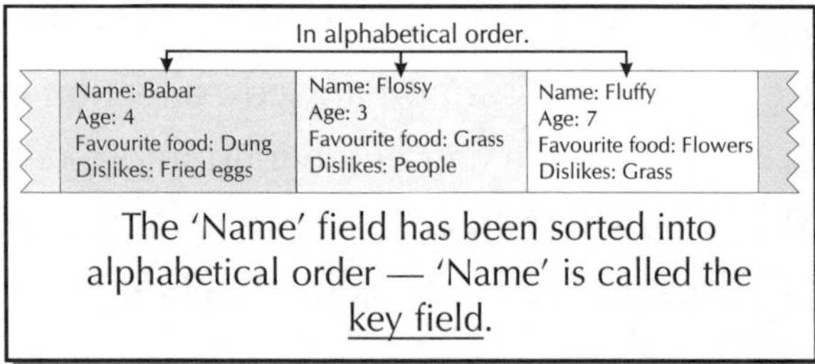

The 'Name' field has been sorted into alphabetical order — 'Name' is called the key field.

3) **DIRECT ACCESS is when the computer can go directly to any record without having to read loads of other data first. This can only be done if the file is stored on a direct storage medium, like a hard disk or a CD-ROM. Direct access files store data in a random order — but the computer has a 'map' of the storage device, so it knows where to find specific records.**

You need to learn all these different types of access

Make sure that you can write about the serial, sequential and direct access. They're quite easy to remember — think about what the actual words mean: "serial", "sequential" and "direct".

Using A Computer System

There are four main ways that computers can process data and turn it into something new. You need to know what they are and when they should be used.

Real-time Processing does it Straight Away

1) Real-time processing is when data files are updated as soon as new information is entered or becomes available.
2) When you book a seat on an aeroplane, your details are entered and the seat is booked straight away — so no other user of the system can book the same seat.
3) Real-time processing should be used whenever it's important to have information processed without delay. However, it can be expensive because of the need to have the processor constantly on-task.

Other examples include in-flight navigation systems, and systems that monitor quality on a production line.

Batch Processing — All in One Go

1) Batch processing is when lots of different jobs are stored up, and then all processed together at the same time. It's often used in large databases where the processing doesn't have to be done immediately.
2) Batch processing should be used whenever there's a large volume of data to be processed at regular intervals.

Large businesses usually work out their employees' wages at the same time every month. This is often done at night or weekends so it doesn't take up processing time during working hours.

Interactive Processing Lets You Talk to the Computer

Interactive processing is when a data file is updated by an operator one item at a time in response to prompts given by the computer.

An example is a cinema ticket booking system. The system might ask for the date and time of a performance, and in response brings up a list of available seats which can then be booked.

Transaction Processing — One-Off Specials

Transaction processing is the opposite of batch processing — individual data files are updated in response to individual requests. The processing is often done by copying data in particular records from the master file, and processing the data on its own.

An example would be if someone wished to cancel their subscription to a magazine, and the publisher processed their file to work out if the customer still owed them any money.

Remember these ways of processing

There's a lot of information here, but it's not so bad if you organise it a bit. You need to be able to list and describe the four types of processing, and give an example for each.

Using A Computer System

*Data can be Updated using **Transaction** and **Master Files***

1) Updating is just the technical word for changing the data in a file. The file will be updated if data is added, deleted or amended.

2) Updating a direct access file is simple — the new or amended data is stored anywhere on the disk, and the computer's 'map' of the disk is altered, so it still knows where to find everything.

3) Updating a sequential file can be trickier. It's like having a cassette full of music, and wanting to add an extra song between two others — you'd have to make a whole new tape. The same thing applies here, but you first need to make an extra file called the transaction file.

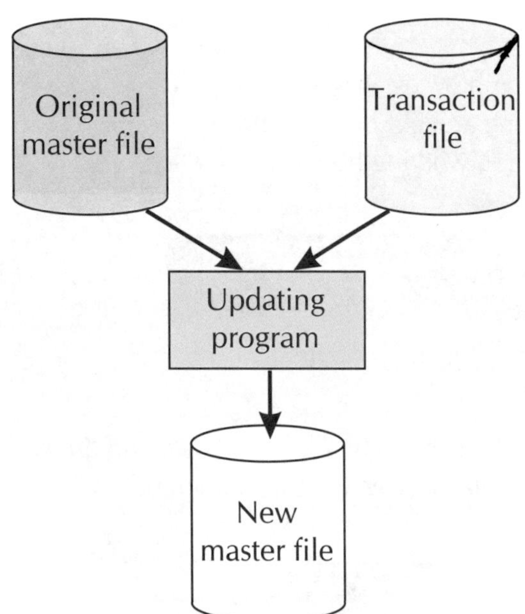

4) The original master file contains all the original data.

   The transaction file contains just the records that have changed, and these are sorted in order of the key field.

5) The old master file and the transaction file are then combined by an updating program to make a new master file. The old master file might become a file in the ancestral back-up system.

Transaction Processing is the opposite of Batch Processing

Transaction processing is relatively easy to understand. It's the fourth processing method, so you have to combine information from this page with what was on the page before. Remember, you'll need to know instantly which is which, so be sure to learn them carefully.

Using A Computer System

Computers can be used to present information in many different ways. Exactly how you do it depends on the data you want to communicate and how you want it to come across.

Information can be **Presented** in **Six** Different Ways...

1) **TEXT** is used to communicate ideas that require the precise use of words. With text, the writer and reader usually share the same meaning of the words — so the message can be passed on accurately. Unfortunately, difficult ideas often need many words to explain them.

2) **SOUND** can be used to communicate, giving the listener a sense of place or mood. The person receiving the message doesn't have to view the screen to receive the message, but they'll need a sound card and speakers (or headphones) to hear it.

3) **PICTURES** (either still or moving) can also communicate ideas and emotions better than words, and communicate directly with the reader. However, the message can be ambiguous — people can interpret pictures in different ways. A general term for all types of picture is graphics.

4) **GRAPHS** show the relationship between two or more sets of numbers using lines, dots and bars plotted between axes. Examples are line graphs and bar graphs. They can accurately summarise complex numerical information, but the reader must possess the mathematical skills needed to read the graph.

5) **CHARTS** are any image that communicates numerical or logical information. Examples include tables, pie charts and flow charts. They have the same pros and cons as graphs.

6) **MULTIMEDIA PRESENTATIONS** combine text, graphics and sound, like in a CD-ROM encyclopedia.

...Using **Two** Main **Output Methods**

1) **SCREEN DISPLAY** is the most common method. The user simply views the information on their VDU or monitor (and also hears any sounds played through a speaker).
2) **HARD COPY** is a permanent printed record of the information — usually on paper.

Each Method has **Pros** and **Cons**

1) With screen displays, information can be seen or edited immediately, and multimedia presentations using sound and moving images are possible.
2) However, some programs do not have WYSIWYG — 'What You See Is What You Get'. In other words, what you see on screen may not look the same as the final printed version.
3) Hard copies have the benefit that they give a permanent record of the information, and can be viewed without a computer. On the other hand, sounds and moving images can't be used.

Charts and graphs are not the same thing

Learn the difference between graphs and charts, and make sure you can list all of those presentation methods. It may all sound like common sense, but if you can't list them now, just think what you'll be like in the Exam. Learn all this, then answer the questions that follow.

Warm-Up and Worked Exam Questions

You must be getting used to the routine by now — the warm-up questions run over the basic facts, the worked example shows you how you should be answering the question, then it's up to you.

Warm-up Questions

1) What is the name for the description .doc or .txt after a filename?
2) What is the name of the categories of data that records of a database are divided into?
3) What type of processing involves data files being updated as soon as new information is entered?
4) What type of data access happens when items of data are accessed 'one after the other'?
5) What type of data access is used on a CD-ROM?
6) What do the initials WYSIWYG stand for?

Worked Exam Question

I'm afraid this helpful blue writing won't be there in the exam, so if I were you I'd make the most of it and make sure you fully understand it now.

1 A bank stores information about its customers in a database.
The database contains a field called surname. This field is a fixed-length field.

(a) State three other fields that the database might contain.

first name; address; telephone number.

Possibly the easiest 3 marks in an exam question ever. Well, pretty easy anyway... *(3 marks)*

(b) Explain what is meant by a 'fixed-length' field.

A fixed-length field contains a specified number of characters. If the surname field had a fixed length of 20 characters, every surname in the database have exactly 20 characters allocated.

(2 marks)

(c) State two benefits and two drawbacks of using a fixed-length field.

Benefits: i) the computer knows exactly where each record will start and end; ii) the field will take less processing time to read and extract data from.
Drawbacks: i) the database will require more memory as even empty characters need to be stored; ii) surnames longer than the fixed number of characters will be truncated.

So it's all about access speed versus memory storage space — <u>variable</u> length fields usually take up less memory, but the computer needs more time to find the files as they aren't arranged neatly.

(4 marks)

Exam Questions

1 A bank stores details of its customers on a database. Customer records are stored on magnetic tape using a serial access system.

(a) Explain what is meant by the term 'record'.

....

....

(2 marks)

(b) Explain what is meant by the term 'serial access'.

....

....

(2 marks)

2 A theatre has an on-line booking system for tickets. Customers can use the internet to book tickets. The computer system is automatically updated each time a customer buys a ticket.

(a) What type of processing does the ticket-booking system use?

....

(1 mark)

(b) Identify one benefit and one drawback of this method of data processing.

....

....

(2 marks)

3 A fashion designer uses a computer to help create new clothes. The designer uses information that is output by the computer to help him create his design.

(a) State the main output method that the designer would use whilst working on the computer.

....

(1 mark)

(b) The designer wishes to send a copy of a new design to a customer, by post. State one appropriate output method that the designer could use.

....

(1 mark)

Exam Questions

4 An electricity company sends its customers a bill every three months.
All bills are processed at the same time.

(a) What type of data processing does the billing system use?

....

(1 mark)

(b) Customer files are stored using a sequential storage system.
Explain what is meant by 'sequential access'.

....

(2 marks)

(c) Explain how the computer system will update the data stored on a sequential access system.

....

....

....

(4 marks)

5 A website designer has created a new multimedia website for Shelley High School.

(a) Explain what is meant by the term 'multimedia'.

....

(2 marks)

(b) The designer has produced a printed copy of the website to show to the Headteacher.
Describe the benefits and drawbacks of producing a printed copy of the website.

....

....

....

(4 marks)

6 A website uses sound to help communicate information to people who visit the website.
Evaluate the use of sound by websites.

....

....

....

(4 marks)

Revision Summary for Section Three

You'll probably recognise a couple of these questions — some are the same as the warm-up questions you did earlier. The most important thing here is that you know all of the answers straight away. If there are any questions that you can't answer without looking them up, you need to keep going through it until you don't need the book any more.

1) What are the two parts to data capture?
2) What's the difference between automatic and manual data capture? Give an example of each.
3) Give two advantages each of manual and automatic data capture systems.
4) What is a turnaround document?
5) How should instructions be written on a data capture form?
   a) Using complex syntax and vocabulary to communicate elementary linguistic structures.
   b) In plain English.
   c) In binary.
6) Explain four other things to remember when designing a data capture form.
7) What's the difference between data validation and data verification?
8) Explain any four methods of data validation.
9) What's a file extension?
10) Explain the difference between a field and a record.
11) Why will a fixed length field be quicker to read than a variable length field?
12) Name the four types of data processing.
13) Which processing method should be used to control the in-flight navigation system on an aeroplane?
14) True or false: Direct access files can't be stored on magnetic tape.
15) Explain the difference between a transaction file and a master file.
16) What do you have to do to sequential data in a transaction file before you use it to update the master file?
    a) Get it in the same order as the data on the master file
    b) Arrange it in random access order
    c) Keep it in the sequence the data analyst asks for
17) Why can't video clips be used on a hard copy?
18) What's the difference between a graph and a chart?
19) Why is WYSIWYG a good idea?

Systems Analysis

Systems analysis is the way that existing information systems are turned into new improved ones. Most ICT coursework gets you to become a systems analyst and solve a problem using ICT. So this section can also provide really useful information for your coursework.

The *System Life Cycle* is a *Summary* of What Needs to be Done

You probably won't need to reproduce this diagram in the exam.
It's still worth learning it though.

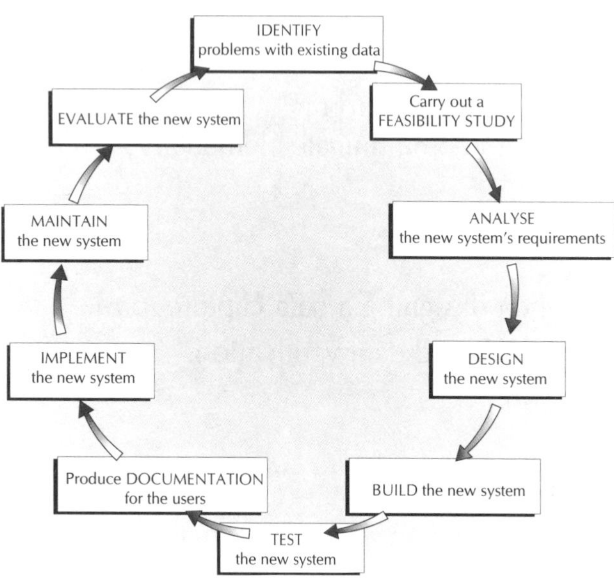

The system life cycle diagram helps you to see how all the bits in this section fit together. It also makes the important point that the systems analyst's job isn't finished when the new system has been implemented.

Identify Means Find Out What the *Problem* is

1) There are two main problems with existing systems:
Firstly, there might be problems with a manual system where introducing a computerised system would make things better. Secondly, there might be problems because the existing computer system is unable to cope with the information processing demanded of it.

2) In order to identify the problems, the systems analyst needs to interview users of the system to find out their experiences; analyse the results of questionnaires given to the users; observe people using the system; study documents such as user guides, printouts and error reports.

3) From this research the systems analyst should understand how the present system works and what the problems are.

4) This information is then used to help analyse the new system and produce the feasibility study.

Systems Analysts have to maintain the systems they create

Learn that circle diagram above. It's a very good summary of the systems analyst's job. That is what this whole section is about.

Systems Analysis

A feasibility study analyses the requirements of the new system and helps decide whether it's going to be worthwhile creating it. You need to know about the four stages of a feasibility study.

Decide on the **Objectives** for the New System

1) Objectives are specific outcomes that can be used to test whether the new system is an improvement on the existing one. They are also called performance criteria and evaluation criteria.
2) An example would be, "to reduce the time needed to process the data by 25%". This is a good objective because it can be tested by measuring and then comparing the time taken on the old and new systems.
3) There should be several objectives for a new system.

Identify the **Hardware and Software** Needed

1) In order to identify the hardware and software needed the systems analyst needs to have an idea of how they think the new system might work.
2) The hardware and software should be chosen by comparing it with alternatives.
   A good example is the decision about whether to use a laser, ink-jet or dot-matrix printer.
3) The decisions made here may be changed once the analyst moves on to the design stage of the system life cycle. But without some guesses at this stage they won't be able to estimate the likely financial cost of the new system.

Carry out a **Cost-Benefit Study**

1) Cost-benefit analysis answers the question: Will the benefits of the new system be greater than the costs? If the answer is yes then the systems analyst will recommend that the new system is implemented. If the answer is no it might be worth looking for a cheaper solution.
2) The benefits are pretty much the same as the objectives.
3) The costs will include the costs of creating the new system — but there might be others as well.

   E.g. the new system might require fewer workers — so the firm may have to pay out redundancy money. Also, new staff may need to be recruited and existing staff retrained.

Make a **Recommendation**

1) The feasibility study and the recommendation need to be presented to the people who will have to decide whether or not to proceed with the new system. These are often company directors or senior managers.
2) Sometimes the analyst will recommend a number of different solutions and let the others decide which system to adopt.

Systems Analysis is really important to learn about

This page is straightforward, but the following ones are going to get a little bit more difficult. Make sure you know what happens at every stage of a feasibility study before you go on.

Systems Analysis

Input — How the Data is Captured

1) The input data might need to be organised into fields of fixed or variable length.
2) The use of codes can reduce the file size. For example, a person's gender can be entered as M or F — reducing the number of bytes needed to store the data.
3) Screen forms should be sketched showing what the user will see whilst they input the data.

Input Checklist

- Decide where the data will come from. ☐
- Design the data capture forms. ☐
- Decide how the data needs to be structured. ☐
- Decide how the data will be input. ☐
- Design the input screen. ☐
- Decide how the data will be validated. ☐

Process — What Happens to It

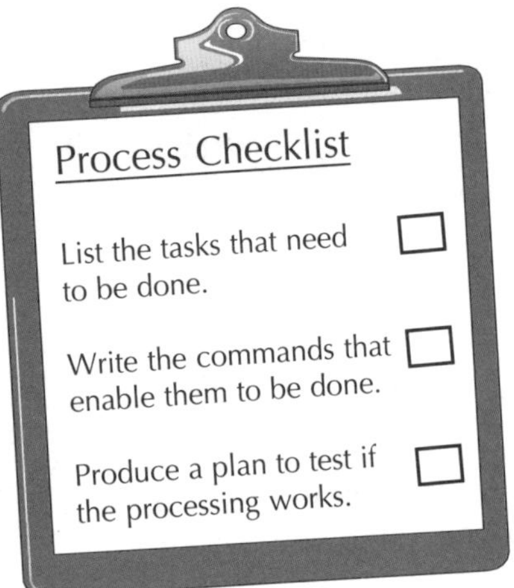

1) The tasks that the system needs to perform should be based on the original problem and objectives.
2) The commands could include spreadsheet formulas, database searches, desktop publishing page design, and word-processing mail-merge routines.
3) The commands could also include exchanging data between different applications. E.g. importing a spreadsheet and using it to create a table in a word-processing package.
4) A test plan for the field 'percentage score' might include typical data such as 76, extreme data such as 100 and invalid data such as Boris. This will test whether the data validation works.

Output — Let it Out

1) The Golden Rule is to be user-friendly. This means that the output must be appropriate for the needs of the audience.
2) Users should only be shown the information that they need — and it should be communicated in a way they will easily understand. Layout is as important as content.
3) The layout of output screens and printouts should first be sketched in rough. They should then be shown to the user to check they are OK.

Output Checklist

- Decide which data needs to be output. ☐
- Decide how to present the information. ☐
- Decide which output devices to use. ☐
- Design output screens. ☐

Don't get stuck, always look things up if you don't know them

If you're stuck, you can look up the following things: bits and bytes (p1), fields and data files (p43), spreadsheets and databases (p87-98), mail-merge routines (p69), data validation (p40).

Warm-Up and Worked Exam Questions

These warm-up questions will run quickly over the basic facts you'll need in the exam — unless you've learnt the facts first, you'll find the exams tougher than stale bread.

Warm-up Questions

1) Draw a rough sketch of the System Life Cycle.
2) State two methods a systems analyst can use to identify problems with an existing computer system.
3) What is a 'feasibility study'?
4) What are the four stages of the feasibility study?
5) Write down the three main stages of the computer system that need to be designed.
6) What is 'extreme data' in a test plan?

Now these questions will give you important practice of actual exam-style questions — and unless you've practised lots of them, you'll find the exams tougher than err... steel bread.

Worked Exam Question

1 A school decides to replace its existing manual filing system with a new computer filing system.

(a) List three activities that a systems analyst should carry out when analysing the existing system.

i) work out the objectives for the new system;

ii) identify the hardware and software required;

iii) carry out a cost-benefit study.

(3 marks)

You could also have answered this question by giving some of the activities the systems analyst carries out to identify the problems (on p52), e.g. interviewing users of the system.

(b) The systems analyst recommends that the codes M or F should be used when entering data about the gender of each pupil. Give three reasons why codes are used to store data.

i) to reduce file size;

ii) to reduce input errors;

iii) to make it easier to search for data.

(3 marks)

It's easy to come up with one reason — getting three is quite tricky. There's lots of common themes in ICT questions — file size, speed, human error are all things which come up again and again in different contexts. Keep them in the back of your mind...

Exam Questions

1 A new computer system is to be introduced in a bank to help staff deal with customer enquiries.

(a) State two possible reasons why a new computer system might be needed.

....

(2 marks)

(b) Describe the steps taken during the input stage of the new system's design.

....

....

....

(4 marks)

2 A computer system is to be installed in a doctor's surgery to replace the existing manual system. There are five stages involved in introducing the new computer system — **analysis**, **design**, **implementation**, **testing** and **evaluation**.
For each of the tasks below, say which stage they belong to:

(a) Interviewing users about how well the new system is working.

....

(b) Carrying out a cost-benefit study.

....

(c) Deciding how information about new patients will be entered onto the system.

....

(d) Interviewing users of the old system.

....

(e) Checking what happens when you create two new patient records with the same name.

....

(f) Transferring data from the existing patient cards onto the new computer database.

....

(6 marks)

3 A bakery wishes to introduce a new computer system to manage its accounts.
The systems analyst decides to carry out a cost-benefit study.

Explain what is meant by a 'cost-benefit study'.

....

....

....

(4 marks)

System Design and Testing

It is important to know how all the bits of the system fit together. The diagrams on the next three pages show how this can be done. Make sure you know the differences between them.

Top-Down Diagrams Set Out the Main Tasks

1) Top-down design looks at the whole system by identifying the main tasks to be done and then breaking them down into smaller tasks.
2) If you read a top-down design from top to bottom, each big task is broken down into smaller tasks. Reading it from left to right tells you the order in which they happen.
3) Top-down diagrams show what has to happen — but they don't always show how they'll happen.
4) The example below shows the tasks needed to create and print a copy of a new database record.

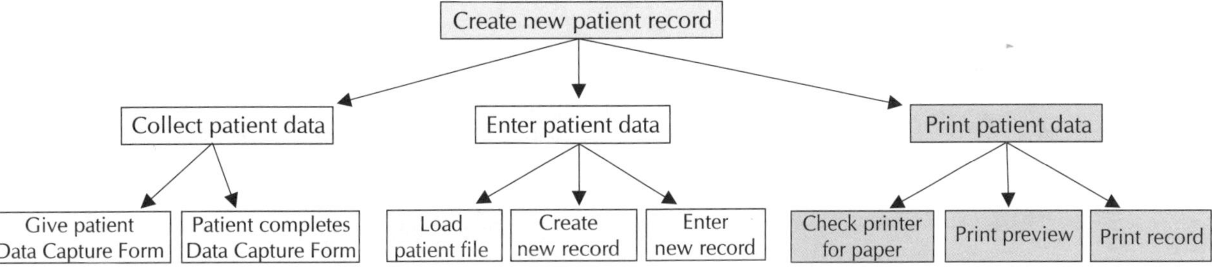

Data-Flow Diagrams Show What Happens to the Data

1) Data-flow diagrams show how data moves around the system — and what happens to it at each stage. There are three main symbols used.
2) The rectangle shows where data has come from. The sausage shows a process such as a search. The square shows where the data is stored — this can include a manual store of a hard copy.
3) Data-flow diagrams show what happens to the data — but they don't show what hardware and software are needed to make this happen.
4) The example shows how an optician can send reminder letters to people who have not had an eye test within the past year.
5) This is a data-flow diagram for just one task. A whole system could be shown by linking together the separate diagrams for each task — rather like linking up different people's family trees.

Customer data file
Produce list of patients overdue for an appointment
Standard letters file
Merge fields into appointment reminder letter
Copy kept in filing cabinet

Learn these diagrams — they show how the system fits together

You will need to use these diagrams if you want to do well in your coursework, although they are not likely to be in your Exam. Make sure you can turn them into a list of written instructions.

System Design and Testing

Most people find system flow charts quite intimidating.
But they're actually quite straightforward once you've learnt what all the symbols mean.

Learn the Symbols...

System flow charts are like data-flow diagrams, except that they use standard symbols to represent different processes, storage mediums, etc.

The symbol for stored data is sometimes replaced by one of the other green symbols if the analyst wants to specify the type of storage medium to be used.

(The colours used here aren't standard, they're just to make it easier to follow.)

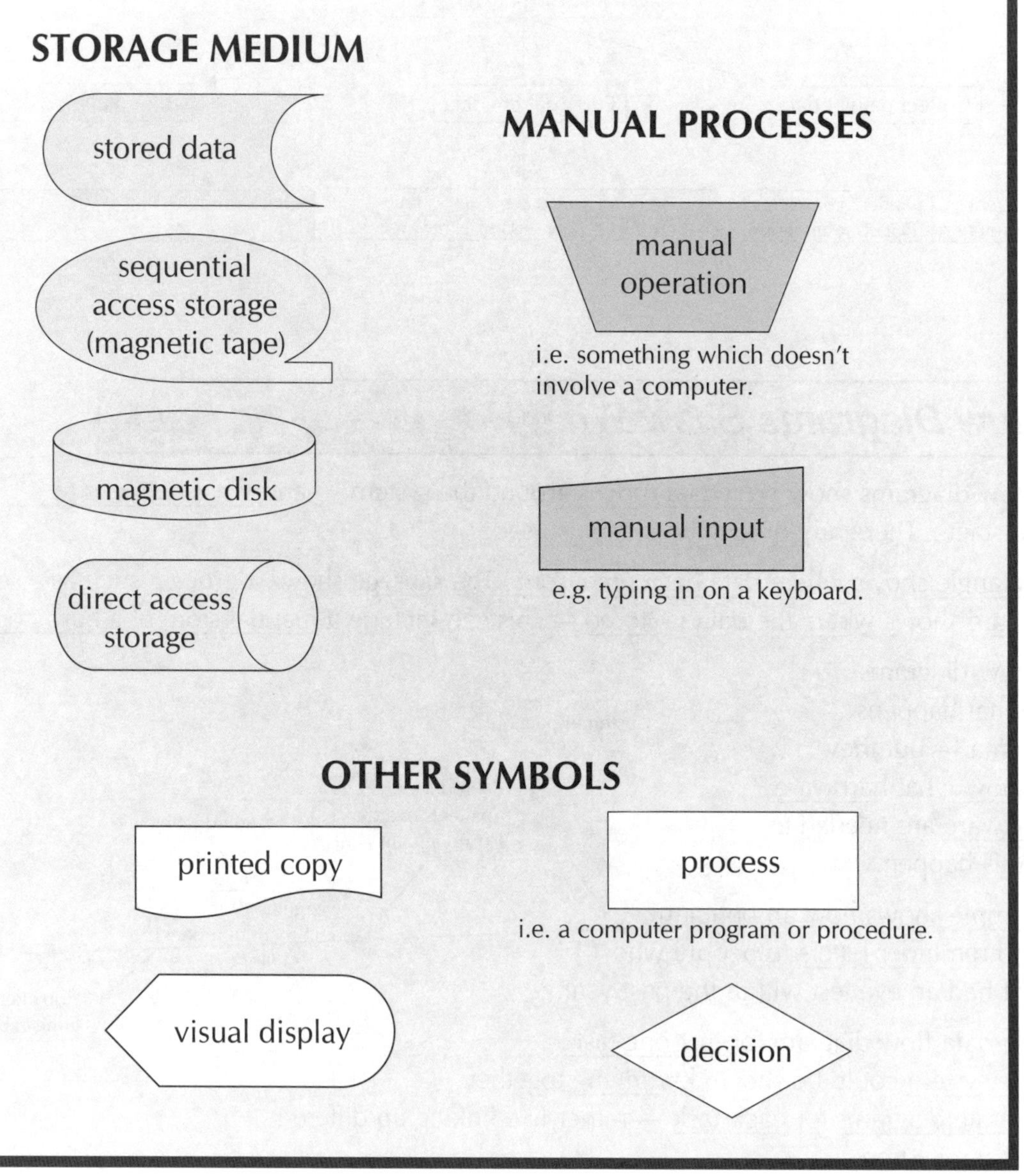

Recognise these symbols by their shape

Copy out all these shapes onto paper, then try and write their names on them. If you can't do some, look them up, and then do it again and again until you've learnt them all.

System Design and Testing

...So you can Use Them

Here's an example of a system flow chart for creating a new patient record at a dentist's surgery:

1) The customer completes a data-capture form.
   This information is then entered onto the patient record file by the receptionist.

2) The new patient record is then used to create a mail-merged letter welcoming the new patient to the surgery.

3) The decision box is an example of an algorithm.
   If the input data is invalid, the receptionist must verify whether the input data is the same as the data on the original data-capture form.

4) If it's the same then the patient needs to be contacted to check the correct details.
   If it's different there has been an input error and the receptionist must re-enter the data.

5) Once the flow chart has been drawn, the programmer will be able to write the commands that will create the system.

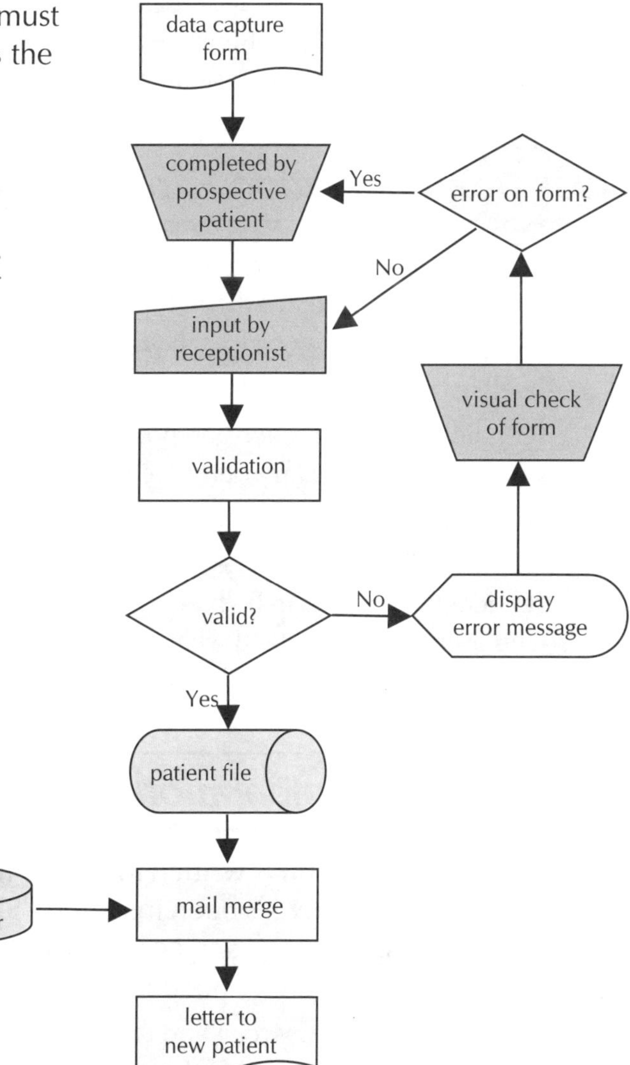

You need to learn about these charts even if they are a bit dull

You need to practise drawing these charts. Learn the symbols, then try and memorise and copy out the flow chart on this page. That will give you a good idea of how flow charts work.

System Design and Testing

A system is tested both during building and after it's built. You need to know what tests are done and why, as well as the different types of documentation that need to be written.

There are **Two Types of Test** to be Done...

1) **System testing** checks whether or not the system will work. Tests are carried out to see if the design has worked. One way is to use test data. There are two types of test data: normal and invalid.

   Normal data is anything that the programmer knows should work in the system.
   Invalid data is anything the programmer knows that the system should reject.
   Any part of the system that doesn't work is said to have a bug — testing enables the programmer to know which parts of the system need to be debugged.

2) **Acceptance testing** checks whether or not the system meets the needs of the intended users. This might involve a trial run with real users operating the system. This can help to make the system more user-friendly.

User Documentation Explains How to **Operate** the System

As the name suggests, user documents are written to help the people who will perform tasks using the system. There are three types of guide — depending on when they might be needed.

1) Installation guides explain how the system should be installed and programs loaded — as well as which peripherals are needed and how they should be installed.
2) User guides give instructions on how to perform tasks using the system — for example, how to carry out searches and print data from a database.
3) Tutorials are short training manuals explaining how the system works. They might include exercises which help the user to practise operating the software.

   User documentation can be hard to write. This is because it needs to be written in simple language so the users can understand what they have to do — but at the same time it needs to use the same technical terms that are used in the software.

Technical Documentation Explains How to **Maintain** it

Technical documentation is written for the computer engineers and programmers who will maintain the system after it's been installed. Since they're computer experts, the guides can be full of technical language and complex system diagrams.
There are two times when it's needed.

1) When something goes wrong and the system needs to be repaired. The technical manual should enable fault finding to take place — in other words tell the engineer what's wrong. It should then explain how to fix it.
2) When the system needs upgrading — for example, installing a better user interface. The computer engineer needs to know how this can be done.

Documentation is vital so you can learn how to fix problems

Make sure you learn everything properly. Try the memorise, cover and copy method. Memorise each section, cover it up — then copy it out. Keep repeating until you've learnt it.

System Design and Testing

You now need to know when each of the three different implementation methods should be used, and how the system can be evaluated.

*There are **Three** Different Ways to **Implement** the System*

Implementation happens when data from the old system is loaded onto the new system — so the new system is ready for use. There are three different ways of timing the introduction of the new system — each with its benefits and problems.

1) Direct implementation is when the old system is decommissioned and the new system started up at the same time. There is no change-over period, so users need to be able to use the new system at once.

ADVANTAGE

The benefits of the new system happen as quickly as possible.

DISADVANTAGE

Any bugs not picked up during testing could have disastrous effects.

2) Phased implementation is when different parts of the system are introduced one at a time. The old system is kept running while this happens.

ADVANTAGE

The new system has time to be fully tested — so fewer problems should occur.

DISADVANTAGE

It can take a long time to introduce the new system this way — so the benefits take a long time to come through.

3) Parallel implementation is when the new system is introduced all in one go — but the old system is kept running whilst the new one is tested. This means that for a while there are two systems.

ADVANTAGE

The new system can be tested very quickly — and problems can be sorted out without important operations being affected.

DISADVANTAGE

All tasks need to be done twice.

Evaluation** Checks if the System **Still** Meets its **Objectives

1) Once the system is installed, its performance will be monitored to see whether it's working properly. From time to time it'll be evaluated. This is a check to see if the system still meets its objectives — in other words whether it still does what it was designed to do.
2) Evaluation is basically repeating the research carried out at the start of the system's life cycle. In other words observing and interviewing users and studying printouts.
3) One reason why the system might not meet its objectives is if the workload increases. The demands on the system may become greater than its ability to cope. In other words it becomes obsolete. This brings the system life cycle full circle and the analyst is brought back to begin work on a new system.

Evaluation is the key

There aren't any diagrams to learn on this page — just lists of advantages and disadvantages. You still have to learn everything here. You might have mini-essays on this in the exam.

Warm-Up and Worked Exam Questions

This isn't the most interesting section, so you'll be glad to know that this is the last lot of questions for it. Don't stop now — the sooner you finish these questions, the sooner you get onto the much sweeter section 5 about graphics and nice things like that.

Warm-up Questions

1) Draw the symbol used in a data flow diagram to represent 'manual input'.
2) What are the two main types of testing carried out on a new computer system?
3) Which document explains how the new system should be installed and programs loaded?
4) Which document describes how to perform tasks using the new computer system?
5) What is 'parallel implementation'?
6) What happens when a computer system is evaluated?

Now for the exam questions. If you don't do these, you'll never make it as a Systems Analyst.

Worked Exam Question

1 A systems analyst has created a new computer system for a cinema. The analyst recommends that an acceptance test is carried out and user documentation is written.

(a) State two reasons why an 'acceptance test' is carried out.

i) to see whether the intended users are able to use the new system;

ii) to help the systems analyst to improve the new system, e.g. make it more user-friendly.

(2 marks)

It's not rocket science, it's just common sense. You need to have learnt what an acceptance test is though...

(b) Describe the user documentation that should be written for the new system.

Installation guides should be written to explain how the system should be installed; user guides will be needed to explain how to perform tasks using the new system; tutorials should be written to teach the users how to use the system using examples and exercises.

There's 6 marks up for grabs — you'll get a mark for each of the three types of document and a mark for each explanation.

(6 marks)

Remember — if you want the full 6 marks, you need to make sure there's 6 separate points in your answer, each worthy of a mark.

Exam Questions

1 A library has installed a new computer system. The systems analyst has written technical documentation and user documentation for the new system.

(a) Give two differences between technical documentation and user documentation.

....

....

(2 marks)

(b) State two occasions when technical documentation might be needed.

....

....

(2 marks)

2 A theatre is installing a new computer system to replace its existing computer system. The new system is installed using phased implementation.

(a) What is 'phased implementation'?

....

....

(2 marks)

(b) State one benefit and one drawback of phased implementation.

....

....

(2 marks)

(c) When is the 'phased implementation' complete?

....

(1 mark)

3 A school has installed a new computer system. The systems analyst has recommended that the new system be evaluated when it is three years old.

Explain why it is necessary to evaluate the performance of a computer system.

....

....

(2 marks)

Revision Summary for Section Four

Well done — you made it to the end of Section Four. Now you know all about systems analysis — or do you? This stuff's really important — if you're doing a full GCSE you can pretty well guarantee that you'll get asked some questions about it. Not to mention your coursework. So, roll up your sleeves, and get stuck into these questions.

1) What comes between analysing and implementing a new computer system?
2) List three ways of gathering information about the performance of an old system.
3) What is the difference between objectives, performance criteria and evaluation criteria?
4) What does a cost-benefit study do?
5) What is a screen form?
6) List three things that should be done when designing a system's input.
7) List three things that should be done when designing a system's processes.
8) List three things that should be done when designing a system's output.
9) What are the three types of test data needed? Give an example for each if testing the validation of data entries for the field "Day of month born".
10) In which two ways do you read a top-down diagram?
11) What does it mean if you see a sausage on a data-flow diagram?
    a) Input b) Process
12) Correctly label each symbol in the box.

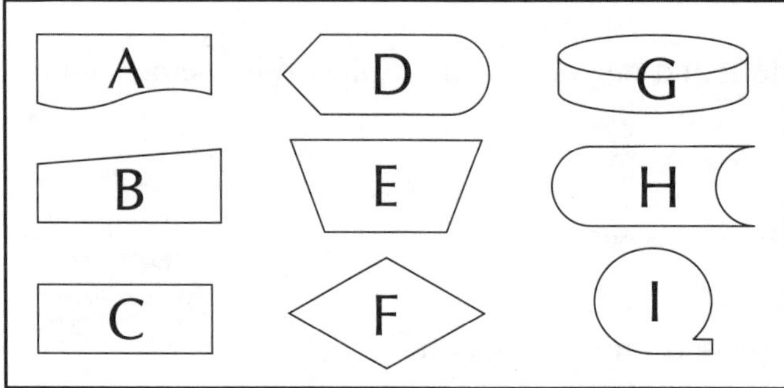

13) Which would be the correct symbol for each of the following events:
    a) A screen prompt to log on
    b) Keying in your user name
    c) The computer checking that your user name is on its list
    d) A hard copy of your filenames
14) What is the difference between system testing and acceptance testing?
15) Explain how parallel implementation is different from direct implementation.
16) Explain how phased implementation is different from parallel implementation.
17) Give one benefit and one problem of each type of implementation.
18) List the three different types of user guide — and explain when each one should be used.
19) What is the difference between monitoring and evaluation?

Word Processing

Revise word processing in the same way as you revise as all the types of software in the next three sections. You need to know what to use it for, its advantages and disadvantages — and how to use it.

Word Processing — it Does More than the Name Says

1) The very first word processors were nothing more than computerised typewriters — they were just used to enter and edit text.
2) Modern word processors are much more powerful, combining graphics with different ways of presenting text and numerical information.

Things a word processor can produce:
Letters, memos, CVs, questionnaires, reports, leaflets containing graphics, newsletters, printed envelopes, personalised letters using mail-merge, worksheets, labels, web pages...

Word Processors have **Four Benefits...**

Written documents and documents produced using a typewriter share the same problem — once created they can't easily be altered. Word processors changed all that, and other things too...

1) Once text is entered, it can be processed (i.e. changed) easily. The appearance can be changed — called text formatting. Also the content can be changed — called text editing.
2) The text can be saved and reused. For example, a standard letter template can be created, and used to send similar letters to different people.
3) Professional-looking documents can be created by just about anyone. That's because it's easy to correct spelling mistakes, and to improve the appearance of the document with graphics and text formatting.
4) Since most people now create their own documents, fewer people are employed as professional typists. But this efficiency gain is reduced a little because most people can't touch-type — so it takes longer to enter text.

...but always remember your **Audience**

1) The big problem with word processors is that because they now contain so many different ways to edit and format information, it's all too easy to get carried away and do things just because you can, rather than because it's useful.
2) The Golden Rule is to keep the layout simple — remember the needs of your intended audience.
3) If possible, design the layout of the document first, and then carry out an acceptance test with the user.

Word processing's better than handwriting 30 copies of your CV...

These things often get overlooked because you spend so much time actually using word processors. Learn the advantages and disadvantages of using a word processor, cover the page and scribble them down. Always remember the Golden Rule: keep the layout simple.

Word Processing

This page covers the basic features of a word processor — you might know some already.

There are Three Main **Text Formatting** Methods...

1) Change the font (the fancy name for the character style).
   There are two main types of font — serif and sans serif.

Serif fonts like this can make long passages easier to read. (Serifs are the little twiddly bits at the tops and bottoms of the characters).	Sans serif fonts (i.e. fonts without serifs) like this are better if the text is arranged in boxes on the page.

2) Change the size of the text. Emphasise headings and sub-headings by making them larger.
   A font size between 10 and 12 point is easy to read for most people (this text is in 12 pt).
   But small children and people with reading difficulties might need a larger font size.
3) Highlight the text. There are four ways to make text stand out. Words can be in:
   (i) **bold type**, (ii) *italics,* (iii) underlined, (iv) colour.
   Again, the golden rule is to keep things simple — be consistent and don't do them all at once.

...and Four **Text Editing** Methods...

As well as changing the appearance of text, you can change content as well — individual characters, words, or whole blocks of text. You just need to highlight the bits you want to change.

1) **New text can be inserted within existing text.**
2) **Existing text can be deleted (by using the delete or backspace keys).**
3) **Text can be moved to another position on the page (e.g. by dragging highlighted text).**
4) **Text can be copied so that it appears more than once on the page. Highlight the text, select 'copy', put the cursor where you want the duplicate text to appear and then select 'paste'.**

...and Four Ways to **Position** Text

1) The TAB key on the keyboard makes the cursor jump one step to the right.
   Use it to start a paragraph away from the side of the page (called indenting).
   You can also use it to make simple tables — but most word processors have a built-in table facility which works much better.
2) Margins fix how far from the side of the page the text starts and finishes. Changing them is useful if you print pages that are going to be bound together — e.g. a piece of coursework.
3) Line spacing adjusts how far apart the lines of text are on top of each other. Double-line spacing is much easier to read than single-line spacing — but it uses up much more paper.
4) Alignment and justification affect how each line of text is arranged. Three different types of alignment are shown in the box. This paragraph has been justified — so that each full line is the same length.

This text is left-aligned.
This text is right-aligned.
This text is centre-aligned.

Text justification — you have to make sure it's really worth it

You might be asked to describe these functions in the Exam. Beware — they won't use terms specific to just one manufacturer's software. So make sure you learn the terms used in this book.

Word Processing

Most of the things on this page should also be fairly familiar — but they are all ways of making a document look more professional and readable. Learn all the key terms.

Tables, *Borders* and *Columns* can Help Readability

1) Tables are a good way to present lists of numerical or textual information, e.g. lists of names and addresses.
2) Putting borders around tables, pictures or blocks of text helps break up the information on the page — which sometimes makes it easier to read.
3) Columns can be created so that the text flows down the page and jumps automatically to the next column. This is great for newsletters and newspapers.

Wordprocessing Weekly News

Typists around the country were staggered to learn yesterday that text can be arranged automatically in columns.

"I'm staggered," said 38-year-old Ian Denting. "If these newfangled word processors keep going at this rate then I'm going to become marginalised."

Nelson Column, of London, said it had "absolutely nothing to do with me."

Choose the Correct **Page Set-Up**

Choosing the page set-up means deciding how the page will look when it has been printed. There are two main things to decide:

1) The layout can be either portrait (tall and narrow) or landscape (short and wide).
2) The size of the paper you want to print on. The page can be A4 (the size of this book), bigger (e.g. A3), or smaller (e.g. A5 or business card size). However it is important to have the right sized paper — and most printers can't print pages bigger than A4.

Portrait

Landscape

(With A3, A4, A5 etc., the page halves in size as you increase the number by 1.)

Watch Out for **Widows** and **Orphans**

Orphans are small blocks of text that don't quite fit onto the bottom of one page, and so get put on a new one. (Widows are the blocks of text they get separated from.) As well as looking unprofessional, they waste paper. There are two main ways of getting rid of widows and orphans.

1) Reduce the font size of the entire text so it fits onto a whole page (but not too small to read).
2) Adjust the margins at the top and bottom of the page. However, a page can look cluttered if text is too close to the edge.

You need to make all your work neat and clear for the examiner

Two good reasons to learn all of these word processing features:
1) You can use the tricks to make your coursework look excellent. 2) It'll be in the Exam.

Word Processing

A WYSIWYG Screen Display Helps

1) WYSIWYG stands for What You See Is What You Get, meaning that a document will look exactly the same on-screen as on a printed page.
2) Not all word processors are WYSIWYG — others have different ways of viewing the document, and only some of these options might be WYSIWYG.
3) Some views might be non-WYSIWYG to reduce the amount of RAM needed — by not displaying graphics for example.

These are the slightly fancier word-processing tools — and they're a bit more difficult.

Headers and Footers are Good for Multi-Page Documents

1) These are blocks of information at the top (header) or bottom (footer) of the page. They're especially useful in multi-page documents where similar information needs to be on each page.
2) The most common examples of information in a header or footer include: filename, date and page number. For example, each page can display that it is page X of a document Y pages long — and this is updated automatically if new pages are inserted.

Find and Change Text Using Search and Replace

1) Search enables a specified word to be located wherever it appears in the document.
2) Replace can automatically replace a selected word with a different word — either individually or every time the word occurs.

Mind Your Language with Spell- and Grammar-Checking

Most word processors can automatically correct your spelling and grammar.
This should improve the quality of your written communication — but there are problems.

SPELL-CHECKERS:

1) They come in different languages. Many words are spelt differently in different parts of the English speaking world — e.g. labor (American English) and labour (UK English). So if you live in the UK, check that you're using UK English.
2) They only recognise misspelt words — not their context. This is a problem with words like 'were' and 'where'. If you use the wrong one, the spell-checker won't find a problem.
3) Sometimes the dictionaries contain mistakes. One well-known word processor's spell-checker contained a misspelling of 'liaise'. (This is an example of 'garbage in garbage out'.)

GRAMMAR-CHECKERS:

Grammar-checkers can be unreliable and give confusing advice. This is because good grammar depends upon context — and most software isn't yet powerful enough to take this into account.

Don't rely on spell- and grammar-checkers

It's very very dangerous to rely on them spotting all your mistakes. You need to learn how to proofread your own work as well. It might take a little longer but it's always worth it.

Word Processing

Check **Word Count** and **Readability Scores**

1) Sometimes you need to know how many words you've written, e.g. in a piece of coursework. Automatic word counting is an option on most word processors.
2) Readability scores are often linked to grammar checks. The computer counts things like the lengths of words and sentences, and uses them to calculate an overall score. One common index is the Flesch-Kincaid Grade Level score — this gives the reading age of the document as an American high school grade.

You're expected to know how word processors work — and for good coursework, you'll need to use them, and use them properly.

Write Junk Mail using **Mail-Merge**

Mail-merge lets you send personalised letters by combining a standard letter with information in a database. They save clubs and businesses loads of time — and there are three steps involved:

1) A database is created containing the information you want to appear in the personalised letter.
2) A standard letter is created containing codes, which are usually based on the field names in the database. An example is Dear <Surname> where 'Surname' is a field in the database.
3) The standard letter is linked to the database, and software merges the data by inserting each database record in turn into the letter. If there are 1000 names in the database then you'll get 1000 personalised letters — and each one will greet the reader by their surname.

Create **Templates** of Standard Documents

1) A template is a standard document containing pre-set formats and layouts. Their main benefit is that once they've been created, they save time — so they're often used for business letters.
2) A letter template contains spaces for the recipient's name, address, and the date. These are already formatted — the user just has to stick in the text.
3) Most word processors include a range of templates for different uses, e.g. newsletters, CVs, faxes, memos, etc.

See page 80 for more information.

Templates are very useful for things like revision guides

All of these features are incredibly useful things to know. This is one bit of the ICT course which might help you on a daily basis. Make sure you've learnt everything on this page.

Word Processing

Use **Macros** to run Routine Operations

A macro is another time-saving device — and they're much simpler than most people think.

1) **A macro is a sequence of commands that have been recorded by the computer and saved, using a short code as a filename. You run the macro by keying in the code — easy.**
2) **A good example is a macro to insert a footer containing the filename, date and page number into all new documents.**

Import Information from Other Applications

See page 73 for more information.

1) Importing means adding data created using a different software application. A good example is the use of clip-art.
2) In order for imported data to work it must have been saved using a common file format that both pieces of software can recognise.
3) It's sometimes possible to embed a spreadsheet into a word-processed document and then activate it from within the word processor. Or you can link the spreadsheet to the document so that when the spreadsheet is edited, the word-processed document is automatically updated.

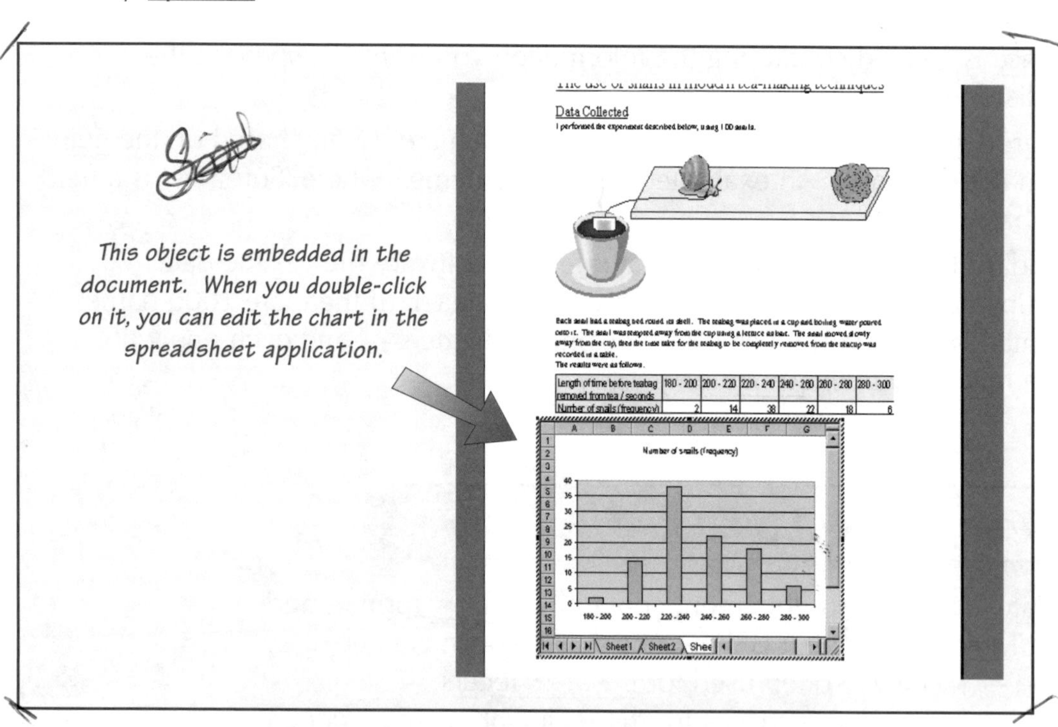

Linking works with other programs as well — not just spreadsheets and databases.

Make sure you place imported files really neatly

Make sure that you are always careful and don't rush any of your work. Here's another hint: make absolutely sure that the file you're importing is completely finished, or else you might have to edit it and then go through the importing process all over again — very frustrating.

Warm-Up and Worked Exam Questions

It's easy to think you've learnt everything in the section until you try the warm-up questions. Don't panic if there are bits you've forgotten. Just go back over that bit until it's fixed in your brain.

Warm-up Questions

1) Explain the difference between spell checking and proof reading.
2) Give two examples of errors that spell checking software would not identify.
3) List three ways in which pieces of text could be made to stand out.
4) What font size would you use for a standard document, e.g. a letter or memo?
5) What problems might arise from using many different font styles in a document?
6) What is mail-merge?
7) What is a macro?

And now... the exam questions. You know the drill.

Worked Exam Question

1 A word processor is much more than just a computerised typewriter, it can produce many different kinds of professional-looking documents.

(a) List three different kinds of information a word processor could combine into a document.

(i) text, (ii) graphics or pictures, (iii) tables

These are probably the most obvious ones, but there's lots more you could have too... *(3 marks)*

(b) List four advantages word processors have over typewriters or hand writing documents.

(i) Text can be easily edited/changed once it has been entered; (ii) the appearance of the text can be easily changed (iii) documents can be reused many times (iv) it is very easy to create professional-looking documents either from scratch or by using prepared templates.

4 reasons may seem a lot, but when you think about all the things word processors can do compared to typewriters, it shouldn't be too hard... *(4 marks)*

Modern word processors include templates to help produce particular documents.

(c) What is a template?

A standard document containing preset formats and layouts designed for a particular purpose.

(1 mark)

(d) Give two examples of standard templates that might be included with a word processor.

Business letters, newsletters

...memos, envelopes, CVs, questionnaires, labels, web pages... take your pick. *(2 marks)*

Exam Questions

1 Word processing software enables users to format and edit text easily.

(a) List three methods of text formatting.

....

(3 marks)

(b) Describe two methods for editing portions of text quickly and simply.

New text can be inserted within the old text.

text can be copied.

text can be Pasted.

(4 marks)

2 Documents can be made to look very professional using word processing software.

(a) Tables can be inserted into word processed documents.
Give two advantages of using a table to display information rather than using a list.

....

....

(2 marks)

(b) Name the two main page layouts and describe how they are different.

....

....

(3 marks)

3 Brisk Industries need to send a lot of letters out to their customers. They want the letter to be the same but for each customer to receive a letter personally addressed to them.

State the word processing function that would be used to do this.

....

(1 mark)

4 Describe the following word processing features and how they can be useful.

(a) Word count

is used to count the word

....

(b) Readability score

....

....

(4 marks)

Graphics

You can draw simple images using a word processor. But for good-looking graphics you need to use graphics software. You need to know the different types of image and how they can be created.

Images are Stored as either **Bitmap** or **Vector** Data

There are two types of graphics software. The main differences are to do with how they store the image, and how the image is edited.

PAINTING SOFTWARE (also known as pixel-based software) *A pixel is a coloured dot. It can take 1000s of dots to make up a whole picture.*	DRAWING SOFTWARE (also called object-based or vector-based software)
1) The graphic is saved as a series of coloured dots (pixels) in a file called a bitmap. These files are large — each dot in a red circle would be saved individually. 2) To edit the image, you basically alter each dot individually, although there are lots of different tools to make this easier.	1) The image is saved as coordinates and equations *(e.g. a red circle might be represented by its radius, the coordinates of its centre and a number for its colour)* — making file sizes a lot smaller. 2) The image is edited by manipulating objects. You can stretch them, twist them, colour them and so on with a series of tools.

You can use **Clip-Art**...

1) Clip-art is graphics that have been created by someone else, but made available for you to copy. Some come free with software packages — others can be bought on CD-ROM.

2) It's possible to treat the Internet as a free clip-art source and copy graphics from web sites. But lots of images are protected by copyright — so using them without permission can be illegal.

...Input **Existing** Images...

Existing images (e.g. photographs) can be converted and stored as a digital image (i.e. data). There are two main ways to do this:

1) Photographs on film or in a book, or hand-drawings on paper need to be converted into a digital image using a scanner. These images are usually stored as bitmap files — so the files can be very large (though they can be converted to other formats, e.g. JPEGs).

> A JPEG is a compressed bitmap. When you convert a bitmap to a JPEG, you lose some of the picture quality, but in a way that's not noticeable to the human eye — e.g. there might be slight colour changes. Compressing the image in this way can massively reduce the file size.

2) New images can be made using a digital camera, and then downloaded onto a computer. Digital photographs are initially stored as JPEG files — which are usually smaller than bitmaps, although the file size will depend on the level of resolution you've chosen.

Resolution = the number of pixels making up the image.

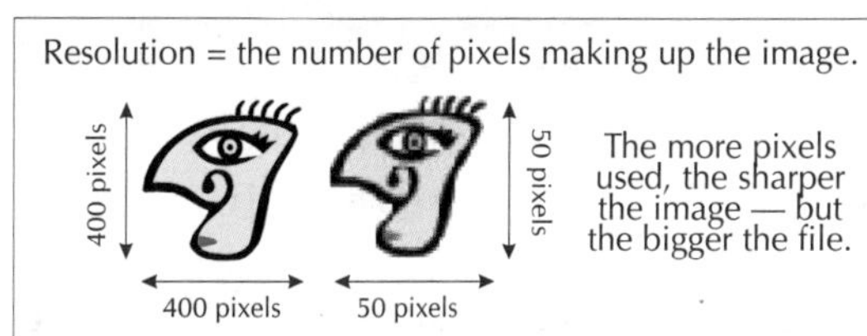

...Or **Create** Your Own

Producing your own graphics by hand using the functions of the software is the most creative and fun way, but it can be very time-consuming — so it's often not worth doing if there's a quicker way.

Graphics

Graphics software is changing rapidly — especially image manipulation software for digital photos. But whatever the technology, the same basic principles still apply. Learn what they are.

Resize the Object — But try not to **Distort** it

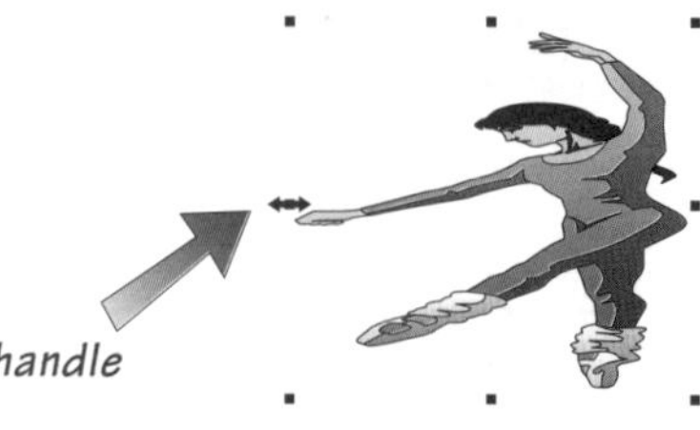

1) Resizing a graphic is often done after the image has been imported into a word processor or desktop-publishing package.
2) It's usually done by selecting the graphic and then dragging one of the 'handles' — outwards to make the image bigger, and inwards to make it smaller.

3) The clever bit is to keep the proportions of the image the same — in other words to keep it the same shape. Otherwise the image gets distorted and it can look pretty bad. You'd be amazed at how many publications contain distorted images.

Cropping Removes Unwanted Bits

1) Cropping removes parts of the image you don't want — e.g. someone on the edge of the shot you want to get rid of. Cropping reduces the size of the image by removing blocks from the edges of the graphic.
2) It's a quick and easy way to remove bits of the image, although it can only remove whole edges — you can't use it to remove something in the middle of the graphic. Fortunately most graphics software has a separate tool to do this.

Group Two or More Images Together

1) If you want to use an image that isn't in your clip-art library — for example a sheep riding a motorbike — but you have separate clip-art of a sheep and a motorbike, you can make a new object by grouping them together so that it looks like the sheep is riding the bike.
2) You can also select which graphics are at the front of the image and which are at the back — this is called layering.

Rotate and **Recolour** Objects

1) Images can be rotated to make them appear upside down, or flipped to appear back to front. Or you could make the Leaning Tower of Bradford by rotating an image just a little bit.
2) Images can also be recoloured — some packages will change the colour of the whole object automatically. With others you have to change it manually, pixel by pixel using a paint spray.

There are some extremely powerful graphics packages around now

You can create some very impressive effects , but you won't always need them.
Think about how much time they'll take, and what the best way to get what you want is.

Graphics

Computer-Aided Design gets its own page because examiners like to test you about it. All it is is very powerful and specialised graphics software. Learn its benefits and problems.

CAD — Computer-Aided Design

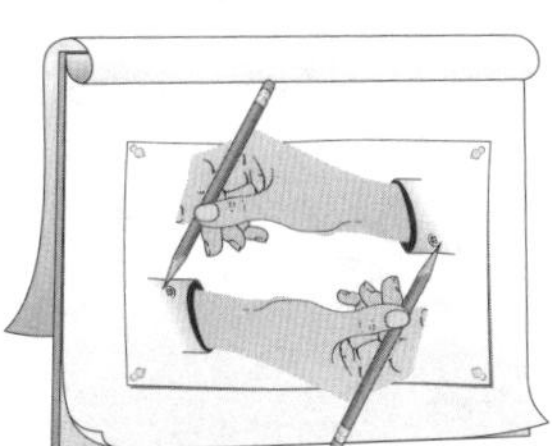

1) Computer-Aided Design is abbreviated to CAD. It's used by manufacturers and engineers to create computerised designs of objects which they will then build.
2) Examples of products designed using CAD include cars, bridges, buildings and toasters.
3) CAD is usually vector-based software — even so, CAD packages are very powerful and often require a lot of memory to run them.

CAD Software can do **Four** Main Things

1) Objects can be designed in two dimensions (e.g. height and width) and then processed into a three-dimensional design. The object can then be rotated to see how it looks from any angle.
2) Calculations can be performed — e.g. calculating the space needed to drive a car in a circle. Another useful calculation is the cost of the object based upon a database of standard costs for the product's components.
3) Some CAD software will suggest suitable materials and components to do a particular job. A good example would be the materials needed to build a greenhouse — the strength of the walls needed will vary depending on the size and weight of the roof.
4) Some CAD software will simulate how the object will perform under certain conditions, e.g. work out how much wind is needed to blow a car onto its side. However, sometimes computer simulations don't work — the Millennium Bridge in London had to close because it wobbled when too many people walked on it, but the simulation hadn't suggested any problem.

Using CAD has **Pros** and **Cons**

Advantages of CAD	Disadvantages of CAD
1) Designs can be created very quickly — especially when the system has a library of standard components. 2) Designs can be changed quickly and easily. 3) Good systems can produce high-resolution images that are almost lifelike. 4) Simulations help design better products first time round. That can save hours of testing, which reduces production costs.	1) Professional CAD systems require powerful hardware such as microcomputers with special chips. 2) CAD software is very expensive. 3) CAD software is complex — users need a lot of training in its use.

CAD is hard to do properly, but learning about it is simple

You've got three sets of lists to learn. Read and memorise everything on this page, cover it up and scribble down all you can remember, then compare and redo it if you missed anything.

Warm-Up and Worked Exam Questions

It's easier to learn about graphics when you're sitting in front of a computer, but doing these questions will still help refresh your memory. Do the quick ones first, to get you limbered up.

Warm-up Questions

1) What are the two main types of graphics packages?
2) List four possible sources of images that could be used to illustrate a document.
3) What is the main difference between a JPEG and bitmap file?
4) What does CAD stand for?
5) Explain the difference between cropping and resizing an image.

Worked Exam Question

I'd like an exam question, and the answers written in — and a surprise.
Two out of three's not bad.

1 New technology now means that many people choose to take photographs using a digital camera rather than a traditional one that uses film.

(a) Describe 3 steps you would follow to get traditional printed pictures into a computer document.

Put the picture into a scanner or scan it with a hand-held scanner, save the file as a bitmap or JPEG file and import it into your document.

Make sure you do have 3 separate stages, it's not enough just to fill all the space. So the 3 different stages are scan, save as bitmap, import into document.

(3 marks)

(b) Describe 3 steps you would follow to get digital pictures into a computer.

Connect the digital camera to the computer, download the images and import them into your document.

Don't worry if you haven't used up all the space provided — the main thing is to be clear and concise.

(3 marks)

For these questions, it's good to NOT use brand names for software and hardware. The examiner wants to know you've understood the CONCEPT...

Exam Questions

1 Using specialist software, it is possible to alter an image to make it suit your needs. Identify the tool or technique you would need to use to carry out the following:

(a) Make a building appear to lean to the left.

rotate

(b) Remove unwanted background from a photograph.

cropping

(c) Make a small picture fill a larger area.

Resize

(3 marks)

2 A graphic designer is considering purchasing a graphics program to help her create accurate technical drawings.

(a) What type of program would you recommend she purchases?

vector based Software.

(1 mark)

(b) Give three advantages of this type of program over other graphics packages.

less file space, accurate.

(3 marks)

(c) Give one disadvantage of your recommended program type.

(1 mark)

3 Jenny wants to scan in a photograph of her family to e-mail to her cousin who lives abroad.

(a) What file format should she save the image as?

JPeg

(1 mark)

(b) Explain the advantage this file type has, considering what she wants to do with the image.

by using this format will save disk space.

(2 marks)

Desktop Publishing

Most of the word processing information is relevant to desktop publishing (DTP) as well. But you also need to know how DTP is different from word processing.

DTP Creates Professional Looking Pages

1) Desktop publishing software is used to build professional looking pages — ones that are good enough to be published.
2) Examples of documents produced using DTP software include newsletters, newspapers, leaflets and posters. But there are loads of others as well.
3) Pages are built up as a series of frames — text frames containing text, graphics frames containing images, and so on.
4) DTP software usually lets the user create text and simple pictures — but it often works best when the source material is created in other specialised software (e.g. a word processor or a graphics package) and then imported into the DTP package.

DTP Software is usually Frame-Based

1) Frame-based software means that information is put on pages in blocks (called frames).
2) Frames can be moved or resized. This means that it is very easy to edit a DTP document by moving pictures or blocks of text around. Frames can also be moved from page to page.

3) DTP works rather like creating a noticeboard — you have a set of different pieces of information which you can move around until you're happy with the overall layout.

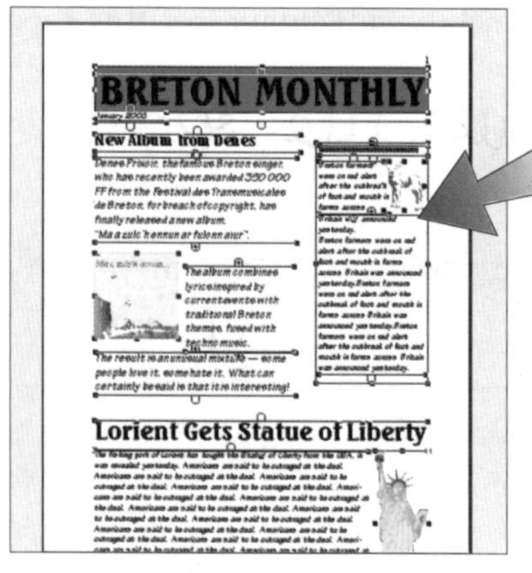

Each block of text or picture forms its own frame that you can drag around separately.

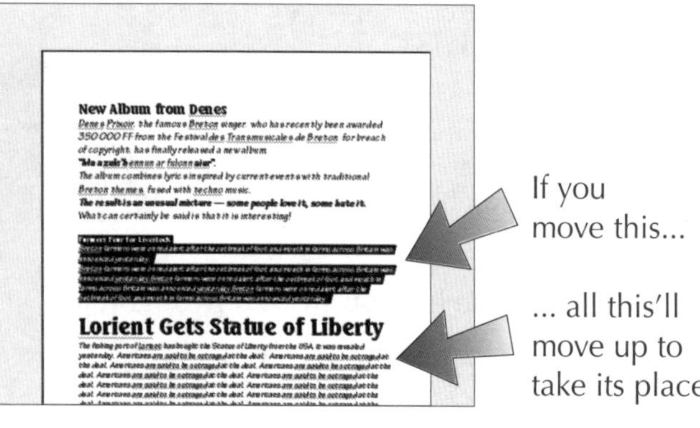

4) Most word processors are not frame-based, so the position of one thing depends on the position of everything else. That means moving one thing might make a whole load of other stuff move as well. This doesn't happen with DTP.

Make sure you know how DTP is different from word processing

Lots of people think they're experts at using DTP — but exam questions are often answered badly. That's because they don't know the basic facts — don't make the same mistake.

Desktop Publishing

DTP has Three Main Benefits

1) You can create very professional-looking documents — even with relatively inexpensive DTP packages. But the quality of the printed document is often limited by the quality of the printer.
2) The layout of the document can be changed more easily using DTP than a word processor.
3) DTP packages contain most features of a word processor but many more, giving you greater power and flexibility.

It's the frames that really make DTP software more powerful than a word processor for some tasks. You need to know how style sheets can improve the layout of a document.

Four Things You can do with a Frame

1) Frames can be lined up in columns — most DTP software can insert column guides or guidelines (lines that appear on screen but not on the printed document) to help position the frames. This keeps the document looking tidy, and the layout consistent.

2) Text frames can be linked together, so any text not fitting inside the first text frame will automatically appear inside the next one. Frames can even be linked across different pages of the document — so they're handy if you want to continue a story on a different page.

3) You can set the text to wrap. Then, if a picture frame is positioned on top of a text frame, the text will wrap around the picture, instead of being covered by it.

4) Frames can be layered — i.e. put on top of each other. This is usually done with picture frames, but it can also be done with text frames. E.g. you could put some text over the top of a picture (but you have to make the text frame transparent first so you can still see the picture).

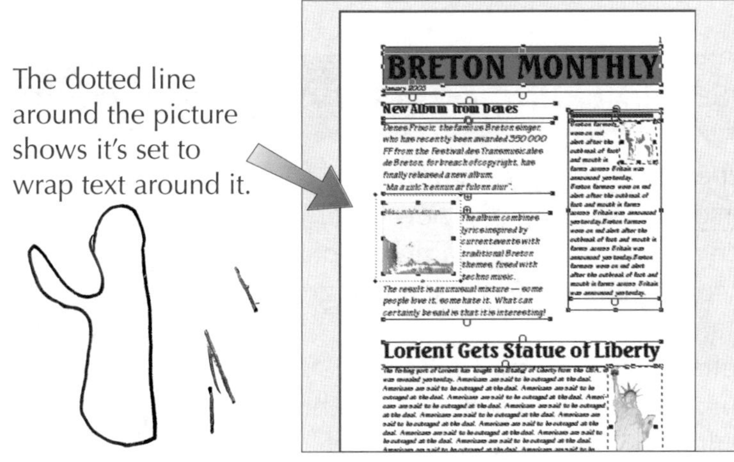

The dotted line around the picture shows it's set to wrap text around it.

Frames are the key to using DTP

DTP can take a while to get used to at first. Once you've understood the basic concept, however, the rest is just about learning all the tricks. So get learning — no excuses.

Desktop Publishing

Style Sheets and Templates Save Time Designing Pages

1) The Golden Rule of good page design applies to DTP as well as word processing — keep the page layout simple, and appropriate for the needs of the audience. Templates and style sheets can make this easier.
2) Templates and style sheets are similar — they're both files containing the basic layout and format for a standard document. Most DTP software has loads of different templates. They save time but if you're not careful, documents can end up looking the same.

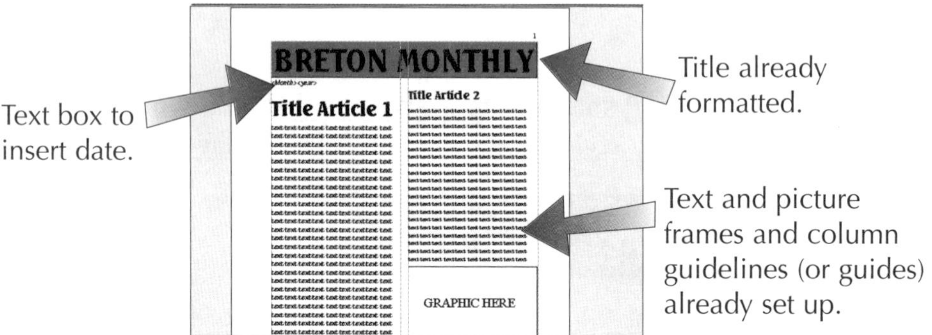

3) A template for a newspaper will have columns, text frames and picture frames. The text frames will be formatted with different fonts for the newspaper title, headlines and main story.
4) Templates can also be designed by the user — e.g. for a school newsletter. At the top of the template's first page would be the school name, address, crest, and a text box for the date. The basic layout of the other pages may also be set — e.g. a page for PE results might contain graphics to represent the main sports, and tables where results can be entered.

Presentation software is being used more and more to give talks and display ideas. You need to know what it is suitable for and what the main features are.

Presentations are used to Communicate New Information

1) Presentations are given either to communicate new information, or to help persuade someone of a new idea. A teacher might give a presentation to introduce a new topic in a lesson, or a salesperson could give one to persuade a group of people to buy something.
2) They can sometimes be quite boring — especially if the speaker just talks on and on. Presentation software can help overcome this by using multimedia and animation effects.

Good presentations need to be interesting

It's true. There is absolutely no point in giving a dull presentation. People will just switch off part way through. You need to find a way to make your information gripping.
Using eyecatching visual aids is a great way to perk up your presentations, and get good marks.

Presentation Software

Presentations can be given *With* or *Without* a *Speaker*

1) The typical way to give a presentation is with a speaker introducing slides projected onto a large screen. The audience can read the information on the screen while the speaker gives them more detailed spoken information.
2) The other way is to give a presentation without a speaker. For this to work well the slides have to be good enough to communicate all the required information by themselves. Multimedia presentation software can help by allowing a commentary to be recorded.

Presentation Software has **Four** Main Features

1) Presentation software creates a series of slides in a single document — and each slide contains a number of frames (a bit like DTP software). This means that text and images — and even movies and sounds — can be put on the slide.
2) The really clever thing about presentation software is that the speaker can decide when each frame on a page appears — so each bullet point in a list can appear on screen at just the right moment.
3) Animation effects can even make the frames arrive on screen in different ways — e.g. a line of text can appear one word at a time, or the whole line can fly into place from either side of the screen.
4) The animation effects can either happen at set times (useful if there's no speaker), or they can be controlled by the speaker as he/she is talking — usually with the click of a mouse or a remote control button.

How Presentations Used to be Done

1) Traditionally, slides were either handwritten or word-processed.
2) Unfortunately, it's easy to muddle up the order of the slides.
3) Another problem is that the speaker sometimes has to cover up information they don't want the audience to see yet.
4) Unless the speaker is very good, a presentation can easily end up looking unprofessional.

Mentioning presentation software can get you good marks

Presentation software is fairly new so it's not always on ICT syllabuses. But you can get good marks by referring to it in questions that ask about presenting information. That makes it an important thing to learn. Learn it and show off a bit in your exam. Examiners will love you.

Presentation Software

It's one thing to have clever software to produce exciting slides, but another thing to know how to use the software to produce a good presentation. Make sure you learn the following rules.

Remember the **Rules** for Giving a **Good Presentation**

1) **PREPARE THOROUGHLY** — make sure you know all about the topic you're presenting. The whole point is to get people interested enough that they'll want to ask questions — so you need to have all the answers.
2) **DECIDE ON THE FORMAT** for the presentation — decide whether you'll be delivering it in person, or making it available as a computer file.
3) **WRITE THE SCRIPT** of the presentation first — then decide how the slides will help put the key points of the message across. The slides should be a summary of the main points to be made.
4) **KEEP THE SLIDES SIMPLE** — don't let background colours clash with the text and pictures. Ideally use the same background for all the slides, and don't use hard-to-read fonts. Use no more than two pictures per slide.
5) **USE OPENING AND CLOSING SLIDES** — start the presentation with an attention-grabbing opening slide. The closing slide should leave people with the main message of the presentation.
6) **KEEP EACH SLIDE'S CONTENT TO A MINIMUM** — the Golden Rule is to have no more than six words per line of text and no more than five lines of text on a slide. Font sizes should be big enough for people at the back of the audience to see — between 30 and 60 point should do.
7) **DON'T USE TOO MANY SLIDES** — if you're giving a commentary, each slide should be visible for about two minutes. That means no more than five main slides in a ten-minute presentation.
8) **TEST ANY ANIMATION EFFECTS** using the hardware that will be used in the presentation. Large movie clips might run very slowly on some systems.
9) **REHEARSE** — then rehearse, then rehearse again.

Presentation Software has **Pros** and **Cons**

Advantages of using Presentation Software

1) *It produces professional looking presentations.*
2) *Use of multimedia can help grab and keep people's attention.*
3) *Presentations can be saved and used again — with or without the speaker being present.*
4) *It's easy to edit presentations and adapt them for different audiences.*

Disadvantages of using Presentation Software

1) *It is very easy to get carried away by the technology and produce badly designed slides.*
2) *The software needs expensive hardware to run the presentation — a laptop computer and an LCD projector can easily cost over £3000.*

Don't rush your presentation — you'll just be throwing away marks

This is a very straightforward page. The trouble is that not everyone bothers learning these rules. Learn all nine rules and you'll be set to make some amazing presentations.

Warm-Up and Worked Exam Questions

DTP and presentation software — 2 smashing topics. DTP is a really big industry. It's how all the books, magazines and newspapers we read are made. And presentation software is just great — it can really liven up a talk and take pressure off the speaker. Anyway, enough rambling and on with the questions...

Warm-up Questions

1) What does DTP stand for?
2) What is the main difference between DTP and word processing packages?
3) List three documents that might be produced using DTP software.
4) List two people who might need to use presentation software.
5) What is each "page" of a presentation called?
6) What feature might be included in a presentation designed to run without a speaker?
7) What multimedia components can be included in a presentation?

Worked Exam Question

1 Patrick McBonbon is going to start producing a weekly newsletter for his local village. He plans to buy a computer with the necessary hardware and software that he needs, but doesn't know whether to produce the newsletter using a word processor or DTP software.

(a) Suggest three advantages to Patrick of producing the newsletter with a word processor, rather than desktop publishing software.

(i) Word processing software is much cheaper than desktop publishing software and may come free with the computer, (ii) word processing software is easier to learn than DTP, (iii) a village newsletter won't need a very fancy layout, so the basic layout features provided by a word processor would be more suitable than those of DTP.

(3 marks)

(b) Suggest two advantages to Patrick of producing the newsletter with desktop publishing software, rather than a word processor.

(i) Desktop publishing software is more powerful — can achieve more interesting and varied layouts, (ii) once the package is learned, it is easier and quicker to manipulate the layout than with a word processor.

Questions like this don't have set answers — any sensible points you come up with will get the marks.

(2 marks)

Exam Questions

1 Documents created using DTP software are built up using text and graphics frames.

(a) Describe one way in which using frames makes editing your document's layout easier.

....

(1 mark)

(b) Sometimes blocks of text are too long to fit in a frame. Describe two ways in which you could adapt the document layout to make all the text fit.

....

....

(2 marks)

2 Brisk Industries use DTP software to create their monthly staff newsletter.

(a) What feature of DTP could they use to create a consistent layout for each issue?

..........frames..........

(1 mark)

When the newsletter is finished, it needs to be printed out.

(b) List one factor that might affect the quality of the finished newsletter.

..........Printer quality..........

(1 mark)

(c) Suggest one way in which Brisk Industries could ensure their newsletters look more professional when printed out.

....

(1 mark)

3 Presentation software contains many clever features to make the show more interesting.

(a) Name one such feature that could be used to liven up a show.

....

(1 mark)

(b) If a show is to be given by a speaker, state one way that they might control when the next slide appears on the screen.

....

(1 mark)

(c) The same show could be set up to run without a speaker, how could this be achieved?

....

(1 mark)

Exam Questions

4 Motham Industries want to produce a presentation for their sales representatives to present to new customers.

(a) To help them decide what type of presentation is most suitable, write a short piece of advice including one advantage and one disadvantage for each of the following presentation methods.

(i) Presentation using hand-written slides.

....

....

(2 marks)

(ii) Presentation using presentation software.

....

....

(2 marks)

Motham Industries have decided to create a presentation using software.

(b) Write a short piece of advice to the presentation designer, including three helpful hints to ensure their presentation looks professional.

....

....

....

(3 marks)

Now that the presentation has been created, the sales representatives need to present it.

(c) Write another piece of advice to the speakers, including two helpful hints to ensure they give a successful presentation.

....

....

(2 marks)

Revision Summary for Section Five

Yet again, you might recognise a couple of these questions from the "warm-up" questions earlier on in this section. You'll know what you're doing by now though — keep going through these questions until you can get all the questions right without having to look the answers up. If you do get them all right, you can consider yourself well-prepared for any Exam questions on text and image software. It's not the most thrilling activity on earth but it's definitely worth doing.

1) List five things that can be produced using a word processor.
2) Explain three benefits of using a word processor to write an essay.
3) Why is it a good idea to keep the layout of a document simple?
4) List four different ways you can change the format of a piece of text.
5) List two different ways that the content of a piece of text can be changed.
6) What is the difference between left, right and centre alignment and justification?
7) Why are borders useful?
   a) To make it easier to read a block of text
   b) To keep customs officers busy
8) Which is the bigger paper size: A4 or A5? How much bigger is it?
9) Why should you avoid having widows and orphans?
10) What does WYSIWYG mean? Explain one benefit and one problem with it.
11) Give one benefit and one problem of using a spell-checker.
12) Explain how mail-merge works.
13) Explain one benefit and one problem of mail-merge.
14) What is a template?
15) Why is a common file format needed to import data from a graphics file into a word processor?
16) What is the difference between pixel-based and vector-based graphics software?
17) Is drawing software pixel-based or vector-based?
18) How can a printed photograph be entered into a computer system?
19) Which type of image file is usually bigger — a bitmap or a JPEG?
20) Explain the difference between resizing and cropping an image.
21) What does CAD stand for?
22) Describe three things that CAD software can do.
23) Give three advantages and two disadvantages of using CAD.
24) What is the main difference between how pages are built up using word processing software and using DTP software?
25) Give two benefits of using DTP software over using word processing software.
26) Explain how animation effects can help make a presentation more interesting.
27) Give three advantages and two disadvantages of using presentation software.

Spreadsheets

Most people find spreadsheets a bit scary — very few people really understand them. But they're basically quite simple. Make sure you learn this page well before moving onto the harder ones.

Spreadsheets are Clever Calculators

1) A spreadsheet is simply a program that can display and process data in a structured way. Most people think spreadsheets can only process numbers — but they can handle text as well.
2) Spreadsheets can be used to:

a) record data,
b) search for particular items of data,
c) perform calculations based on data,
d) produce graphs and charts.

3) Examples of uses include keeping records of patients in a doctor's surgery, calculating the exam results of a group of pupils, and producing graphs based on the results of a questionnaire.

Data is Entered into Cells

1) A spreadsheet is made up of rows and columns. These divide the sheet up into individual cells.
2) Each cell can be identified using the column letter and row number as coordinates.

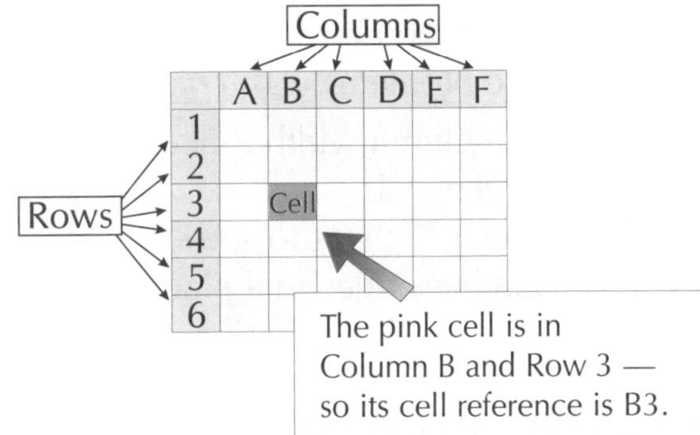

Each Cell can contain One of Three Things

Each cell can contain one (and only one) of three things...

NUMERICAL DATA
e.g. numbers, dates and money.
Most spreadsheets recognise dates and money and convert them into a suitable format — so if you enter 23-6, it's converted to 23 June.

TEXT DATA
e.g. people's names, titles of CDs.
1) Column headings usually contain text.
2) One process that can be carried out on text is sorting it into alphabetical order.
3) The ICT term for a piece of text is a text string.

FORMULAS
1) These allow results of calculations to be displayed inside a cell.
2) E.g. you could get the computer to add up all the numbers in a column and display the answer in a cell at the bottom of the column.
3) The great thing about spreadsheets is that if any numbers are changed, the formulas are automatically updated.

You need to learn the basics of how spreadsheets work

Once you've learnt everything on this page, you'll be set to move on to the next page. The most important thing to understand is that cells can only contain ONE of the three types of data.

Spreadsheets

The Golden Rule is to put only one piece of data in a cell — this means that you shouldn't mix any types of data.

1) If you enter the weight of a kilo of fish as '1000g', you have numerical data (1000) and text data (g).
2) Spreadsheets treat cells with any text in them as though they contain only text data, which has a numerical value of zero.
3) This means the spreadsheet will read '1000g' as having a numerical value of zero.

Three Ways to *Improve* the *Design* of a Spreadsheet...

1) Put the title of the spreadsheet at the top — normally in cell A1.
   a) If the title's too big to fit in A1, it'll spill into cells A2, A3 etc. — this isn't a problem.
   b) If a spreadsheet's going to be used as the data file for a mail-merge, the first row has to contain field names — so put the title into a header.
2) Next enter the column and row headings.
   a) Don't leave any columns or rows empty — they cause problems with charts and graphs.
   b) Increase the column width if necessary.
3) Enter data into the cells.
   a) Change the cells' format to show numbers to a certain number of decimal places, or with a currency symbol if it's money.
   b) Most spreadsheets let you enter data validation formulas — so if you enter someone's age as 1290, you get an error message.

See page 68 for more about headers.

	A	B	C
1	ICT Club — membership fees owing		
2	First Name	Last Name	Amount owing
3	Teresa	Wood	£8.00
4	Tanya	Hide	£5.52
5	Arthur	Brain	£0.00
6	Willie	Winn	£0.00
7	Betty	Wont	£33.67

...and Three Ways to *Improve* its *Appearance*

1) Format the data in similar ways to a word processor.
   Use italics, bold type, different fonts, colours, sizes etc. to make data stand out.
2) Some spreadsheets allow conditional formatting.
   The format of a cell is changed if the contents of a cell meet certain conditions, like if a number's negative. Here, the cells turn red if the person owes money.

	A	B	C
1	ICT Club — membership fees owing		
2	First Name	Last Name	Amount owing
3	Teresa	Wood	£8.00
4	Tanya	Hide	£5.52
5	Arthur	Brain	£0.00
6	Willie	Winn	£0.00
7	Betty	Wont	£33.67

3) Some spreadsheets let you insert graphics, movies and sounds. This is quite a useful feature.

This information about cells is a bit dull, but really important

Spreadsheets are used to process data and then communicate the information. You'll need to use them lots. That means that you have to know how to set up a spreadsheet properly.

Spreadsheets

Spreadsheet Data can be **Imported** and **Exported**

1) **If the data you want to put in a spreadsheet is in another file somewhere else (like in a database or a data-logging device), you can import it directly into the spreadsheet — but only if the data is in a common file format such as CSV. This saves you the bother of typing it all in again.**
2) **CSV stands for Comma-Separated Variable. When the data is saved, a comma is inserted between each piece of data in a row, and a line break is inserted between the last piece of data in one row and the first in the next row. CSV data can be transferred easily between spreadsheets, tables and databases.**
3) **Integrated software suites that combine spreadsheets and word processors can transfer data between the applications by using copy and paste. This is simpler but is still based on CSV.**

See page 70 for more information about all this.

Without formulas, spreadsheets are just fancy tables.
You need to learn how to use them if you want to do well.

A **Formula** is a Simple Computer **Program**

1) A formula is an instruction to the computer to process data held in specific cells — using functions which you can either type in or select from a list.

STEP 1 — Click on the cell where you want the answer.

STEP 2 — Type an equals sign (=).

STEP 3 — Type in the formula. Here, it would be C3+D3+E3.

The equals sign tells the computer to expect a formula.

	A	B	C	D	E	F
1	Exam Marks for 1st Year Mocks					
2	First Name	Last Name	Maths	ICT	English	Total
3	Teresa	Wood	63	45	89	=C3+D3+E3
4	Tanya	Hide	32	54	78	
5	Arthur	Brain	33	53	95	
6	Willie	Winn	24	54	75	
7	Betty	Wont	64	53	88	

2) The simplest functions are +, –, * (for multiply) and / (for divide), but there are usually loads of others, e.g. to find an average, or the sine of an angle. You can usually choose these from a list.
3) Once you've entered a formula, you can copy it to other cells. So the formula in F3 could be copied to cells F4 to F7 — and the computer would automatically insert the correct formulas for the totals of these rows. This makes spreadsheets an easy way to do lots of similar calculations on a large set of data.

C	D	E	F
Maths	ICT	English	Total
63	45	89	=C3+D3+E3
32	54	78	=C4+D4+E4
33	53	95	=C5+D5+E5
24	54	75	=C6+D6+E6
64	53	88	=C7+D7+E7

The computer changes all the 3's to 4's, 5's, 6's and 7's. when you copy and paste cell F3.

Find the formula for success

If you still don't know all of these things, get yourself on a computer, load up a spreadsheet and try doing all the things described on this page. Learning by doing is definitely a good idea.

Spreadsheets

Formulas can have **Absolute** or **Relative Cell References**

1) In the example on the last page, the formula in F3 (=C3+D3+E3) tells the computer to add together the data in the three cells to the left. If you copy this formula to cell F4, it still adds together the contents of the three cells to the left, so F4 becomes '=C4+D4+E4'. That's why they're called relative cell references — the data used is in the same place relative to the answer cell.
2) Sometimes part of a formula always needs to refer to one particular cell — and you don't want the computer to change the cell reference. In this case, you need to use an absolute cell reference — one that won't be changed. The usual way to make a cell reference absolute is to put a dollar sign in front of the cell's coordinates. So B12 is a relative cell reference — but B12 is an absolute cell reference.
3) The spreadsheet below uses an absolute cell reference (to represent the % commission a letting agency charges on its properties).

Once you've entered the formula for C2, you can copy and paste it to cells C3 to C6 and it will automatically insert the correct formula.

	A	B	C	D
1	Property	Monthly Rent	Letting Agent's commission	Amount to Landlord
2	Oak Vale	£450	£45	£405
3	The Old Post Office	£300	£30	£270
4	Ash House	£250	£25	£225
5	Lilac Cottage	£150	£15	£135
6	Low Wood	£500	£50	£450
7			£165	£1,485
8				
9	Letting Agent's Commission (%):		10	

Column C:	Column D:
=B2 / 100 * C9	=B2 – C2
=B3 / 100 * C9	=B3 – C3
=B4 / 100 * C9	=B4 – C4
=B5 / 100 * C9	=B5 – C5
=B6 / 100 * C9	=B6 – C6

Logic Functions let the Spreadsheet Decide What to Do

Logic Functions are quite scary — but dead useful.

1) Logic functions do different things depending on the data in other cells — e.g. if the number in a cell containing a temperature is negative, the output of the logic function could be "Chilly", while if it's positive, the output could be "Warm".
2) In this spreadsheet, the percentage scores from a maths exam are in column C. Students with 40% or less have to take the exam again. The logic function in column D tells the spreadsheet to display the word "Yes" if the number in column C is 40 or less, and "No" if it's above 40.
3) This uses the logic function IF. The output cell will display a specific output if a condition is met.
4) Logic functions can save a lot of time, and reduce the chances of human error.

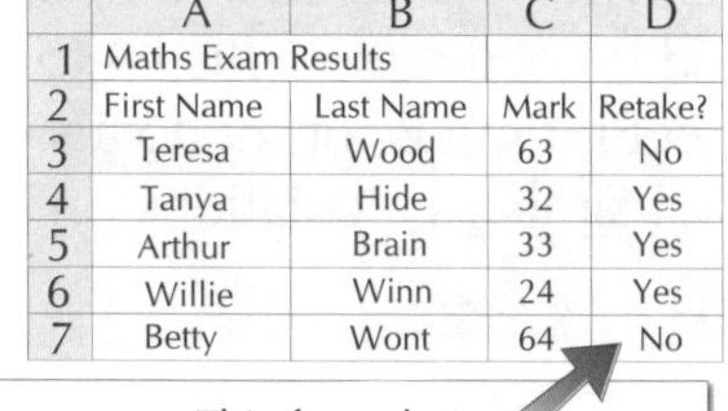

	A	B	C	D
1	Maths Exam Results			
2	First Name	Last Name	Mark	Retake?
3	Teresa	Wood	63	No
4	Tanya	Hide	32	Yes
5	Arthur	Brain	33	Yes
6	Willie	Winn	24	Yes
7	Betty	Wont	64	No

This formula is '=IF(C7>40,"No","Yes")' — meaning if the condition 'C7>40' is met, then display "No", otherwise display "Yes".

Don't confuse IF logic functions with What-If Analysis. What-If Analysis is covered in Section 7 (page 112).

Don't give up yet — learn all these things to get a good grade

Make sure you understand all the formulas. You need be able to write them all down exactly how you'd type them, and you should know the difference between absolute and relative cell references.

Spreadsheets

Look-Up Tables Display Specified Data

1) A look-up table is a bit like a database. Data is stored in a table in one part of the spreadsheet, and in another part, you can display data from that table.

2) Here, a shop selling vampire supplies has listed its products at the bottom of the spreadsheet. At the top, the user enters a product code into cell B1 — the spreadsheet then automatically displays the product name in B2 and the price in B3.

3) The formulas in cells B2 and B3 are pretty scary — but basically they search the data in cells A6-A12, and display the data next to the relevant product code.

4) Look-up tables are pretty useless for small data sets like this one because you can just find the information yourself. But they're really useful for large data sets such as supermarket stocklists.

Enter a product code here...

...and the details appear here.

	A	B	C
1	Product Code	26346	
2	Product Name	Garlic repellent	
3	Price	£0.50	
4			
5	Product Code	Product Name	Price
6	12532	Black capes	£25.99
7	65489	Sharp teeth	£5.50
8	26346	Garlic repellent	£0.50
9	57243	Sunglasses	£15.99
10	53289	Assorted bats	£25.99
11	12489	White face paint	£5.99
12	23412	Light meter	£34.50

Creating a Chart is Easy

All modern spreadsheets can produce graphs and charts — but each one uses a slightly different method. The basic idea is always the same though.

Step One: Get all the data you want to put into a graph into a single block. It's best if the data is arranged in columns.

Step Two: Highlight the data you want to use — you might need to highlight the column headings as well.

Step Three: Select the type of chart you want — be sensible and make sure it's suitable.

Step Four: Choose a meaningful title for the chart — one that summarises the contents of the chart, and label any axes.

Step Five: Decide whether the chart needs a key (also called a legend).

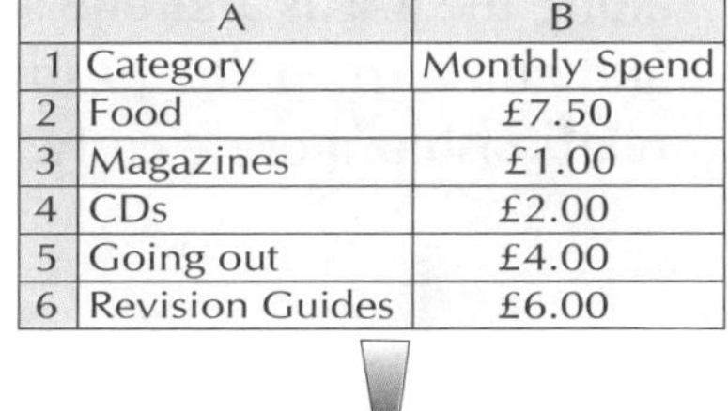

	A	B
1	Category	Monthly Spend
2	Food	£7.50
3	Magazines	£1.00
4	CDs	£2.00
5	Going out	£4.00
6	Revision Guides	£6.00

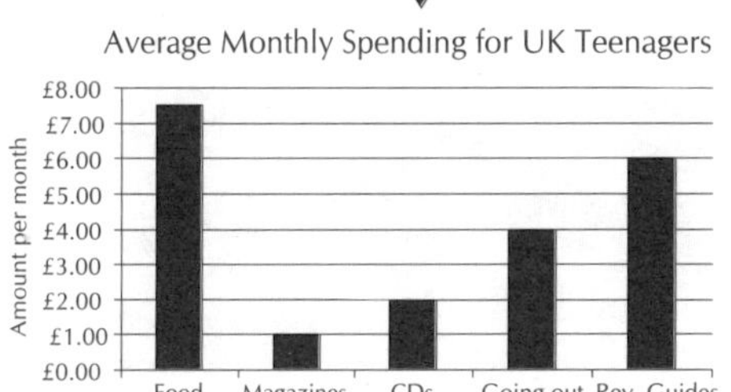

When you find a table, 'look up' and you'll learn something useful

Two tricky things on this page. Knowing about the stuff on this page can get you valuable extra marks in the exam. Make sure you can explain how look-up tables work and how to do charts.

Spreadsheets

*You need to know which charts are **Appropriate***

Spreadsheets can create so many different types of graph — but you need to choose the right kind. Sometimes it's just a matter of taste, but sometimes there are definite rights and wrongs.

1) **BAR GRAPHS display a category on the x-axis and a value on the y-axis. Use a bar graph when each category is discrete (i.e. separate from the others) — e.g. the number of people who take certain shoe sizes.**

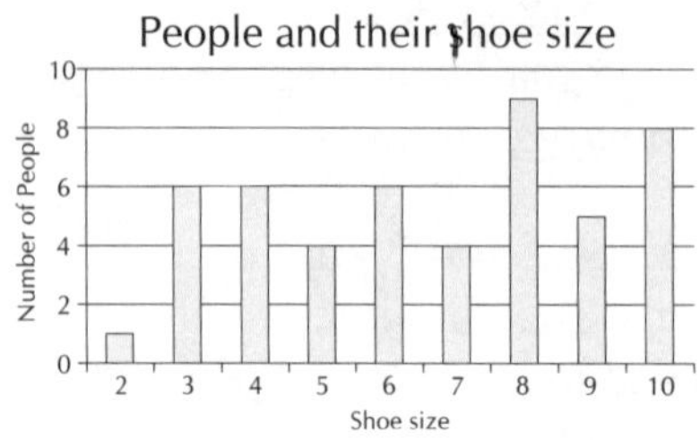

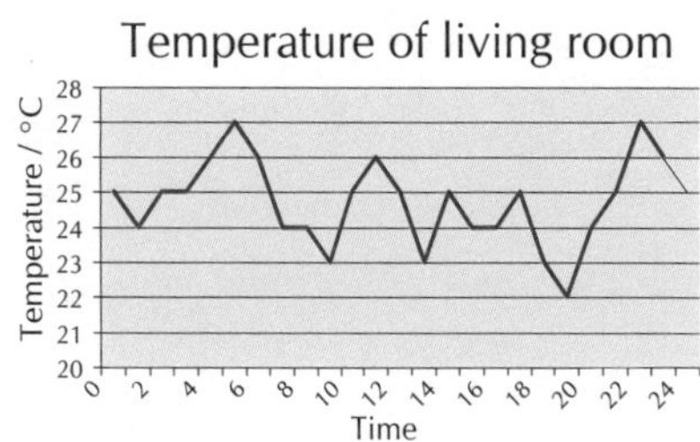

2) **LINE GRAPHS are similar, but are used when the data on the x-axis isn't in categories — like 'time' when you show the temperature of a room over a 24-hour period.**

3) **SCATTER GRAPHS show the relationship between two sets of data — plot one set along the x-axis and one set on the y-axis, and add a trend line to show the relationship more clearly.**

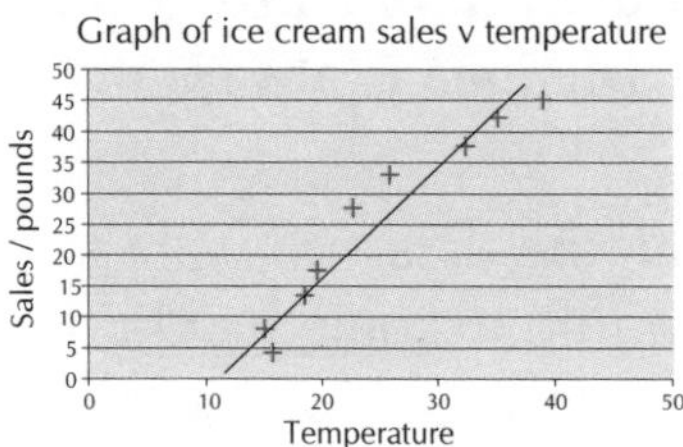

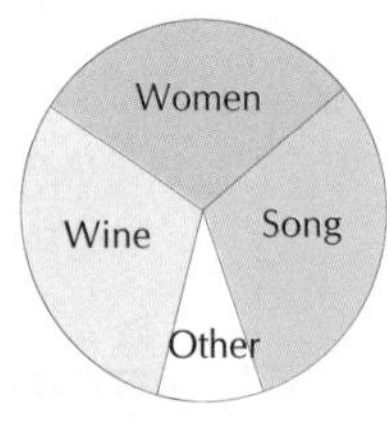

4) **PIE CHARTS show the contributions of categories to a total — e.g. a chart showing what I spend my money on.**

It's tempting to try to be too clever and use impressive graphs that aren't really any clearer than something basic. Again the golden rule is keep it SIMPLE — make sure the graph gets its point across and, if possible, test your graph by showing it to an intended user.

I used to have a pi chart but it just went on forever

Make a table with headings for 'type of chart', 'what it is' and 'when to use it' then fill it in. That's the best way revise the information that's on this page.

Warm-Up and Worked Exam Questions

So that's spreadsheets. Time to take a breather and check you know it all. The usual drill — some quick easy questions, a nice worked example, then some exam questions for you to try.

Warm-up Questions

1) Name three types of data that can be stored in a cell.
2) What do the initials CSV stand for?
3) What is meant by importing data?
4) What is a spreadsheet formula?
5) What type of graph would you use to show how the temperature of a swimming pool varies during a day?
6) What's the difference between a relative and absolute cell reference?

Worked Exam Question

Look — an exam question — with the answers helpfully written in. It must be your birthday.

1 Oaklands School tuck shop keeps a record of sales items on a spreadsheet. Part of this spreadsheet is shown below and the amount of money taken for each item is calculated using a formula.

	A	B	C	D
1	Tuck Shop Sales			
2	Item	Sales	Cost	Amount
3	Apples	16	£0.10	£1.60
4	Chocolate bars	35	£0.40	
5	Cream eggs	23	£0.40	
6	Crisps	23	£0.35	
7	Peanut bars	32	£0.40	
8	TOTAL			

(a) What formula has been entered in cell D3?

*Formula is = B3 * C3*

*Remember * for multiply, / for divide...* *(1 mark)*

(b) What is the most efficient way of entering the formulas in cells D4, D5, D6 and D7?

Copy cell D3, highlight cells D4 to D7 and paste.

There are other variations depending on the spreadsheet package used e.g. highlight cell D3 and fill down into cells D4 to D7. *(1 mark)*

(c) The cell D8 could be given the formula D3 + D4 + D5 + D6 + D7.
Suggest a better formula to enter for this cell.

SUM (D3:D7)

(2 marks)

SUM is about the most simple of the functions, so you should definitely know about it. You should also learn some of the others like Max, Average, Count and all those logic ones. The best way is to have a play with them when you're on a computer.

Exam Questions

1 Hightown Drama Club are putting on their annual production and selling tickets for the five performances of their play. A spreadsheet is used to keep a record of ticket sales and this is shown opposite.

	A	B	C
1		Ticket Sales	
2	Ticket Cost	£2.50	
3			
4	**Day**	**Number of tickets sold**	**Total**
5	Monday	101	£252.50
6	Tuesday	120	
7	Wednesday	105	
8	Thursday	98	
9	Friday	120	
10	Total		
11	Average		

(a) The formula B5 * B2 is entered in cell C5 to calculate the total sales (in pounds) for Monday night. However when this formula was copied and pasted into cell C6 it gave a value of £0.00.

(i) Explain why this happens.

....

(1 mark)

(ii) How would you change the formula in cell C5 so that when it was copied it gave the correct answer?

....

(1 mark)

(b) The organisers are interested in how the number of tickets sold varies from night to night and wish to see the data in a chart. What type of chart would be most suitable and why?

....

(2 marks)

2 Miss Keeley is a Maths teacher and she keeps a record of the examination marks for her class on a spreadsheet. Part of this is shown. A logic function is used in column C to work out whether the pupil has passed or failed the exam. The pass mark is given in cell B2. The formula in cell C4 is IF(B4>50, "pass", "fail").

	A	B	C
1		**Marks in Exam**	
2	Pass mark	50	
3	**Name**	**Mark**	**Grade**
4	Chloe	56	pass
5	Davina	76	
6	John	45	
7	Patel	49	
8	Sam	95	

(a) Explain in your own words, how this formula works out if a pupil has passed or failed.

....

(2 marks)

(b) The pass mark can change, so the formula in cell C4 needs to be changed so that it automatically takes this into account. It also needs to be copied into cells C4 to C8. What should the formula in cell C4 be?

....

(2 marks)

Here is a bonus question for those with really good eyesight: (Got a bit short of space on this page...)

3 A travel agent has details of average temperatures in January and July for various cities around the world. The data is stored in a spreadsheet and an extract is shown. Suggest three ways in which the appearance of this spreadsheet could be improved.

	A	B	C
1		Weather	
2	City	Temp (Jan)	Temp (July)
3	Sydney	23	12
4	Cape Town	24	16
5	London	10	21
6	Moscow	-5	25
7	New York	4	28

....

(3 marks)

Databases

Some of the basic stuff about databases was covered on pages 43 and 44.
You might want to re-read those pages before tackling this one.

A Database is a **Store of Data**

1) A database is an organised collection of data.

2) Use a database when you need to store lots of data.

In this table, each column is a different field... Key field

.. and each row is a record.

Item of data

First Name	Last Name	Department	Payment Number	Date of Birth	Salary	Favourite Fruit
Doug	Witherspoon	Catering	100345	26/09/64	£19,000	Peach
Neil	Beforem	Customer Service	100346	12/08/76	£15,000	Banana
Anita	Dear	Marketing	100347	23/05/83	£18,000	Passion Fruit
Phil	Ordabuk	Sales	100348	30/03/77	£17,000	Strawberries
Bill	O'Verdue	Finance	100349	22/05/79	£15,000	Banana
Stan	D'Alday	Porter	100350	06/11/80	£8,000	Guava

3) Data is organised into fields and records. The key field contains an item of data that is unique to that record — so no records have the same value in the key field. Here, the payment number is the key field.

4) The big benefit of databases is that you can search them quickly to find specific data, or use them to generate reports — e.g. which books in a publisher's database have sold the most.

Well-Structured **Fields** are Very Important

1) The first step in creating a database is to decide on what fields you need. Then each field needs a name, a description of its contents, a data type and a format.

2) The data type is dead important, as different processes can be performed on different types of data. The most common data types are in the box — most programs allow others.

TEXT e.g. Banana
INTEGERS i.e. whole numbers such as 25
REAL NUMBERS e.g. 25.67
DATES e.g. 26-09-82 or 26/09/82

3) One way to reduce the file size of the database is to use coding — e.g. use 'M' and 'F' for gender instead of 'male' and 'female'. This uses fewer characters and so takes up less memory.

Databases need to be learnt — that's the bottom line

Databases are probably the dullest part of the ICT syllabus, but you have to learn how to use them. Learn what a key field is and make sure you understand why it's useful to know about.

Databases

Databases can be *Flat-File* or *Relational*

Flat-file Databases

1) Flat-file databases are the ones normally used in GCSE ICT coursework.
2) All the data's organised into one table, which can be viewed by opening one data file.
3) Flat-file databases can be created using all database programs and most spreadsheets.

Relational Databases

1) Relational databases store the data in separate tables and files.
2) All the data's linked together by key fields and a database management system (DBMS).
3) The DBMS also controls who can access what — e.g. a firm's customers might be allowed access to information about a firm's products, but not the cost of making them.
4) Relational databases are used a lot in large organisations.
5) A good piece of GCSE coursework might use a simple relational database.

As well as knowing how to create a database you need to know how to interrogate one. Make sure you learn all the main methods explained on these two pages.

Database Records can be *Sorted*...

1) A sort is the simplest process you can do with a database. You choose a field, and the records are then sorted into order using the entries in that field.

First name	Last name	Team	Value
Boris	Batley	Blood and Thunder	£60
Basher	Best	Workington Warriors	£40
Freddy	Beech	Joshy's Giants	£15
Knuckles	Borissov	Higgie's Hairy Men	£5
Smasher	Bentley	Burton's Brigade	£3.50

These Fantasy Tiddlywinks League players are sorted in order of transfer value — most valuable first.

2) Sorts can be done using text fields and numerical fields. With text fields, the entries are sorted into alphabetical order by giving all the letters a numerical value (e.g. A = 1, B = 2, ... Z = 26).

3) Sorts can either be in ascending order (with the lowest value first), or descending order (with the highest value first).

Flat-file databases are the ones you're most likely to be using

Even though this is the case, it's still important for you to know the difference between a flat-file and a relational database. You might need to use a simple one in your coursework.

Databases

...and Searched

1) A search is when the computer looks for data meeting certain conditions. To do this, you use a query — which is basically a list of the things you want the computer to look for.
2) Simple queries tell the database to look for records that meet just one condition.

SIMPLE QUERIES...

This could be to list all the records of players whose transfer value equals £40 — the query is:

Value = £40

=	**finds values equal to the amount specified.**
<	**finds values less than the amount specified.**
>	**finds values greater than the amount specified.**
<>	**finds values not equal to the amount specified.**
<=	**finds values less than or equal to the amount specified.**
>=	**finds values greater than or equal to the amount specified.**

3) It's also possible to do wildcard searches. These are where you only know part of the value to search for — maybe you can remember that a tiddlywinks player's last name begins with 'Be', but can't remember the full name.

WILDCARD SEARCHES...

Use * to stand for anything.
In the query

Last Name = "Be*"

the asterisk can stand for anything (or nothing).
So the results will include Best, Bentley and Beech, but not Batley or Boris.

4) You can also do complex searches — these are when you use AND, OR and NOT to find records that meet more than one condition.

COMPLEX SEARCHES...

These search for data meeting more than one condition. You might need to find all the tiddlywinks players called either Boris or Beryl. So your search criteria would be:

First Name = "Boris" OR "Beryl"

Or maybe you need to find players called Boris who also have a transfer value over £50. In this case the search is:

First Name = "Boris" AND Value > £50

Or maybe you're looking for people not called Boris whose transfer value is not over £20 (you never know...).
You could use:

NOT (First Name = "Boris") AND Value <= £20

Since CD-ROM encyclopedias and Internet search engines work like large databases, most of the ways of searching listed here can be used on them as well.

5) AND, OR and NOT are Boolean Logic operations.
They're used in expressions which can only be either true or false.

If you don't know your search criteria, you'll never find what you want

This page about search criteria is not very difficult. You probably know a bit of it already — but make sure you read and learn it all thoroughly. You don't want to miss anything out.

Databases

A report is the result of a database query that is intended to be seen by someone else.
Make sure you know about the different types of report possible, and their benefits and problems.

*Reports can be in **Record** or **Column Format***

Reports can either be screen-based or printed depending on what the user needs.

1) Record-format reports display each record of data completely separately. They're useful if you want to view each record on its own.

   This record format report has been designed to be used as a reminder slip to send to customers whose payments are overdue.

   You can format reports by using different font sizes, colours and so on. If the database format options are limited, you could export the data into a word processor or desktop publishing package where you have more options.

Mortgage Payment Reminder Notice

Name and Postal Address | **Account No.**

Yoda
Murky Swamp District
Dagobah System
MS5 6RP

07293

Date of Issue: 23 June 01

Amount due 26p

We have still not received payment of the amount shown above.
Please pay this bill immediately.
If you are having difficulty paying, call us on 1236329012.

Your hut may be at risk if you do not keep up with payments.
Offer subject to status. Terms and conditions apply. May the force be with you.

2) Column-format reports display the data in a big table, with all the information shown underneath the field headings. This is more useful if you're interested in comparing values in particular fields across different records.

Account No.	First Name	Date of Issue	Amount Due
07293	Yoda	23 June 01	26p
26438	Darth	4 May 01	13p
14472	Luke	23 April 01	68p
91772	Han	5 June 01	84p
02379	Obiwan	23 Dec 01	45p

Most database software lets you specify which fields will be displayed in the report.

3) The results of a database query can also be used to create mail-merged letters. For example, an optician could send reminder letters to all people on their database who have not had an eye test for over 12 months.

Mail merge is described on page 69.

4) Most database software will allow calculations to be performed on the data, and the results displayed as part of a report. For example, a publisher might use a database to store details about the weekly sales of books, with each week's sales in a separate field. The database could then add together the weekly sales for each book and display this on a report as Total Sales.

PROS OF DATABASES

1) They're a fast and efficient way of storing and accessing large volumes of data.
2) Much less storage space is required, compared to a paper based system, and data is less likely to get lost.
3) Searching for specific data is quicker and easier than using paper records.
4) It's easier to perform calculations and use the database to create other documents.

CONS OF DATABASES

1) Large databases require expensive computer hardware and software.
2) Users need to be trained in how to use them properly.

That's the database bit all finished now

Databases are on the syllabus and you need to learn about them. It's hard to summon up any enthusiasm, but it'll really help your exams and coursework if you know how to use them well.

Warm-Up and Worked Exam Questions

It's hard to get really excited about databases, but you're definitely going to get questions on them in your exam, so you might as well just get on and learn it. Starting with the WUQs...

Warm-up Questions

1) What is a database?
2) Name two data types that can be used to describe a field.
3) What is meant by a key field?
4) Why is coding used when storing some items of data?
5) What is meant by a "wildcard" search?
6) What is the difference between a flat-file database and a relational database?

Worked Exam Question

Take your time to really absorb everything in these questions. Practice really will make a big difference — exam questions always ask the same things, just in different ways.

1 Peynton School uses a database to store details of all the students in the school.

(a) Give four fields that could be used in this database.

student ID; surname; first name; student's form.

Or if you needed more... date of birth, address, emergency telephone number, year of entry...

(4 marks)

This is a very standard question — you should be armed with lots of examples, ready for the exam.

(b) Suggest four ways in which the school database might be used.

i) to contact parents or guardian in an emergency by finding the emergency telephone number from the database; ii) to print out form lists by searching for a particular form; iii) to send personalised letters home to parents using mail-merge; iv) to record daily attendance and calculate percentage attendance for the year.

(4 marks)

Remember, databases are just a big store of information about something (often people). So all you need to do is think of situations where you'd need to access bits of that information and what you'd do with it.

(c) Mrs Patterson wants to search the database to get the records of all the girls in form 2a. Write a query that could be used to extract the correct records.

Form = "2A" AND Sex = "F"

You're not told what the fields are, so you can just guess what they might be.

(2 marks)

To get the marks you need 2 separate conditions — one to find the correct form and one to get the correct gender, linked with a logic function. The exact syntax isn't so important — this varies from software to software.

Exam Questions

1 Viking Videos keeps details of all the videos for hire on a database, along with details of all the customers. They can then contact customers who have not returned videos.

(a) All the customer details are stored in a table.
Suggest a suitable key field for this table.

....

(1 mark)

(b) All the details of videos are stored in another table.
Suggest three fields that would be used in this table.

....

(3 marks)

(c) Is this database a flat-file or relational database? Give a reason for your answer.

....

(2 marks)

2 Downtown Garage keeps details of all cars for sale on a database so that the staff can search to find out if there are cars which fit the needs of particular customers. An extract is shown to the right.

Year	Type	Engine size (cc)	Colour	Mileage
2001	4X4	2200	Black	12000
2002	Estate	1600	Grey	14000
1999	4X4	2000	Red	34000
2000	Saloon	2000	Green	35000
1999	Estate	1600	Blue	40000
2000	Saloon	1800	Green	54000
2001	Mini	1200	Red	55000
1999	Estate	1700	Green	66000
1998	Hatchback	1400	Red	123000

(a) How many fields and how many records are shown?

....

(2 marks)

(b) On which field is the table sorted? Say whether it is ascending or descending order.

....

(2 marks)

(c) How many cars would the following searches find from the extract above?

(i) Colour = “Red” OR “Blue” .... cars

(ii) Colour = “Green” AND mileage < 60000. .... cars

(iii) NOT (Type = “4X4”) AND Year >= 2000. .... cars

(3 marks)

3 Jenny Smart owns an art gallery that sells paintings by local artists. At the moment she stores all the details about the paintings on paper, but she is considering storing it on a database. Give three advantages and one disadvantage to Jenny of using a database.

....

....

....

(4 marks)

Revision Summary for Section Six

You're used to revision summaries by now. This one is no different — all you've got to do is answer every one of these questions then check back to the section to see if you were right. If you get any wrong — just do them again. Off you go then.

1) What is the smallest part of a spreadsheet called?
   a) Sell b) Smell c) Cell
2) Which row is cell G14 in?
3) What is a text string?
4) How many different items of data should be entered into a single cell?
5) When creating a mail-merge data file — where should the field headings be put?
   a) In the first row b) In the second column c) Somewhere in Millom
6) Explain fully what conditional formatting is.
7) What does CSV stand for? Why is it useful?
8) What formula will Farmer Kevin put into cell B5?
9) Is C6 an absolute or a relative cell reference?
10) What does "absolute cell reference" mean?
11) What are logic functions?

	A	B
1	Cow	Selling price
2	Daisy	£48.26
3	Buttercup	£58.69
4	Boris	£2.50
5	Total income	

12) What does the function =IF(C2>£15,000,"No pay rise","Pay rise") mean?
13) Explain fully how a look-up table works.
14) List three things that should be found in any graph.
15) Explain the difference between a bar graph and a line graph.
16) The types of graph and the examples in the box below have been jumbled up. Put them back into matching pairs.

Pie Chart	Relationship between age and number of teeth
Line Graph	Goals scored by each player in a netball team
Bar chart	Average daily temperature in Millom
Scatter Graph	Number of vampires with particular shoe sizes

17) What is a database?
18) What is a key field?
19) What might be the key field in a database listing information about different books?
20) What's the difference between an integer and a real number?
21) Give one benefit of entering an item of data using a short code rather than in full.
22) Explain the difference between a flat-file and a relational database.
23) Who will appear at the top of a list sorted in descending order of Last Name — Alice Zybrynski or Zack Alphonsus?
24) What's the difference between > and <>?
25) What is a wildcard search? How could one be used to search for all people whose last name begins McD?
26) What is Boolean logic? How can it be used to generate complex searches?
27) What are the two main ways of setting out a report? How are they different?
28) Explain three benefits and one problem of using databases.

Measurement and Control

This section is about different ways of recording, responding to and controlling events, either in the real world or in a model of it. Even if you have not had a chance to carry out this sort of ICT in your school, make sure you learn it because it's in the exam.

Data Logging means Recording Data Automatically

1) Data logging means capturing and storing information using sensors.
2) The information is first stored as data, and then downloaded into a computer package for analysis.
3) Data logging is best used whenever large amounts of data need to be collected over very long or short periods of time, or from hostile environments.
4) Examples of data logging activities include collecting weather data via satellite, radioactivity data from nuclear power stations, and temperature data from inside a pizza oven.

Data Logging needs the Right Hardware and Software

1) Data is collected by an input sensor. Most sensors work by converting environmental signals into electrical energy — producing either an analogue or a digital signal.

Sensors are often used to measure...
Light: Light-dependent resistors are used to determine when to switch street lights on.
Radioactivity: Geiger counters measure the amount of radioactivity in an object.
Temperature: Thermistors can be used to control an air-conditioning system.
Sound: Sensors can be used to check that aircraft noise keeps within agreed levels.
Pressure: Pressure pads are used in burglar alarms to detect unwanted visitors.
Infra-red: A sensor can detect a break in an infra-red beam.
Air pressure: Sensors can be used to control emergency oxygen masks on aircraft.

Data Logging will certainly be in your exam

You have to learn all of this section very thoroughly, because it's something that you might not have been able to cover much in school. Learn all the different types of data logging.

Measurement and Control

2) A pressure pad at a set of traffic lights produces a signal whenever a vehicle passes over it. This is a digital sensor since it's either on or off.
3) A thermistor is a resistor whose resistance changes with temperature — the hotter the thermistor, the more easily electricity flows through it. Output from a thermistor can take a range of values — it's an analogue signal.

Digital v Analogue	
Analogue:	An analogue signal can take any value in a certain range.
Digital:	A digital signal can only take certain values.

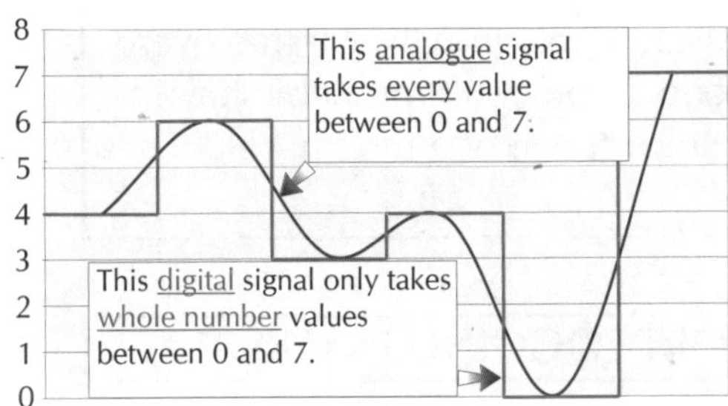

4) Before an analogue signal can be stored and downloaded onto a computer system, it needs to be converted into a digital signal — using an analogue-to-digital converter (ADC).
5) An ADC is often part of the interface board (the device that lets you connect the sensor to the computer).
6) Once the output's been converted into digital data, it's often stored in CSV (comma-separated variable) format. This means that it can be exported into a spreadsheet for data analysis. The output from this analysis can be screen-based or paper-based, and will probably include graphs.

Choose an Appropriate **Logging Period**

1) The logging period is the total length of time you're going to collect data for. If this is too long, you can waste valuable time. But if it's too short, you might miss some important data.
2) The logging period depends on the thing that's being monitored. For example, an experiment to investigate the cooling of a cup of coffee should not take measurements over a two-year period — one hour would be better.
3) If you're not sure what logging period to use, do some preliminary research — for example, leave a cup of coffee to cool and see roughly how long it takes.

Converting analogue to digital — easy as ADC

This stuff isn't the most exciting stuff you'll ever learn, but you're guaranteed to get a question or two on it in the exam. So do the decent thing, and learn it well. You know it's right.

Measurement and Control

This stuff's just common sense — but that doesn't mean you don't have to bother learning it. Make sure you know how to decide on a suitable logging period and logging interval.

You Also Need a Decent **Logging Interval**

1) The logging interval is the time between one measurement and the next.
2) As a general rule, the longer the logging period, the longer the logging interval can be.
3) Once you've decided on a logging period and logging interval, you can work out the number of readings you'll have — be careful not to make this too small.

USE A LONG LOGGING INTERVAL...

If you're measuring the growth of a tree over a two-year period, you could probably have a logging interval of a month.

USE A SHORT LOGGING INTERVAL...

On the other hand, measuring the temperature of a chemical reaction which lasts only a couple of seconds might require a logging interval of a fraction of a second.

$$\text{Number of readings} = \frac{\text{Logging period}}{\text{Logging interval}}$$

Data Logging has Four **Benefits**

1) Data logging can record information in places where humans find it hard to operate — e.g. the bottom of the sea, outer space, and inside nuclear reactors or pizza ovens.
2) Data can be collected over very long or very short periods — you could record the growth rate of a tree, or the changing temperature of a melting ice cube.
3) Intervals between measurements can be more accurate than when a human's doing the measuring — for example, a temperature reading taken every 27 seconds will be exactly that.
4) Data loggers don't need tea breaks, lunch breaks or sleep.

Sometimes data logging is better done by machines

There are more examples of this. Think some up for yourself. Volcanos are a good example — scientists don't have to risk their lives taking readings as machines can do it for them.

Measurement and Control

Control Systems are Dedicated or Computer-Controlled

A control system is a system of hardware and software that's used to control the operation of a piece of equipment. There are two main types of control system.

1) Dedicated control systems are basic systems that carry out a pre-programmed set of instructions, e.g. a traffic-light system where the lights change at fixed time intervals.
2) Computer-controlled systems use a computer to control the output device, and this computer can be connected to a sensor — making the system more flexible. These are used in traffic-light systems where the time between changes needs to alter depending on the volume of traffic.

Most Computer Control Systems use Feedback Loops

1) A feedback loop is when information from a sensor is used to control the output of a device. The sensor is sometimes in a different place from the output device. For example, in central heating, input from a thermostat (the sensor) is used to control the output of the radiators.
2) Sometimes the feedback data comes from a sensor attached to the output device itself.

E.g. a robot used to check for leaks inside a sewerage system will send data about its position inside the sewer to a computer, which then uses it to guide the robot's forward movement.

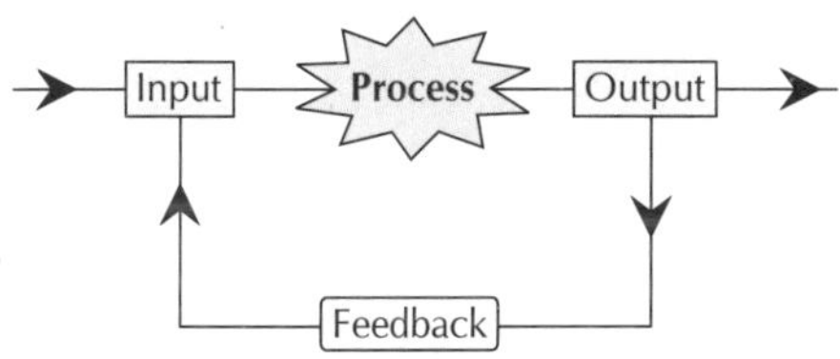

Computer Control Systems need Hardware and Software

1) Sensors are connected to the computer via an interface such as an analogue-to-digital converter (an ADC), or a control board (also called an interface board). This allows the two devices to communicate with each other.
2) The computer then processes the data according to a set of instructions.
3) The output signal from the computer is then sent to the output device. The output will be a digital signal but the output device might only operate using analogue signals — so an output interface containing a digital-to-analogue converter (DAC) might be needed.
4) The output device used will depend on the specific task — but could include a switch or a motor.

E.g. — making a lamp brighter or dimmer depending on how much natural light there is:

1) A light-dependent resistor is used as the sensor.
2) As less and less light falls on it, its resistance increases.
3) The changing resistance affects a voltage, which is an analogue signal.

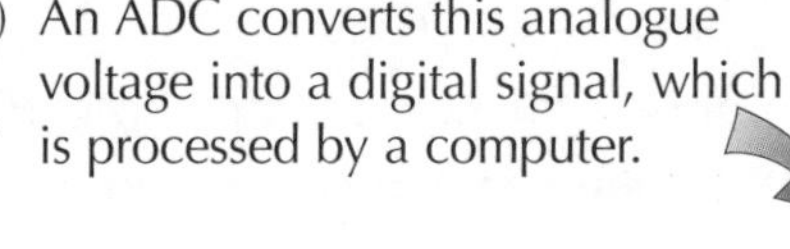

4) An ADC converts this analogue voltage into a digital signal, which is processed by a computer.

5) The computer's digital output passes through a DAC.
6) The DAC converts the digital output to an analogue voltage.
7) This analogue voltage determines the brightness of the lights.

Sensors need to be learnt

Once you've passed your exam, you can forget lots of these things. But — imagine what a nightmare it would be to fail and have to resit and revise all this again. Don't fail. Learn it now.

Measurement and Control

The two examples of control systems on this page should prepare you for the different types you might get asked about in the exam. There are some other examples in Section 9.

Greenhouses Control Environmental Conditions

1) In this diagram of a control system, a heater is controlled by the computer in response to readings from a temperature sensor.
2) When the temperature falls below a certain level, the computer sends a signal to the interface board to switch on the heater. When the desired temperature is reached, the heater is switched off — this is an example of a feedback loop.

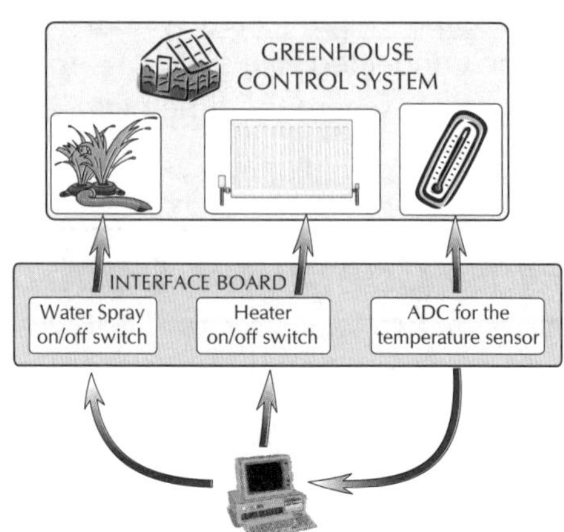

3) The water spray is controlled by a simple timer — once the timings have been programmed into the computer, the water spray will be switched on and off at regular intervals.
4) The water spray could be controlled using a feedback loop from a humidity sensor in the soil — but this would make the system more expensive. Other things that could be controlled include opening and closing windows, and the feeding of nutrients to the plants.
5) Fully automated systems are very expensive, so only large greenhouses will have them.

Robots are Usually Computer-Controlled

1) A robot is an automated piece of equipment designed to carry out routine repetitive tasks.
2) Simple robots are designed to carry out a pre-programmed set of operations — like spraying paint onto the bonnet of a car on an assembly line. There are two different ways to develop these instructions:

① The Teach-And-Learn Method

a) The programmer writes a set of instructions.
b) The robot is observed as it carries these instructions out.
c) The instructions are improved if necessary.

② The Do-It-Once-And-Remember-It Method

a) The robot is guided through the correct movements.
b) It then automatically produces the correct programming instructions to carry out the task.

3) Robots without feedback systems are a potential safety hazard — if a robot can't detect that someone's walked in front of the bonnet, the person ends up getting sprayed, not the bonnet.
4) Robots can be programmed to carry out a number of different tasks. E.g., a robot could be programmed with different instructions so it can spray different-shaped car bonnets.

Robots

a) are cheaper to operate than paying people wages,
b) don't get tired or make mistakes,
c) carry out tasks that humans can't or won't perform.

Robots
a) can't think for themselves, and so can't respond to new situations as well as humans can,
b) are very expensive to buy.

Robots need feedback systems to work well

The best thing to do is to learn this page and scribble down two mini-essays all about the joys of greenhouses and robots. As with all of this book, you have to get into robot mode and L-E-A-R-N.

Measurement and Control

Process control is all about, well, controlling things. It could be something industrial, or it could be a small turtle that draws shapes on the screen.

Process Control *doesn't need Human Operators*

1) Process control means using sensors, computers and automated devices to control an industrial process. But people are still needed to check the computer works properly.
2) Processes in industry controlled this way include the mixing of paint, the flow of gas or water along a pipeline, and the production of paper and chocolate.
3) Like many other computerised systems, process control is potentially more efficient than humans, but requires precise programming and is very expensive to install.

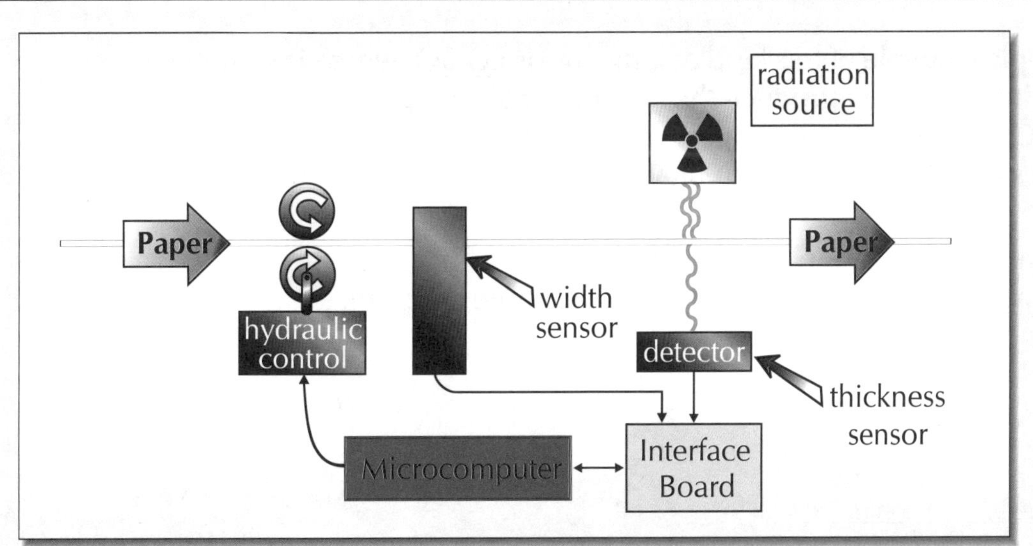

EXAMPLE

A paper manufacturer might use process control with radiation to make sure their paper is made to the correct thickness.

1) Radiation is directed towards the paper, but the amount that passes through will depend on how thick it is.
2) Sensors on the other side of the paper detect the amount of radiation getting through, and compare this with a 'target' figure in the computer's memory.
3) If the figure is too high or too low, the machine automatically adjusts itself to make the paper thicker or thinner. This is an example of a feedback loop.

At the end of the day, humans are still the cheapest labour around

Computer systems like process control are great in theory (and practice) — but they're generally just too expensive for people to be able to buy and install.

Measurement and Control

The Simplest Control Language is LOGO

1) Devices are controlled using special programming languages.

> **PROGRAMS AND LANGUAGES**
>
> A program is a sequence of instructions that a computer can carry out.
>
> A programming language is basically the list of commands that the computer will accept.
>
> Programs are eventually translated into machine code — the sequence of 0s and 1s that the computer understands. This is usually done automatically.

2) A simple example of this kind of language is LOGO, which is sometimes used in schools to introduce the idea of control programs. You can use LOGO to move a turtle on a computer screen — and the trace of the turtle's movements is used to draw an object such as a shape or a letter.

3) You might get asked in the Exam to list some of the simple commands used in LOGO, or to write a simple program. So have a look at this lot...

Some LOGO commands:

FORWARD X Move turtle forward X units

BACKWARD X Move turtle backward X units

LEFT X Rotate turtle X degrees to the left

RIGHT X Rotate turtle X degrees to the right

REPEAT n (Y) Repeat instruction Y, n times

PEN UP Stop drawing a trace

PEN DOWN Start drawing a trace

A simple sample LOGO Program:

```
PEN DOWN
FORWARD 40
REPEAT 3 (RIGHT 90 FORWARD 20)
LEFT 45
FORWARD 14
PEN UP
```

Learn about LOGO — but check with your teacher FIRST...

Luckily (for some at any rate), not all syllabuses need you to know LOGO commands, so it's probably worth asking your teacher before you start learning them all. Think of the fun you can have with a turtle that draws things — everlasting joy, surely.

Warm-Up and Worked Exam Questions

You <u>will</u> get a question on data-logging in the exam. Of that there is little doubt. Probably a big one too. There's some practice questions here. You know what you have to do.

Warm-up Questions

1) What is data logging?
2) Name three types of sensors used for data logging.
3) What is the difference between an analogue signal and a digital signal?
4) What is meant by the logging interval?
5) What do the initials ADC stand for?
6) What is meant by a feedback loop?

Now, the exam questions. When you've been through enough of these, you'll get used to the format and they'll start looking a lot friendlier.

Worked Exam Question

1 Wheels and Co is a company that makes cars. At the moment, all the work is done with manually-operated machines, but the management are thinking of using robots instead.

(a) Give four advantages to the company of using robots.

i) Robots are cheaper to operate than paying people wages; ii) robots do not make mistakes; iii) robots can carry out tasks that humans cannot perform; iv) robots can work continuously without a break.

(4 marks)

(b) Give three disadvantages of using robots.

i) robots are very expensive; ii) robots need to be programmed to carry out tasks; iii) robots cannot think for themselves and cannot respond to new and different situations.

(3 marks)

Even though this question is set in a specific context, the answers are just all the standard robot issues.

You need to be careful — sometimes questions will expect you to answer more specifically in the context. But this time, the standard robot things work just fine...

Exam Questions

1 Greenfingers garden centre are going to use a computer-controlled system in their greenhouses to make sure that the plants are kept at the right temperature. A heater is used to heat the greenhouse and this can be switched on and off by the computer.

(a) Name a sensor that could be used in this situation and state, with reasons, whether it is an analogue or digital sensor.

....

....

(3 marks)

(b) Explain how the system would work, outlining the steps involved.

....

....

....

(3 marks)

(c) Give the name of another sensor that could be used to control when the plants needed watering using a water spray.

....

(1 mark)

2 Dollywaggle school are setting up an automatic weather station which will record the outdoor temperature at regular intervals using a data logging system.

(a) Name three items of hardware that are needed for this system.

....

(3 marks)

(b) Give two advantages of using data logging compared to using pupils to measure and record temperatures.

....

....

(2 marks)

(c) How could the temperature readings be analysed to produce a graph showing changes of temperature during a day?

....

(1 marks)

3 A simple LOGO program to draw a shape on the screen is shown below. Sketch the result, giving the length of each line. It does not have to be drawn to scale.

```
PEN DOWN
FORWARD 50
REPEAT 4 (LEFT 90 FORWARD 30)
PEN UP
```

(3 marks)

Models and Simulations

Modelling and simulating usually crop up at least once in a GCSE ICT exam.
They're related, but subtly different, so get your head around this before you move on.

A **Simulation** is carried out **Using a Model**

1) A model is an artificial re-creation of an object or phenomenon, and should behave in the same way as the real thing — e.g. a model of a sports car built for testing in a wind tunnel.
2) A simulation is when the model is used to carry out an activity that mimics real life — like when bridge designers use a model to simulate what'll happen when the bridge is actually used.
3) A computer model is created using programmed instructions and equations. An example would be a computer model of the way an aircraft behaves when in flight.

Limitations of Modelling

1) Any model or simulation is only as good as the rules, programs and equations it's based on.
2) It's important to test the model, using situations where the actual results are known.
3) In this way the model and simulation can be improved.

There are **Four Main Types** of Computer Model

1) Simple models can be made using a spreadsheet, where equations are used to build the model.
2) Computer-aided design (CAD) is used to create a graphical image of an object, based on data fed into the package by the user. CAD is covered on page 75.
3) Virtual reality (VR) aims to give the user a more complete experience. The user might experience noise, movement and views (using a special visor) similar to what would happen in the real thing. Virtual reality models tend to be large and complex.
4) Expert systems model the knowledge of a human expert. They contain a 'knowledge bank' of data about a particular subject, as well as a set of instructions for processing the knowledge. The idea is that the computer asks the user a series of questions, with the answer to each question helping to determine what the next question should be. Eventually the computer has enough information to suggest a solution to the problem. Expert systems can be used to give advice about illnesses that match certain symptoms, or advice on tax/welfare benefits etc.

Some people call an expert system an IKBS — Intelligent (or Information) Knowledge Based System.

The Ups

1) Dangerous events can be studied, e.g. the effect of a nuclear explosion.
2) The model can be used to make predictions, e.g. the speed at which a car loses control on a bend.
3) Running a simulation may be cheaper than using the real thing, e.g. crashing a car.

The Downs

1) The model might not be an accurate representation of the real world — so the simulation might give misleading results.
2) Producing an effective model might be time-consuming — and running the simulation might require expensive hardware and software, like with virtual reality.

Learn the ups and downs of modelling

To simulate being in an exam, you could write down an explanation of how models and simulations are different, and the advantages and disadvantages of using them.

Models and Simulations

You could get asked about any kind of model or simulation in the exam. But, boring as they are, spreadsheets come up more often than the others. You have been warned.

***Three Reasons** why Spreadsheets make Good Models*

1) Spreadsheets use formulas to try to describe the rules that a real-world phenomenon seems to follow. Input values can then be processed using these formulas to produce output values.
2) Spreadsheets can be used to carry out a what-if analysis. This is when the user changes input values to see the effect on the output of the model. So companies can ask a question like, "What would be the effect on profits if I invested this much money on new machinery?"
3) The output can be in the form of graphs and charts to make the predictions of the model easier to understand.

*Example 1 — **Queues** in a School Canteen*

1) A school canteen manager could build a model to represent the relationship between the number of pupils wanting to eat in the canteen, the number of staff and the queuing time.
2) The model could be used to find out the number of staff needed to keep waiting times to a minimum. Taking this one step further, it could be used to find out the minimum number of staff needed to serve all meals in less than an hour.
3) The formula in cell B5 is =B1*(B3/60)/B2. This says the total time needed for one person to serve all the pupils is equal to the number of pupils multiplied by the time taken to serve each pupil. This is then divided by the number of staff to find how long it takes for everyone to be served, using four people. The assumption is that two people can serve a meal twice as quickly as one person.
4) A weakness of the model is that the assumption about serving times is questionable — the time saved by having extra serving staff may not be this simple. The model also assumes that serving staff can be added forever — but having 100 serving staff would create obvious problems.

	A	B
1	Number of pupils	600
2	Number of staff	4
3	Average time to serve a meal (seconds)	20
4		
5	Total serving time (minutes)	50

*Example 2 — **Profitable** Pizzas*

1) A pizza business could build a model to show its profit from selling pizzas. The owner enters data into cells B1 to B4, then the model calculates the data in cells B5 to B7.
2) The firm could then change any of these variables to see the impact of these changes on its profit — e.g. the effect a reduction in sales to 400 and an increase in production costs of 50p per pizza would have on profits.
3) This could be extended to give a direct link between the price of pizzas and the number sold.

	A	B
1	Production cost per pizza	£2.00
2	Other business costs	£1,000
3	Selling price per pizza	£6.00
4	Number of pizzas sold	500
5	Total costs	£2,000
6	Total profit	£1,000
7	Profit per pizza	£2.00

=B2+(B1*B4)

=(B3*B4)-B5

=B6/B4

Watch out for weaknesses in your models

Spreadsheets are quite useful, once you understand how they work. If you find yourself struggling with them, go back and have a look at Section 6 — there's more explanation there.

Models and Simulations

Flight simulators are the opposite of simple spreadsheet models. They aim to simulate, as closely as possible, the experience of being a pilot in a real aircraft.

***Flight Simulators** are Just Like the Real Thing*

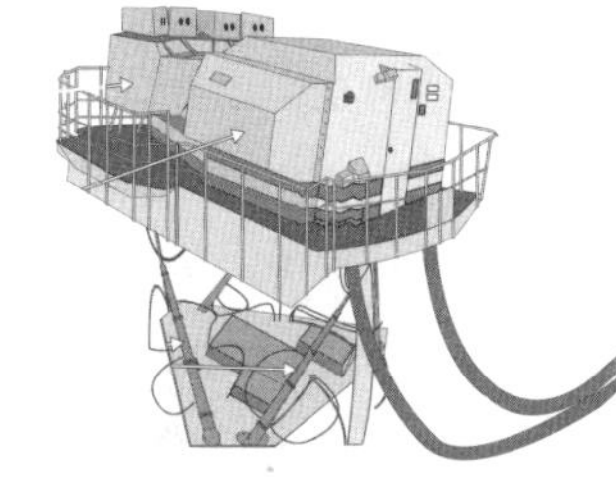

1) Flight simulators were developed to simulate the experience of flying a large jet aircraft — without the risk of a real plane crash. They're used to train pilots, and are built around a full-scale model of a cockpit.
2) Instead of windows there are high resolution computer screens that display computer-generated images. The images work in real time — meaning they respond exactly to the cockpit controls.

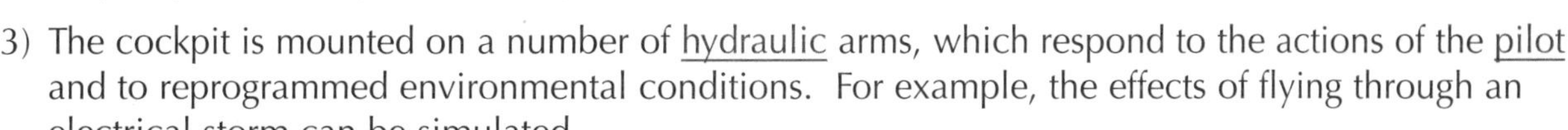

3) The cockpit is mounted on a number of hydraulic arms, which respond to the actions of the pilot and to reprogrammed environmental conditions. For example, the effects of flying through an electrical storm can be simulated.
4) The cockpit can be a closed environment — allowing things like cabin pressure and light levels to be as they would in reality. This means that some of the effects of a cabin fire can be simulated.
5) The system makes use of feedback loops. When the pilot alters the controls, signals are input into the computer, which then changes the output of the simulation, e.g. the image screens, hydraulic arms and cockpit environment controls.

Computer Monitor (where window should be — to make it *look* real).

Full-size cockpit (Made out inside to look and respond like a real flight deck — to make it *seem* real.)

Hydraulic Pistons which control the elevation and physical position of the simulator's cockpit. They help make the simulation *feel* as real as possible.

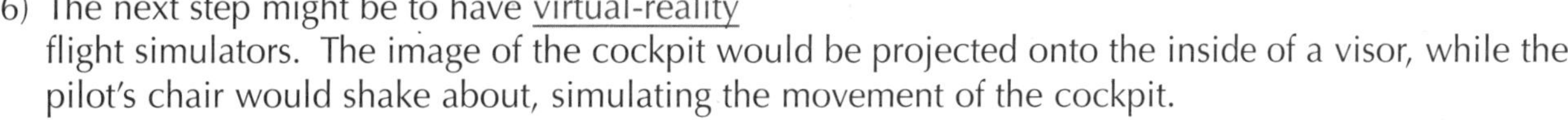

6) The next step might be to have virtual-reality flight simulators. The image of the cockpit would be projected onto the inside of a visor, while the pilot's chair would shake about, simulating the movement of the cockpit.

*Using a Simulator has **Four Advantages***

1) Flight simulators are much safer than teaching a pilot to fly in a real plane. After a 'crash landing', the pilot can simply begin again.
2) Flight simulators, despite being very expensive, are cheaper than flying a real aircraft.
3) They can carry images of many different airports — so they can train pilots to land in different conditions all over the world.
4) Pilots can still train even when the weather is too bad to take off and land a real plane.

Flight simulators are also available as computer games. The image quality can be good, but viewing it on a small computer screen is not as realistic.

Flight simulators are complex but the idea behind them is simple

There are four main features — real-time images, hydraulic arms, a closed environment and feedback loops. Learn these, and what effect each one of them has on the final experience.

Warm-Up and Worked Exam Questions

Take a deep breath and go through these warm-up questions one by one.
If you don't know these basic facts there's no way you'll cope with the exam questions.

Warm-up Questions

1) Explain the difference between a model and a simulation.
2) Name four types of computer model.
3) Give three benefits of using a flight simulation to train pilots.
4) What is meant by virtual reality?
5) Explain what is meant by a 'what-if' analysis.
6) Name the two parts of an expert system.

Worked Exam Question

I've gone through this exam question and written in answers, just like you'll do in the exam. How kind of me. Before you read the blue bits, try to answer them yourself.

1 The British Electricity Board have decided to make a computer model which simulates what might happen in the event of an accident at a nuclear power station.

(a) Give three possible advantages to the company of using this model.

i) the situation can be studied without putting anyone in danger; ii) the model can be used to find ways to minimise the danger of an accident and work out the best action to take in the event of an accident; iii) the conditions can be easily changed to see the causes and effects of different types of accident.

(3 marks)

This is a question where most of the answers are just general things you should know about simulations, but you have to look at them all in the context of the question.

(b) Give two possible disadvantages to the company of using it.

i) the model may not be a totally accurate representation of the situation and may give misleading results; ii) the model will be much simpler than real-life and will not take into account all factors; iii) if the model is to be effective it may take a very long time to produce.

(2 marks)

Remember the general points — Simulations are good for predicting what will happen, especially for things that you wouldn't want to test for real, and good for testing lots of different situations.

The drawbacks are they're not always accurate enough and can be expensive and time-consuming to produce.

Exam Questions

1 The Olympic Games organising committee aims to raise money by selling T-shirts with the Games logo shown on the back. The predicted sales results and profits are stored in a spreadsheet. Part of this is shown in Figure 1.

	A	B	C
1	T-shirt sales		
2	Month	Sales	Profit
3	April	250	£250.00
4	May	360	£360.00
5	June	350	£350.00
6	July	500	£500.00
7	August	210	£210.00
8			£1,670.00
9	Cost of making T-shirt £3.50		
10	Selling price of T-shirt £4.50		

Figure 1.

	A	B	C
1	T-shirt sales		
2	Month	Sales	Profit
3	April	250	£375.00
4	May	360	£540.00
5	June	350	£525.00
6	July	500	£750.00
7	August	210	£315.00
8			£2,505.00
9	Cost of making T-shirt £3.50		
10	Selling price of T-shirt £5.00		

Figure 2.

(a) What formula is stored in cell C3?

....

(2 marks)

(b) Using this model, the selling price of a T-shirt could be increased to £5 and the profit would increase to £2505. This is shown in Figure 2. However, this may not happen in real-life. Explain why.

....

(1 mark)

(c) What is the best way to show how the predicted monthly sales figures rise and fall over time?

....

(1 mark)

2 A flight simulator is used to train pilots to fly. Give three of the main features of this type of simulator and explain what effect each has on the final experience.

....

....

....

....

....

....

(6 marks)

Revision Summary for Section Seven

That's another section of this guide over. You'll already have a fair idea from the practice exam questions on how you're doing. Use this revision summary as a guide to the whole section, to work out whether you need to go back and study more of it or not. Keep doing the questions until you know the answers to all of them without having to look any up. The modelling and simulation bits are probably the most difficult. The rest should (hopefully) be fairly straightforward. Remember to check with your teacher whether you need to learn about LOGO or not.

1) Give a definition of data logging.
2) Explain how a thermistor works.
3) What do the initials ADC and DAC stand for and why are they needed?
4) What does CSV stand for? Why is it useful?
5) Explain the difference between a logging period and a logging interval.
6) Give three benefits of using data logging.
7) What are the two types of control called? How are they different?
8) What is a feedback loop? Explain how a feedback loop might work in a smoke alarm.
9) Name three sensors you might find in a greenhouse and explain what they might be used for.
10) Some buildings have automatic sprinkler systems that spray water in the event of a fire. Explain how sensors and output devices could be used in such a system.
11) Give three reasons why robots might be used in preference to human workers.
12) Give and explain two problems with robots.
13) What is process control? Give two examples of where it might be used.
14) Explain the difference between a programming language and machine code.
15) List four commands used in LOGO and explain what they mean.
16) Explain the difference between a model and a simulation.
17) What could make the difference between a good model and a bad model?
18) What are the two main parts of an expert system?
19) Explain how an expert system could be used to help pupils choose their GCSE subjects.
20) Explain two advantages and two disadvantages of using models and simulations.
21) Dave wants to use a spreadsheet to help him model the profits from his second-hand balloon business. Give one way he could do this.
22) What is "what-if" analysis? How could it be used to help model the effects of an increase in patients on waiting times at a doctor's surgery?
23) Explain fully how a flight simulator works.
24) Explain three benefits of using a flight simulator.

The Internet

The Internet — known by everyone. It's the biggest growth area in ICT at the moment, so you can expect to see it in the exam.

The *Internet* is an *International Network* of Computers

1) The Internet is basically a very big Wide Area Network (WAN).
2) The Internet was originally developed by the US Government to improve communication between its military computers. But it's since grown into what we all know today.

See page 6 for more about WANs.

To Connect you need *Special Hardware* and *Software*

1) Most people access the Internet using a PC connected to a normal telephone line. Computers are attached to a telephone line via another piece of kit called a modem — this converts digital computer signals into the analogue signals carried over telephone lines (and the other way round).
2) To connect to the Internet, you use your modem to dial up a computer owned by an Internet Service Provider (ISP) — these companies have computers permanently connected to the Internet. All the information sent from your PC goes via the ISP.
3) The two most important pieces of software you need are a web browser to display web pages, and an e-mail client, which transmits and receives e-mail from a PC.
4) Web browsers sometimes need plug-ins — extra little bits of software — before they can play certain types of multimedia files, like videos for example.

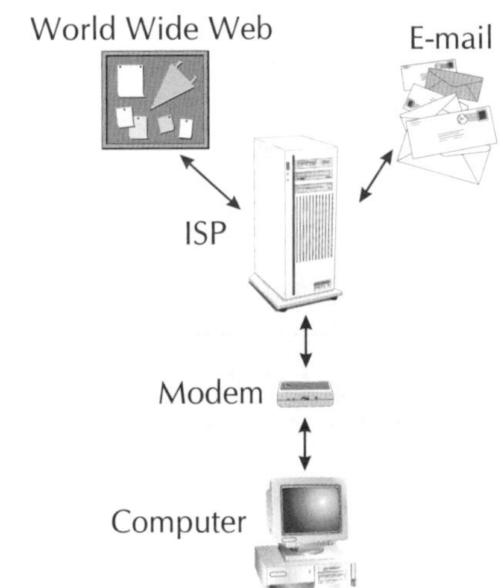

The Internet has *Two Main Parts*

1) The World Wide Web (WWW) is the part that contains web pages. It's like an incredibly large notice board — anything posted onto the Web can be read by anyone else (although you can restrict access to sites by using user IDs and passwords).
2) Electronic Mail (E-mail) is the part where messages are sent from one person to another — it works a bit like sending a letter.

People are already forgetting what life was like before the Internet

You probably know quite a lot about the Internet. It's still worth scrutinizing this section. There will be some things in it you didn't already know, and they'll get you marks in the exam.

The Internet

Speed of Access depends on Three Things

The speed of an Internet connection is measured in kilobytes per second — Kbps (i.e. how much data is transferred per second). Three things determine the speed of access:

1) **Modem Speed: Most PC modems work at either 28 Kbps or 56 Kbps (higher numbers usually mean faster connections), but the speed of the modem at the other end also matters.**

2) **The Telephone Line: Standard analogue lines are the slowest. But newer digital lines such as ISDN and ADSL speed up the transfer of data between the user and the ISP.**

3) **The Volume of Traffic: The more people using the Internet, the slower the speed of access. In the UK the Internet is slower in the afternoon because that's when it's morning in the USA — peak time for Internet use.**

You can also measure the speed of an Internet connection using the response time — the average time it takes for a remote computer to reply.

The WWW is enormous — so you need to know how to navigate your way around, which means knowing how web site addresses are structured and how to locate them.

Find Pages Using Search Engines and Portals

Search engines are web sites that help you search for other web sites.

1) **The basic type of search is a keyword search — you type in a keyword and the search engine lists a load of websites containing that keyword. Or you can do a complex search using more than one keyword and linking them together with AND and OR.**

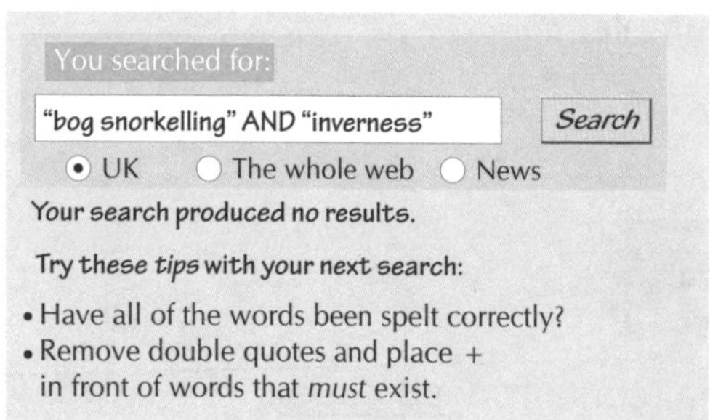

Most search engines work by storing details or keywords of different web sites. However, no single search engine will have data on every web site — so it's worth using more than one.

2) **Portals are web sites offering lots of different services — like search engines, e-mail, on-line shopping and so on. Originally, portals were dedicated to a particular theme (e.g. cheese, so all links were to sites about cheese) but they're usually more general nowadays.**

Portals can be useful, but they don't open doors to other dimensions

Don't assume that if you use the Internet there's nothing to learn here. Examiners want to know if you've got a detailed understanding of how it works. Learn all this stuff — properly.

The Internet

You Can Also Type in the URL

1) URL stands for Uniform Resource Locator — in other words, the address of a web page. They look a bit confusing at first — but they're easy enough once you get used to them.
2) URLs can't contain capital letters or spaces or certain types of punctuation. But some full stops, colons and slashes are necessary, and they have to be in exactly the right places.
3) Type URLs carefully — pretty obvious really — otherwise you'll either end up looking at the wrong web site, or more likely you'll get an error message.

Example: http://www.cgpbooks.co.uk/whatsnew.htm

This is the URL of the CGP "What's New" web page.

http	This stands for hypertext transfer protocol, which is the language the Web uses. You don't have to type it usually, as most web browsers add it automatically.
www	This means that it's a web site.
cgpbooks	This is the domain name — it's usually the name, nickname, initials etc. of the company, organisation, government department or whatever.
.co	This is the domain type — 'co' means the web site is run by or for a company.
.uk	This bit tells the computer that the web site is held on an ISP in the United kingdom.
/whatsnew	This tells the computer exactly which page within the cgpbooks.co.uk web site you're after.
.htm	The "htm" means the page is written in html (see page123).

Common country codes:

- uk – United Kingdom
- irl – Ireland
- fr – France
- de – Germany
- nz – New Zealand

The USA doesn't have a country code, which is a bit weird considering they invented the Internet in the first place. Just assume that if there's no country code in the web address, it's American.

Main domain types:

- com - business (mainly USA)
- co - business (non-USA)
- gov - government
- ac - university/academic
- sch - school
- net - general, often business
- org - other organisations e.g. charities

Make sure you learn all the URL details on this page

There's nothing hard to get your head round on this page, just lots of codes to learn. It's like a page of French vocab. Learn the parts of a URL, the country codes and the domain types.

The Internet

You can also find pages using hyperlinks and favourites / bookmarks. Even when you find a good page, it can take an eternity to download anything, which is where file compression comes in.

You can follow **Hyperlinks...**

Hyperlinks are the bits on a web page that you can click on to go somewhere else.

The pointer  changes to a hand when you hover over a hyperlink.

They're often coloured blue and underlined. They're usually displayed in a different colour (e.g. red) if you've followed them before.

1) Hyperlinks connect the different parts of the Web.
2) To the computer, they're an instruction to open a specified file, which is located along a particular path — to us, we click on a hyperlink and that's where we go next.
3) You can create them in other programs too, to link documents together, e.g. between two word-processed documents on an office network, or from a spreadsheet to a web site.

...or use your **Web Browser**

These are standard features of web browsers to help your Internet navigation:

BOOKMARKS
Browsers can save URLs you use often, so you don't have to type them — a feature called 'bookmarks' or 'favourites'.

If you want, you can save 'bookmarks' in groups, which makes it easier to find the one you want — e.g. you might want to put all your favourite cheese web sites together.

HISTORY
Browsers usually keep a list of all the web sites you've visited — this is called the history. If you want to revisit a web site, you can get the URL from the history list.

BACK and FORWARD buttons
If you've followed a series of hyperlinks but want to go back to a page you saw earlier, then the browser can 'retrace its steps', and go back one page at a time. And once you've gone backwards like this, you can also go forwards again.

Downloading Files can take **a Long Time**

1) Downloading web pages can take ages, especially if they've got lots of graphics. So the computer usually saves all web pages you view onto its hard drive. Then if you want to see a page again, the computer can use the version on disk rather than reload everything down the phone line. This store of temporary web pages is called a cache.
2) Other files like software updates or music files can be compressed to reduce their size, and this means they'll take less time to download. To actually use the file once you've downloaded it, you need to have the correct software to decompress it.

Don't assume you already know everything about the Internet

Just because you can buy t-shirts on-line, it doesn't mean that you know everything about the Internet. Learn everything in this mini-section and have a go at the practice questions.

Warm-Up and Worked Exam Questions

The Internet is a huge topic because it's a fairly recent thing and it's had such a big impact. You're bound to get a question on it. Don't assume that because you use the Internet, there's nothing you need to learn. Anyway, it's time to test yourself, starting with some easy questions...

Warm-up Questions

1) What is a hyperlink?
2) What do the initials ISP stand for?
3) Explain the difference between a search engine and a portal.
4) What is the purpose of a modem?
5) What is a 'cache' used for?
6) What do the initials URL stand for?

Now that you're warmed up, you're ready to gently ease yourself into some exam questions...

Worked Exam Questions

1 A local company wishes to be able to access the Internet to find out information about stock market prices.

(a) Name three items of hardware that will be required to do this.

i) computer (PC); ii) modem; iii) telephone line.

(3 marks)

(b) Name an item of software which will also be required.

a web browser

Other possible answers... e-mail client, plug-ins e.g. to play videos. *(1 mark)*

(c) Explain why the company will need to register with an Internet Service Provider (ISP).

The company's computer won't be able to access the internet directly. Their computer will need to connect to an ISP which will provide access to the internet through its server.

(2 marks)

2 Polly is able to access the Internet at home but sometimes finds that the connection is very slow.

(a) Name three things that could affect the speed of access to the Internet.

(i) The type of telephone connection, i.e. whether it is analogue or digital, (ii) modem speed, (iii) number of users accessing the Internet at the same time.

(3 marks)

(b) How could Polly access the Internet much faster?

Part a) gives the answer here...

Use a faster connection such as ADSL or Broadband.

...or a faster modem, or use the Internet when there's less traffic. *(1 mark)*

Exam Questions

1 Softsell is a company which has its own website where customers can buy software on-line. The address (URL) of this website is http://www.softsell.co.uk/home.htm.

Identify four parts of this URL and explain what each means.

(4 marks)

2 John regularly downloads music from a particular site on the World Wide Web. He finds it difficult to remember the address (URL) of this site so he uses the facilities of his web browser to help him. He is able to download the music fairly quickly because of the way that it is stored.

(a) Name two features of a web browser which would help John remember the address of the web site, explaining what each feature does.

Favorite and bookmark.

(4 marks)

(b) How can music files be organised and stored so that they take less time to download?

By compressing the files.

(1 mark)

3 The following standard buttons are found on the navigation bar of most web browsers. Explain what each button does.

Back It takes to back page.

Stop It stop the current page from further downloading.

History It show all the web sites you have been visited.

Home It display your home page.

(4 marks)

Web Sites and E-Mail

Some syllabuses ask you to design web sites as part of your coursework. As well as having the technical knowledge, you need to know what makes a good web site.

Well-Designed *Web Sites follow* ***Five Golden Rules***

Web sites need to follow the same design rules as any document you want other people to read — but when you're making a web page you need to think about hyperlinks and download time as well.

1) Remember the needs of the intended audience — if possible test the design on the target users.
2) Keep backgrounds simple, and choose text formats that will contrast with it. This makes the pages easier to read on the screen, and on paper as well.
3) Keep the overall design simple — and use a similar layout on all the pages, so it's easier to navigate through the site.
4) Keep graphics to a minimum — they increase the file size and make download time longer. Most people don't wait more than seven seconds for a page to download — they just find another web site.
5) Keep the number of hyperlinks needed to reach anywhere to a minimum. Ideally, it shouldn't take someone more than four links to get to anywhere on your web site.

Web pages are Written in ***HTML***

1) Web pages are written in a language called HTML (hypertext mark-up language). Most word-processing and DTP software can convert documents into HTML format.
2) You can also get web-design programs that let you create a web page and save it as an HTML file.

Web sites can contain ***Forms***, ***Web-bots*** *and* ***Counters***

As well as hyperlinks, text and images, there are three other features you need to know about:

Forms are places where the user can input information. If you book a plane ticket on the Web for example, there'll be a place for you to input your destination and date of travel.

Web-bots are programs that retrieve data from other locations on the Internet, such as search engines and counters.

Counters show how many visits (or hits) the site has received. They avoid counting people twice by searching for the cookie that was placed on someone's computer when they first visited the site. If the web-bot finds the cookie, that person's already been counted.

COOKIES

These are small text files placed onto a computer by a web page. They're mostly harmless but if you want, it's possible to stop your computer accepting them.

Don't hyphenate "web sites" either — it annoys people

There's a fair bit of detail on this page — so make sure you learn it properly. Learn the golden rules of good web page design. Then explain what forms, web-bots and counters are.

Web Sites and E-Mail

Examiners love asking questions about e-mail — make sure you know all this inside out.

Five Steps to Sending an E-Mail

Electronic mail (e-mail) is a way of sending messages (and documents) from one computer to another. The messages are often text-based, and are usually sent via a PC connected to the Internet. But you can also use a WAP mobile phone or a digital television.

STEP 1: Create the message e.g. using a word processor or the e-mail software on a computer.
STEP 2: Connect to the Internet.
STEP 3: Press the 'send' button
...then the machines take over...
STEP 4: The message is sent from the sender's ISP to a 'mailbox' in the computer system of the recipient's ISP.
STEP 5: The recipient later connects to the Internet, opens their e-mail account, and finds the new message — which they then download and open.

You can also use web-based e-mail, which means you don't have to be connected to a particular ISP. You get an e-mail address by registering at a web site. Then you can e-mail from any on-line computer in the world — ideal if you're planning a round-the-world trip.

For web-based e-mail, steps 1 and 2 might have to be reversed.

Take Care Opening Attachments

1) As well as text, it's also possible to send other files via e-mail — these are called attachments. For example, you could e-mail a picture or a music file to a friend.
2) Unless you're expecting to receive an attachment, treat any you receive with suspicion — it's easy to get a virus from an infected attachment. Viruses are covered on the next page.
3) It's possible to view an attachment without fully downloading it, or you can use virus-checking software to scan it before downloading. Both help to reduce the risk of getting a virus.

E-Mail has Benefits and Problems

E-mail PROS

1) It's quick — e-mails take seconds to send, compared to days for a letter.
2) It's cheap — e-mails are cheaper than posting or faxing, especially for large documents.
3) The same message can easily be sent to loads of different people — and if you group addresses, sending a message to lots of people is as easy as sending it to one person.

E-mail CONS

1) The sender and receiver both need Internet access and e-mail accounts.
2) The hardware and software needed is expensive if you just need e-mail.
3) Get a single letter of an e-mail address wrong, and the message won't be delivered.
4) The message will sit in the recipient's mailbox until they next look at their e-mail account.

Never open an attachment unless you trust its source

There's no way to stress that enough. Viruses and all sorts of annoying things happen if you just open any old attachment. Make sure you learn this lesson now, and not the hard way.

Web Sites and E-Mail

A big problem with the Internet is that data is transmitted using telephone technology, which means unauthorised users can intercept the data relatively easily.

On-Line Shopping uses ***Encryption Software***

1) On-line shopping (or e-commerce or on-line retailing) has got much more popular recently.
2) The basic idea is that the retailer puts details of their products on a web site. Customers can put the stuff they want into an electronic shopping basket (by clicking on a button). They then pay using a credit card, and the goods are delivered soon after.
3) Some people don't like on-line shopping because they're worried that their credit card details might be intercepted and used to make unauthorised purchases. Encryption software can reduce this risk.
4) Sensitive information — like credit card details — is encrypted by the web site into a code which can only be decoded with the right software and a special password called a key. In theory, only the retailer's web site can access the information, so even if someone intercepts the transmission, they won't be able to use the data.

Web sites that encrypt details like this are called 'secure', and display a padlock icon at the bottom of the browser.

Passwords *give* ***Restricted Access*** *to some Web Sites*

1) Some web sites restrict access to authorised users only. Schools allowing pupils and parents to access material on their intranet might do this to prevent other people accessing the information. On-line magazines also do this, so they can charge people for access.
2) The usual way to restrict access is to issue user names and passwords.

An intranet is like a private mini-Internet that can only be viewed by people connected to a particular organisation.
E.g. a hospital might use an intranet to circulate information to its employees.

Get Protection from ***Hackers*** *and* ***Viruses***

1) Hacking means accessing a computer system and its files without permission. It's totally illegal, and once inside a system, the hacker might be able to view, edit, copy or delete important files, or plant a virus. Organisations can protect themselves by using passwords, encrypting files and using hacking-detection software.
2) A virus is a program deliberately written to infect a computer, and make copies of itself. They often corrupt other files — and even operating systems. They move between computer systems by attaching themselves to harmless computer files and e-mails.
3) The main way to reduce the risk of viruses is to use anti-virus software — but it's important to use an up-to-date version because new viruses are detected practically every day.

*Use encryption software to $MUK))G@Ff*E your data...*

It's a pretty scary world out there. So make sure you know how to protect yourself. Learning the different ways on this page will help you in the exam as well as on the Internet.

Warm-Up and Worked Exam Questions

As with most of the sections in this book, it'll help loads if you've actually used the software and tried things for yourself. Either way, you've got to learn all the facts and practise the questions...

Warm-up Questions

1) What is a cookie?
2) What language is used to produce web pages?
3) Why should care be taken when opening e-mail attachments?
4) Define the term 'hacking'.
5) Name three ways of sending and receiving e-mails.
6) What is meant by data encryption?

Worked Exam Question

Time for another worked question. Remember — the best way to learn is to cover up the answer and have a go for yourself, then compare at the end.

1 The owner of a local cycle shop wants to make his own website to advertise the shop.

(a) Suggest two ways of producing this site and give a benefit and drawback of each way.

Method 1: *He could program (write) it directly as HTML.*

Benefit *No specialist software required.*

Drawback *Can be very slow, especially to do complex features.*

Method 2: *Using a web-design program, e.g. Dreamweaver .*

Benefit *Very quick and easy to produce professional-looking web pages.*

Drawback *Software can be very expensive.*

You won't get the mark for just naming a computer package like "Dreamweaver" — you have to say what it is.

(6 marks)

(b) Write down four pieces of advice that you would give the owner about producing a well-designed site.

i) keep the background simple and ensure the text can be easily read; ii) use a similar (consistent) layout for each page; iii) keep the graphics to a minimum to ensure a fast download time; iv) remember the needs of the user and ask for feedback about your design.

(4 marks)

This kind of question is quite common — you could easily get a question on web page design worth 8 marks or more. There's loads of possible answers — just anything that is sensible. (But it's still worth learning reasons to make it easier in the exam...)

Exam Questions

1 Becky uses her computer to send an e-mail to her friend Brad in Canada to give him all the latest news and gossip.

(a) Write down the five steps that are involved in sending and receiving this e-mail.

....

....

(5 marks)

(b) Give two advantages and two disadvantages of using e-mail in this situation rather than writing a letter.

....

....

....

(4 marks)

2 Katherine is concerned that her computer might be infected by a virus and wishes to take precautions to prevent this happening.

(a) Explain what a virus is and what it can do to Katherine's computer.

....

....

(3 marks)

(b) Give one way in which her computer could become infected with a virus.

....

(1 mark)

(c) Give two things that she can do to stop her computer being infected with a virus.

....

....

(2 marks)

3 Oak Vale school has its own website and on it there is an intranet for staff and students. Students can access this intranet from home to look up homework and other school tasks.

(a) Explain what is meant by the term 'intranet'.

....

(1 mark)

(b) How can the school ensure that only students at the school can access the intranet?

....

(1 mark)

(c) The school wishes to keep track of the visits the site has received.
How could this be done?

....

(1 mark)

Exam Questions

4 Shoprite is a large supermarket that offers its customers the facility to shop on-line from home using the Internet.

(a) Write down three steps that the customer will have to go through before the goods can be packed up and delivered by the supermarket.

....

....

(3 marks)

(b) Some customers do not like shopping on-line because they are concerned that personal details might be intercepted and then used by another person to make purchases.
What can the supermarket do to reduce the risk of this happening?

....

....

(2 marks)

5 French football team, Brereton FC, has a website which contains all the latest information on the team. You can also use the site to buy tickets and merchandise on-line.

(a) The website contains several forms.
Give an example of how a fan might use one of these forms.

....

(1 mark)

(b) The site also has several web-bots.
Give an example of a web-bot and what it would be used for.

....

(2 marks)

(c) If the domain name of the club is brfc and it is registered as a business in France, write down the likely web address (URL) for this website.

....

(4 marks)

6 (a) Charley is going to use his computer to access the Internet via an ISDN connection.
Will his computer require a modem? Explain your answer.

....

....

(2 marks)

(b) A modem is advertised as working at 56 Kbps. What does this mean?

....

(1 mark)

(c) Many websites require plug-ins before you can access everything they contain.
What is a plug-in? Give an example of a type of plug-in.

....

....

(2 marks)

Revision Summary for Section Eight

Well that was a nice little section but it's not over yet. Now comes the moment you've been waiting for — the test. Pit your brain and all its new knowledge against this batch of questions and see how you do. But watch out — there's some real tough cookies in there. Remember the way to learn — go back and repeat any questions you get wrong.

1) Explain one reason why you might need a modem to connect to the Internet.
2) Draw a diagram to show how a user connects up to a web site.
3) What are the two main parts of the Internet called?
4) What do the letters kbps stand for and what does it measure?
5) Explain three factors that affect speed of access to the Internet.
6) Explain the difference between a search engine and a portal.
7) Explain what a URL is and how it is constructed.
8) Which country has the code 'dl'? What is the country code for the USA?
9) Explain what a hyperlink is and what it does.
10) What is found in a history folder?
    a) a plan of the Battle of Hastings
    b) history coursework
    c) links to recently visited web sites
11) Explain how web pages that have already been visited can be displayed more quickly.
12) What's the name for the process of making a file smaller?
    What's it called when the file is expanded back to its original size?
13) Give five rules of good web site design.
14) What programming language are web pages written in?
15) What are web-bots?
16) Explain how a counter on a web site works.
17) Explain fully how an e-mail is sent and then read by the recipient.
18) What are attachments? Describe one potential problem with opening attachments.
19) Explain two benefits and two problems of using e-mail.
20) Explain how a shopper makes a purchase from an on-line retailer.
21) What does encryption mean? Describe one of its benefits.
22) Explain the difference between the Internet and an intranet.
23) List some of the problems that hackers can cause.

Computers in Shops

All syllabuses get you to look at how ICT is used in everyday life. This section covers most of the applications you need to know about. But there are lots more than this.

Computers Make **Stock Control** Easier...

1) Bar codes are the patterns of thin and thick black lines you find on most products — like tins of beans, clothes labels, and the back of this book. The bar code contains details about the product and ends with a check digit, so the computer can validate that the data is correct.
2) EPOS stands for Electronic Point of Sale — the fancy high-tech tills in supermarkets. What usually happens is that the bar code details are scanned into the system by a laser scanner on the till, which is connected to the store's computer system. This computer system contains the current price of the product in its database — so the price is passed back to the till, which processes and prints the customer's itemised bill and receipt.
3) The really clever bit is that the computer then reduces the recorded stock of the product. And when stocks fall to a pre-set amount called the reorder level, an order for more stock is automatically sent to the shop's warehouse or supplier.

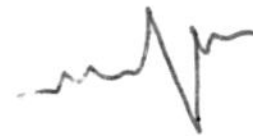

...Reduce the Need for **Cash...**

1) Most tills allow customers to pay for their shopping using a debit card instead of cash. This is called Electronic Funds Transfer at the Point of Sale — or EFTPOS for short.

2) Debit cards have a magnetic stripe (or strip) on the back of them. They're read by swiping the card through a magnetic reader, which tells the computer which bank account the money will come from. A request for the payment is then automatically sent via the telephone network. If the card is valid, the payment is authorised, and the funds are transferred from the customer's account to the shop's.

3) A potential problem is card fraud — paying for goods using someone else's card. To reduce the risk of fraud, the card has a space for the customer to put their signature. This is checked by the shop against the signature the customer puts onto the receipt. Both keep a copy of the receipt.

...and Find Out **Exactly What** Each Shopper **Buys**

1) Some large shops such as supermarkets have introduced loyalty cards. These contain details of the customer and their loyalty scheme account number. The card is swiped when the customer buys something, and details of their purchases are stored on the computer system.
2) The customer is usually 'rewarded' with discounts and vouchers when their spending rises above a certain level. But there's another reason for loyalty cards.
3) The shop's customer database is linked to the product-sales database by the loyalty scheme account number. In other words the store knows exactly what each customer has bought. They can use this information to send personalised mailshots — e.g. someone who buys dog biscuits every week could be told about a special offer on flea collars.

Learn how computers make everyday life easier

You've seen and heard ICT being used in shops loads of times. EPOS, EFTPOS and store loyalty cards don't exactly get the pulse racing, but you need to know why they caught on.

Computers in Banks

ICT is used in banking in three main ways — make sure you know about them. You could also be tested on the impact it has on the customers, banks and their employees. I bet you can't wait.

Computers are used to *Process Cheques...*

1) At the bottom of a cheque are three sets of numbers, printed using magnetic ink:
   (i) Cheque number.
   (ii) Sort code — contains details of the bank and branch where the customer's account is held.
   (iii) Customer's account number.

Here they are...

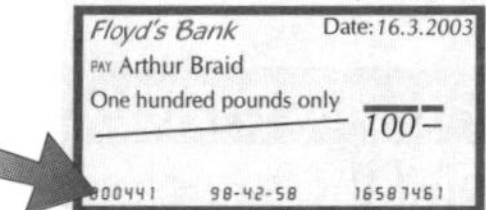

2) You write on the cheque the amount of money to be debited (i.e. taken) from your account and credited (i.e. put into) the payee's account. The cheque is sent to the payee's bank, where the amount of the cheque is typed at the bottom using magnetic ink.
3) All cheques go to a clearing house, where they are read using MICR (see page 15). All that day's cheques are processed to find how much the banks need to pay each other. The cheques are then sent to the customers' bank branches, and the amounts deducted from their accounts.
4) The main benefits — this system is quicker and more accurate than processing the cheques by hand. Also, the magnetic ink characters are difficult to forge, and can be read even if the cheque is damaged or the characters have been overwritten.

...Operate ATMs...

1) ATM stands for Automatic Telling Machine — a.k.a. 'cash machines' or the 'hole in the wall'. By putting in a bank card (like a debit card, a credit card, or a special cash card), a person can withdraw money from their bank account.
2) On the back of the card is a magnetic stripe containing the customer's account number, bank sort code, the maximum amount the person can withdraw in a single day, and their PIN (Personal Identification Number). The PIN works like a password — the user enters it onto the ATM keypad to verify that they are the account-holder. The PIN helps to reduce fraud.
3) The details on the card are read by a magnetic reader in the ATM and, providing the card and the required amount of cash are valid, the machine counts and issues the money.
4) Banks like ATMs because they can employ fewer cashiers and offer a 24-hour service. Customers like them because they can get cash where and when they need it, pretty quickly.

...and allow Home Banking

Home banking uses the Internet or telephone to give customers access to their bank accounts 24 hours a day.

PROBLEMS for the banks

1) High level of system security needed.
2) Still not secure — accounts are still broken into and used by hackers.

BENEFITS for the banks

1) Fewer local branches needed and less staff need to be employed, so costs are reduced.
2) Less storage space and paperwork needed.

You can make payments and transfer funds into and out of your bank account at any time.

Cheques, cash machines, home banking — it doesn't get better than this...

This 'computers in banks' stuff is really interesting. Yes, it's great. Only joking — it's as dry as old sticks. But... it comes up in ICT exams, which makes it worth knowing.

Computers at Work — The Electronic Office

Five ways to help create a *Paperless office*

The effects of new technology on employees are covered in Section 10.

A paperless office is one where computers are used to communicate information instead of printed documents. At the moment it's just a goal (or pipe dream) for most businesses.

1) **E-MAIL** can be used instead of a written document (e.g. a memorandum).

2) **PRESENTATIONS** can be produced and given using computers — less paper gets used and the same presentation can be changed easily to meet the needs of different audiences.

3) **INTRANET** — Documents can be produced in electronic form and made available to other staff on an intranet. Any documents (e.g. brochures) intended for people outside the organisation can be put onto a web site for them to download. This means that only the most relevant pages need be to be printed — the rest can be read on screen.

4) **ELECTRONIC DATA INTERCHANGE (EDI)** — Organisations often need to exchange data with one another — for example, schools need to tell exam boards the names of pupils to be entered for an exam. But instead of sending the information on paper for the exam board to key into its computer system, they can transfer the data direct from the school's computer system onto the exam board's. This is usually done via the telephone network.

5) **DIGITAL COPIERS** are basically hi-tech photocopiers, but you can also connect them to your computer system. And they often have extra features, like being able to add watermarks, page numbers and the like.

BENEFITS of a paperless office
1) Paper costs are lower and less storage space is needed.
2) Searching for things should be quicker.

PROBLEMS of a paperless office
1) Cost of installing, operating and maintaining the computer system.
2) Data might be less secure.

Teleconferencing Reduces the Need for *Business Travel*

1) Traditionally, meetings have usually taken place in person. Teleconferencing could make that a thing of the past.
2) Teleconferencing uses a camera connected to a computer, which is connected to the telephone network or Internet. Voices and moving images are relayed in real time, so that the participants can watch each other whilst they speak. It's also possible for lots of different people to be connected at the same time.
3) The main benefit of teleconferencing is that it reduces the costs of business travel (e.g. transport and hotel bills). And because people spend less time travelling, they can spend more time in the office — which should improve productivity.

An Intranet is just like a mini-Internet that's run over a network

The key things here are to know how ICT is changing the workplace, and what the effects are for organisations. List all the ICT examples mentioned and explain what each one's effects are.

Computers in Schools

CMIS Reduces the Burden of Administration

Schools produce lots of information (e.g. attendance figures and exam results). Computerised Management Information Systems (CMIS) can help produce and process it.

1) Pupil records can be stored in a computerised database. Details are usually stored in a number of related files, the key field usually being the pupil's admission number.
2) A computer program can generate timetables, given details of available teachers and rooms etc.
3) The pupil database and the timetable can be linked to automatically generate class lists.
4) Some schools have computerised attendance registers.
   There are two main types:
   (i) The teacher completes an OMR (Optical Mark Recognition) attendance sheet, which is then input using an OMR device.
   (ii) The teacher inputs data into a portable keypad. This is then transmitted by radio signal to a central computer.

   Both systems can process the data to produce absence lists and other reports.
5) Pupil reports can be written using standard software by mail merging information from a file of examination results. But some schools use specialised report software, which takes information from the pupil database, and allows teachers to insert individual comments from a central comment bank.

BENEFITS of CMIS
1) Schools spend less time producing management information.
2) This means more time can be spent on teaching and learning.

PROBLEMS of CMIS
1) Financial cost to the school.
2) Teachers need to have access to computers and the data.

There are Three Main Features of an Electronic Classroom

① COMPUTER-AIDED LEARNING (CAL) uses software to generate on-screen learning materials and computer-aided assessment. The two go together — the idea is that pupils get an individualised learning programme that's decided by the expert system.

② INTERNET — Computers are connected to the Internet, which can be used as a source of information, or allow pupils to exchange data and ideas with pupils from other schools via e-mail.

③ INTERACTIVE DISPLAY BOARD — All the computers in a class can be connected to an interactive display board at the front of the classroom, so that everyone can watch a presentation by one pupil. The board can also convert the teacher's board notes into a computer file — which can be saved and used again.

The electronic classroom is like the paperless office — great in theory, but not perfected yet.

The main potential benefit is an improvement in the quality of pupils' learning, and hopefully an increase in motivation. The basic problem is the cost of the technology.

Electronic classrooms are great in theory, but are not perfected yet

CMIS has similar advantages and disadvantages to computerised admin systems used in other industries. The major drawback is the actual cost. Learn all the drawbacks and the plus points.

Warm-Up and Worked Exam Questions

Learning facts and practising exam questions is the only recipe for success. That's what the questions on these pages are all about. All you have to do — is do them.

Warm-up Questions

1) What do the following abbreviations stand for: MICR, CAL, EFTPOS?
2) What does ATM stand for. And what is an ATM?
3) Why does a bar code end with a check digit?
4) Give one advantage and one disadvantage of home banking.
5) Give three features of a 'paperless office'.

Worked Exam Questions

Sometimes it's not very clear exactly how to answer exam questions.
These worked examples are here to show you the way...

1 Mrs Plink runs a newsagent. She has just bought a new computer system to help run her business. Suggest three different types of software that the business should buy and give an example of how each one could be used.

(i) Word processor — to write letters to customers who haven't paid their bills, (ii) Database — to keep a record of which newspapers should be delivered to which customers, (iii) Desktop Publisher — to produce leaflets to advertise the shop.

(6 marks)

Don't use the names of specific software packages. It's the type of software that's asked for. And don't forget to explain how each software package would be used.

2 Mr Fribble runs a grocers which uses an EPOS system.

(a) What does EPOS mean?

Electronic point of sale

(1 mark)

(b) Mrs Batty takes her groceries to the counter. Explain how the EPOS system would be used to process her shopping.

Each item would be scanned with a bar code scanner. The computer system will contain current prices of all stocked items. The price of each scanned item will be retrieved and added to work out the total amount. The recorded stock level of each item will be reduced by 1 as it is scanned.

(4 marks)

You have to judge how much to write based on the allocated marks. There's 4 marks here, so that's 4 points to make. If it was worth 8 marks, you'd need to go into more detail and mention more features of EPOS. But you'd still need to make 8 points — you don't get extra marks for waffle...

Exam Questions

1 A large company has four regional offices and a headquarters in London connected through a wide area network. The company has decided to install a teleconferencing system rather than holding monthly meetings in London for the regional managers.

a) Give three advantages for the company of installing a teleconferencing system.

....

....

....

(3 marks)

b) Give two possible disadvantages of the company using teleconferencing.

....

....

(2 marks)

2 Girish has to do a project on space travel for his Physics teacher. He has decided to use the Internet to do his research. His teacher would prefer him to use the reference books in the school library.

a) Give three reasons why it would be a good idea to use the Internet to find information rather than books.

....

....

....

(3 marks)

b) Give two reasons why his teacher might prefer him to use books for his research.

....

....

(2 marks)

3 Sheppersons Supermarket is planning to introduce a customer loyalty card system.

Explain the benefits to the supermarket of a loyalty card system.

....

....

....

(3 marks)

Cars and Traffic Management Systems

Car Records are stored in the **DVLA Database**

1) The Driver Vehicle and Licensing Agency (DVLA) manages a large database containing data on all cars registered in the UK, as well as details of individual drivers.

Data held about drivers includes: Name, address, and the year they first qualified to drive.

Data held about cars includes: Make, model, engine size, registration number, year of first registration, and the registered keeper of the vehicle.

2) Cars over three years old have to pass a test called the MOT every year. The DVLA process the vehicle data and send out a notification to the registered keeper just before the test is due.
3) The DVLA database can be accessed by the Police. This means, for example, that if a car with a certain registration number is seen near the scene of a crime, the police are able to identify the owner.

Car Use is Controlled by **Three** Main Control Systems

1) **TRAFFIC LIGHTS** — The sequence and speed in which a set of traffic lights changes at a particular road junction. These are controlled in two main ways:

FIXED-TIME MODE: The system changes in a fixed, non-varying way — no matter how much traffic is on the road.

VEHICLE-ACTIVATED MODE: The system responds to changes in the flow of vehicles using data from a sensor in a feedback loop — e.g. the lights might stay green for longer at times of heavy traffic.

2) **SPEED CAMERAS** use light sensors to measure the speed of a moving vehicle. That speed is compared with a reference speed set by the programmer. If the vehicle's going too fast, a signal is sent to a camera which photographs the vehicle's registration number. This is then used to retrieve the name and address of the registered keeper of the vehicle from the DVLA database. They'll probably then get sent a letter telling them they've been fined.
3) **CAR PARK MANAGEMENT SYSTEMS** exist in some busy towns and cities. Sensors at the entrances and exits of car parks are used to calculate how many spaces are left in each car park. This data is sent to signs next to nearby roads, which update their display in real time. This means motorists shouldn't have to waste time driving to a car park that's already full.

GIS Helps Drivers **Plan Better Journeys**

Geographical Information Systems (GIS) combine information in a database and mapping software to produce an output that is in map form. GIS helps drivers in two main ways:

1) Drivers can input where they want to start and end a journey — the database then produces a map showing the quickest or shortest route.
2) Drivers can pay for a service that updates this information in real time while they're driving. This means they can be warned of traffic delays ahead and have alternative routes displayed.

A few web sites provide this service for free.

GIS is a very useful development — remember it

Another page of how the ICT you've learnt in the rest of the book gets applied in practice. It's important that you learn both why ICT is used for these purposes, and how it works.

Computers in the Home

A PC has **Many Different Uses**

More and more households now own a Personal Computer (that's a PC).
The most common uses include connecting to the Internet, playing computer games, running education software, word processing, spreadsheets and databases.

Burglar Alarms use **Feedback**

Feedback loops were covered on page 105.

1) Burglar alarms are a good example of a computer control system that uses feedback. Basically, the system constantly collects data from an input sensor, and when the data suggests that an intruder is present the system sends a signal to an output device.
2) The input sensor might be an infra-red beam or a noise sensor. Expensive systems guarding banks and museums might have pressure sensors on the floor. The input from the sensors is processed by the computer software, and when the data from one or more sensors exceeds a pre-programmed limit, a signal is sent to an output device.
3) Common output devices include loudspeakers or sirens. The alarm will sound continuously until the computer sends a signal to turn it off.

Some systems are connected to the local police station or security centre via the telephone network. This means there should be a response even if there's no one around to hear the alarm.

Embedded Computers are **Everywhere**

1) An embedded computer is one where the input, process and output devices are all contained inside the machine they're meant to control. Examples include microwave ovens, video recorders and modern washing machines.
2) Sometimes these devices can also be operated using a remote control — the most common is a handset for a TV. The output signal is transmitted from the handset to the TV as an infra-red signal of digital data, where it's received as an input signal.

Things might be **Different in the Future**

Household computer systems may well be different in the future.

1) It might be possible to control all household devices from a single central control, and then connect to this control via the Internet. So you might be able to set the video from anywhere in the world using your mobile phone.
2) The central control might be able to store details of products that have bar codes. The bar code can be scanned when the product is taken out of the fridge or thrown away. This means that the computer can calculate when to send an order to the retailer. The order can then be sent automatically via the Internet.

Things are already different — the future is now

This is the kind of thing that examiners like. Everywhere you look you see examples of ICT being applied — from gym machines to toasters in kitchens. ICT is everywhere.

Computer Applications — Other Stuff

Modern **Weather Forecasting** *needs* **ICT**

1) Meteorological data such as rainfall or air pressure is usually collected from an automated data logging system using sensors. The data is either sent immediately to a central computer, or stored within the data logging device before being downloaded.
2) The data is processed, and a weather map of the area can be produced using a geographical information system. It's also possible to combine the images collected at different times to create the effect of a moving image of the weather systems. The same can be done for data collected by a weather satellite — this is usually a photographic image which has been converted into digital data.
3) The data can also be fed into a computer model of the way that weather patterns change and interact. This enables detailed weather forecasts to be made.
4) In this way, more data can be collected and analysed than is possible with a manual system. And using a complex computer model, the predictions are also more accurate.

Estate Agents can provide **Virtual House Visits**

1) People selling a house usually use an estate agent, who collects details of the property and advertises it. Anyone interested in the house can then go and look around it.
2) But it's often hard to tell from the written details what the house is really like. As a result, lots of wasted visits get made.
3) To solve this problem, some estate agents have recently started using digital cameras and interactive software to produce virtual tours of properties. This means that buyers can view the property from the estate agent's office, or even at home via the Internet.
4) This saves the estate agent time, as he or she doesn't have to show as many people round the actual house. And as the house details are available on-line, they're quicker to get hold of, and less paper gets wasted.

Interior Designers can **Simulate** *a House* **Make-over**

1) Before people start decorating, they can never be totally sure how a room will turn out. But by the time it's finished, it's too late to change it if it's not what they wanted.
2) This problem can be solved using software that takes a digital image of the room and then manipulates it (by changing the colour of walls, placing images of new carpets etc.). The buyer can see how different types of decoration would look in their house. And when they're happy with the result the goods can be ordered and the decorating done.

Learn the differences between simulation and data logging

Some more examples of ICT in real use. Modern weather forecasting uses both data logging and simulation — so you need to make sure you understand the differences between them.

Warm-Up and Worked Exam Questions

If you've come all the way from section 1 to get here and you've done all the questions along the way, well done. The end is getting near now.

Warm-up Questions

1) What does GIS stand for?
2) What is an embedded computer?
3) What is a sensor?
4) Make a list of data that the DVLA stores about cars.
5) List 4 examples of where ICT can be used in the home.

Worked Exam Questions

There's a knack to be learnt in using the facts you've stored away in your brain box in the right way to get marks in the exam. These worked examples will help you see how...

1 A local computer shop has a burglar alarm to protect the premises and stock from thieves. The system uses a number of sensors and output devices in order to operate fully.

Suggest three input sensors / devices that might be used and state their purpose.

i) a pressure sensor — this would identify when somebody entered the shop by the external door; ii) a movement sensor — the beam would be broken if somebody entered the shop; iii) a contact sensor — this would detect when a window was opened.

To get all the marks you've got to think about how each sensor would be used. E.g. if you put temperature sensor as an answer, you'll need to think of a sensible way it could be used...

(6 marks)

2 Describe how a computer system would control entry to a multi-storey car park.

Cars would approach the car park and a pressure sensor or movement sensor would detect the presence of a vehicle. If a space was available in the car park, a barrier would be raised allowing access. The total number of cars in the car park would increase by 1. When a vehicle left the car park, a movement or pressure sensor would detect the vehicle approaching the exit and again a barrier would be raised. The total number of cars in the car park would decrease by 1.

(4 marks)

To be sure of getting all the marks, you must explain what happens when cars come in and when they leave and explain how the computer keeps track of the number of spaces. As always, if there's 4 marks available, you have to make sure you've made 4 good points.

Exam Questions

1 Sandy Beach Caravan Park is thinking of putting details of their holiday caravans on their web site. This will enable holidaymakers to view different types of caravans before booking their holiday and to take a virtual tour.

(a) What is meant by a virtual tour?

....

....

(1 mark)

(b) Identify two benefits to future holidaymakers of being able to take a virtual tour.

....

....

(2 marks)

2 Kevin's haulage company has a fleet of lorries that are used to transport goods all over the United Kingdom. The company makes extensive use of a computer system and has access to a GIS.

(a) What is a GIS?

....

(1 mark)

(b) Suggest two uses of a GIS to the haulage company.

....

....

(2 marks)

3 Explain how ICT is used in modern weather forecasting.

....

....

....

....

....

....

....

(5 marks)

Revision Summary for Section Nine

You've got through another section — and there's only one more to go. But don't get carried away just yet. You've still got a tricky set of questions to get through before you start the last lap.
The basic idea of this section is to get you to apply your ICT knowledge to some real-world examples. So this section is a bit like a summary of the whole book.

1) What is the final digit of a bar code number called? What is it used for?
2) What does EPOS stand for?
3) Explain how an EPOS system can automatically reorder stock.
4) What does EFTPOS stand for? What hardware do consumers and retailers need for it to work?
5) How can the risk of card fraud be reduced?
6) Explain one reason why retailers have introduced loyalty cards.
7) What four pieces of information are found at the bottom of a cheque? When and how do they get put there?
8) What is used to read the data at the bottom of a cheque?
9) Explain two benefits for the banks of this system.
10) What does ATM stand for?
11) What data is stored on the back of a bank cash-withdrawal card? How is it stored?
12) Explain a benefit to banks and a benefit to customers of ATMs.
13) Explain a benefit to the banks and a benefit to customers of home banking.
14) What's the main difference between a normal office and an electronic office?
15) What does EDI stand for? Explain one example of its use.
16) Describe two other features of an electronic office.
17) What is teleconferencing? How does it work?
18) Explain two advantages to a business of using teleconferencing.
19) What does CMIS stand for? Explain three features of a CMIS in a school.
20) Explain one benefit and one problem of using a CMIS in any organisation — not just schools.
21) Describe two features of an electronic classroom.
22) What is stored in the DVLA database?
23) What is the difference between a fixed-time mode and a vehicle-activated mode traffic light system?
24) How does a speed camera work?
25) What does GIS stand for? Explain how GIS can help motorists plan better journeys.
26) Explain in words how a burglar alarm system works.
27) Draw a system flow diagram to illustrate the burglar alarm system.
28) What is an embedded computer? Find a household device with one inside and describe how it works from input through to output.
29) Explain how an automated data logging system can collect weather data.
30) List all the hardware and software an estate agent might need in order to provide virtual house visits on the Internet for its clients.
31) Explain how computer simulation can result in nicer bedrooms.

Computers and Society

Computers are increasingly being used to store and process important data.
It's very easy to transfer data electronically — so there are laws to control computer use.

The Data Protection Act Controls the Use of Personal Data

1) The Data Protection Act was introduced in the UK in 1984. It gives rights to data subjects (i.e. people who have data about them stored on computer systems). The Act was updated in 1998 to take the increasing use of computers, and changes in European Union law, into account.

2) The Act consists mainly of eight data protection principles — summarised here

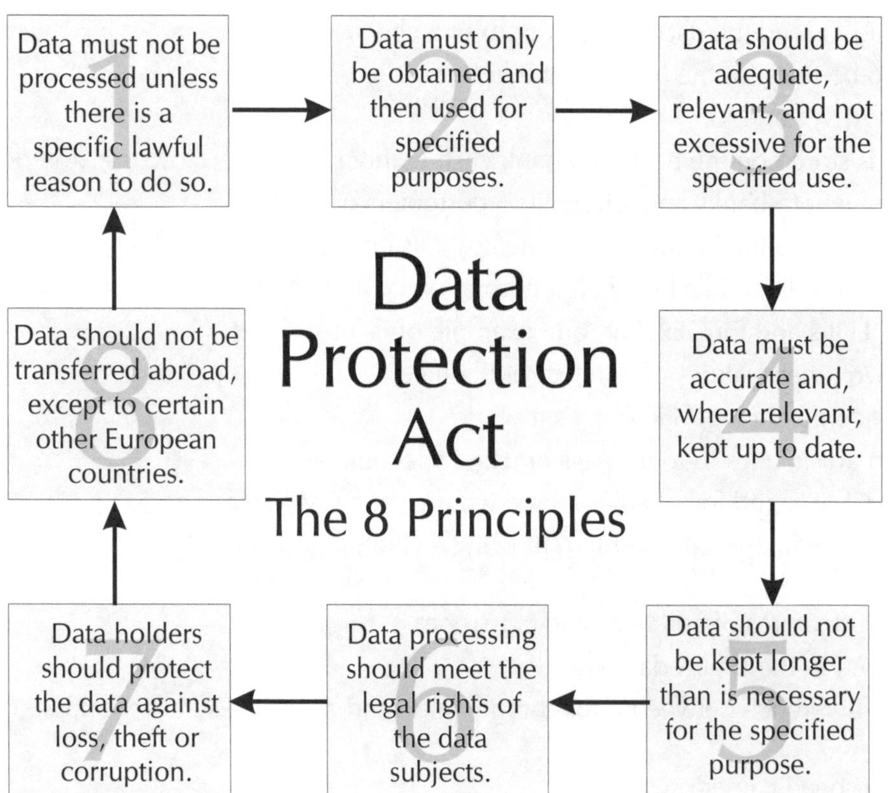

3) The law entitles data subjects to see the personal data about them that's held by an organisation. If an organisation breaks the law, they can be fined and made to pay compensation to the data subject.

Make sure you learn about the Data Protection Act

It means that anyone can look at data about them that's being held by any organisation. This is useful if you fail an interview — you're allowed to see their notes explaining why.

Computers and Society

The *Copyright, Design and Patents Act* controls *Illegal Copying*

This law was introduced in 1989, and makes it illegal to copy a file without permission from the owner or copyright holder. Individuals and organisations who break this law risk an unlimited fine. There are three ways that the law is often broken:

1) Using software without the proper licence. So if you have a licence to use a word processor on one stand-alone computer, but you then install it on all the machines in a network, you're breaking the law.

2) Downloading text or images from the Internet and using them without saying where you got them, or without receiving the copyright owner's permission.

3) Copying a computer program you use at work and running it on a computer at home, without permission from the copyright holder.

The *Computer Misuse Act* prevents Illegal Access to Files

This law was introduced in 1990 to cope with the problems of computer hackers and viruses. The Act made the following three things illegal:

1) Unauthorised access to computer material (e.g. hacking). This includes viewing parts of a network you're not permitted to see, and the illegal copying of programs — software piracy.

2) Gaining unauthorised access to a computer to carry out serious crimes like fraud and blackmail.

3) Unauthorised changing of computer files — including planting viruses, and deleting files. If convicted, the offender can face an unlimited fine and a five-year prison sentence.

These Acts make sure your files are safer

For each law, they'll want to know what it prohibits and all the details about how people can break it. Make sure you know about them thoroughly, so that you don't get flustered in the exam.

Computers and Society

ICT is changing the types of jobs that humans are employed to do, and the way they perform them. It's not just the electronic office — there's much more to it than that.

ICT has ***Replaced Some Jobs*** *but* ***Created Others***

Computers have completely replaced humans in performing some jobs, and reduced the number of people needed to do others. The need to build and operate computers has resulted in new jobs being created and new industries emerging.

JOBS BEING REPLACED BY COMPUTERS	JOBS BEING CREATED BY COMPUTERS
1) Manual jobs replaced by robots, e.g. some car-assembly jobs. 2) Manual jobs replaced by computer systems, e.g. manual print-workers replaced by DTP. 3) Office jobs replaced by computers, e.g. filing clerks and typists.	1) Jobs involved in the design and manufacture of computer hardware. 2) Systems analysts and programmers to design systems and write software. 3) Network managers and technicians to maintain computer systems.

ICT enables ***Teleworking*** *and* ***Hot-Desking***

1) Rather than travel to an office, Internet technology makes it possible for employees to telework (i.e. work from home), uploading and downloading work as necessary.

2) Hot-desking is when an employee sits at any free desk in an office, rather than having their own special place. It could be at their employer's office, or in a work-centre shared by people who work for other organisations.

3) Teleworking and hot-desking reduce the amount of office space needed by an employer, reducing costs. But it can make it harder to keep confidential information inside the business.

4) Teleworking means employees spend less time commuting and can fit their work more easily around home life. But it can be very lonely, as there is less personal contact with colleagues. Hot-desking can also be stressful — never knowing where you are going to be working.

Machines aren't always better than humans

You'll almost certainly get asked about this in the exam, in some shape or form. Just remember to keep your ear to the ground for recent developments, so you can impress the examiner.

Computers and Society

*ICT is increasingly used by **All Workers***

Workers in general, and particularly those in office jobs, are being required to spend more and more of their working day using computers. This has pros and cons for both employers and employees:

PROS

1) Employers benefit because computers can increase the amount of work done. This makes businesses more productive and so more competitive.
2) Workers benefit if computers can do the boring, repetitive work and leave them to do the interesting jobs.

CONS

1) It's expensive to keep investing in the latest and most efficient technology and it takes time and money to retrain staff.
2) There may be job losses as computers replace people for some tasks, such as car-assembly.

Computers weren't originally designed to be used all day. Make sure you know about the health risks of continuous computer use and what can be done to reduce them.

*Computer Use can cause **Three Main Problems***

There are three main problems — connected either with poor design of the equipment, or from not using the equipment properly. In each case the risk is small, but the effects can be serious.

1) **Repetitive strain injury (RSI) is a general term for aches, pains and muscle or tendon damage resulting from overuse of a keyboard or mouse. Some people call it upper limb disorder (ULD).**
2) **Spending too long in front of a VDU can cause eye strain and headaches. The glare from the screen and poor-quality images on some old monitors can make it hard for the eyes to focus properly.**
3) **Circulation, fitness and back problems might result from sitting all day in front of a computer rather than walking around. This is more of a long-term health problem.**

Stay healthy — learn everything on this page now

All of this is very important. Especially the section on the three health problems that are caused by computer use. You'll need to remember this for your whole life, so that you stay healthy.

Computers and Society

There are **Three Main Solutions** to the Computer Use Problems

1) Take regular breaks from computer work. Looking away from the screen, walking around and exercising your fingers and hands can also help to reduce the health risks.

2) Use the correct equipment. You should have:
   a) a proper computer chair with backrest,
   b) an ergonomically-designed keyboard that makes it easier to touch-type without straining fingers,
   c) good background lighting,
   d) a screen filter to reduce VDU glare.

3) Arrange the equipment properly. Adjust the chair and VDU to find the most comfortable position to work.

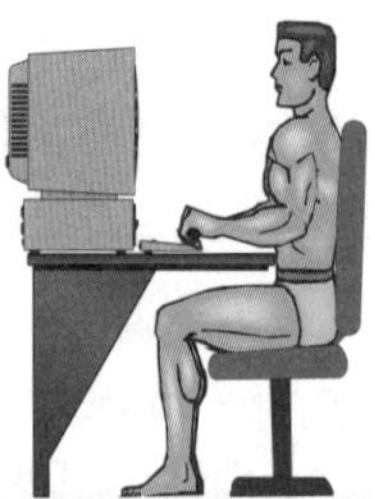

As a general rule:
1) *Your forearms should be roughly horizontal.*
2) *Your eyes should be level with the top of the VDU.*

Employers need to **Follow the Law**

The main law covering computer use at work is the Health and Safety (Display Screen Equipment) Regulations 1992. The law says that employers need to do five main things:

1) **Analyse workstations, and assess and reduce risks:**
Employers need to check that computer equipment (and the area around it) is safe, and if it isn't they need to take action to make it safe.

2) **Ensure workstations meet minimum requirements:**
This includes providing proper computer chairs and good lighting.

3) **Plan work so there are breaks or changes of activity:**
Employers mustn't expect workers to work at a computer all day.
They must provide regular breaks or allow them to do non-computer work.

4) **Provide free eye-tests:**
To all staff who regularly use VDUs as part of their job.

5) **Provide health and safety training and information:**
So that employees can take action themselves to reduce the health risks.

Don't spend too much time at a computer — remember the sun

Sitting down all day will never be as healthy as running around in the fresh air. Cover the page, make a table with one column for problems and another for solutions, then fill it in.

Warm-up and Worked Exam Questions

The impact of computers in society is a really big topic — and it's one which often gets a big essay question in the exam. So make sure you're prepared, starting with these questions.

Warm-up Questions

1) How is it possible to break the Copyright, Designs and Patents Act using a computer? Give two examples.
2) What is a 'data subject' according to the 1998 Data Protection Act?
3) If you deliberately plant a virus in someone's computer, which law have you broken? How?
4) What is meant by hot-desking? How does ICT make this possible?
5) What does ULD stand for? How is it caused?

Worked Exam Question

Have a good read through this question, covering the blue bits to start with.

1 Mrs Musson has started work as a school secretary. After a month or so she complains of back pain, eye strain and unsteadiness in her hands at the end of the working day.

Give **THREE** pieces of advice which would help avoid these problems in the future:

(a) to Mrs Musson.

1) Take regular breaks from computer work. 2) Make sure your chair is at the correct height and the back rest is properly adjusted. 3) Make sure that your VDU is at a comfortable distance from your eyes.

(3 marks)

Advice to Mrs Musson should focus on what she should do, not what her boss should provide for her.

There's plenty more answers you could have given on the page opposite — make sure you know those ones too.

(b) to her employer.

1) It's your responsibility to provide health and safety training. 2) Ensure that the secretary's work place is adequately lit. 3) Provide ergonomically designed keyboards with wrist supports.

(3 marks)

If you've learnt all the points on the page opposite, this part should be easy.

Remember to use the information in the question — your advice has to be relevant to her specific problems (back pain, eye strain and hand / wrist problems.)

Exam Questions

1 A mail order company keeps personal data on its customers. It must comply with the 1998 Data Protection Act. Look at the statements below. Only **FOUR** are correct.
Tick the box after each correct statement.

a) The company cannot transfer the data outside the United Kingdom. ☐

b) If the data is accidentally destroyed, the company has to pay compensation. ☐

c) The company must protect the data from damage or theft. ☑

d) It's the company's responsibility to ensure the data is kept up to date. ☑

e) The company must destroy all personal data immediately after it has been used. ☑

f) The customers can ask to see the personal data held about them. ☐

g) The company must ask its customers for permission if it wants to pass their personal data on to other businesses. ☑

(4 marks)

2 Rebecca is a web-designer. She works at home and uses e-mail to send the web pages she creates to her company's office.

Give **ONE** advantage and **ONE** disadvantage of teleworking in this way:

a) for the company.

Teleworking reduce the amount of space in office

b) for Rebecca.

She can upload her work at home

No social interaction

c) for society as a whole.

disable can

(6 marks)

Social, Moral and Ethical Issues

Social, Moral and *Ethical issues*

1) Social issues are those concerning how computers are affecting the way society is organised, and how people act and behave towards each other.
2) Moral and ethical issues are to do with right and wrong.

There are Four Main Moral and Ethical Issues

These issues are what people generally agree are the most important ones. But there are others. Remember the golden rule — it's up to you to form your own opinion about these issues.

1 Unrestricted Internet Access

There are very few controls on what can be posted on the Internet, and very few controls on what can be downloaded (although it is possible to filter out unwanted sites).

Some people think free access to material that is racist, sexist or offensive will distort people's (especially children's) sense of right and wrong, and that we need more censorship on the Internet.

But who'll decide what's okay and what isn't? Some governments like to control the information available to their citizens.
This censorship is undermined by the Internet, which can be seen as good if it increases the power of the individual at the expense of government.

2 Ease of Copying Computer Files

It's dead easy to copy computer files — but some of these will be covered by copyright and licensing rules. Unauthorised copying is illegal — but it still happens.
As a result, some people worry that this is turning most people into criminals.

3 Computers are Replacing People at Work

New technology means that firms can reduce costs and remain competitive in today's global economy by employing fewer people.

But some people worry about the jobs that are lost and wonder if it is right that computers result in an increase in the standard of living for many people, while others are losing their jobs.

4 Increased Government Surveillance

Every time an e-mail is sent, the ISP could (in theory) keep a copy of the file. In the future, governments could request (or demand?) access to this permanent record of every e-mail.

1) Some people claim this might help to catch criminals.
2) Others worry that this intrusion into people's personal lives is a threat to their civil liberty.

Censorship — a controversial topic

Make sure you understand the issues by covering them up and scribbling down the main points. Then write a mini-essay on the moral impact of computers.

Social, Moral and Ethical Issues

The increased use of computers is changing the way that society works.

There are **Five Main Social Issues**

Once again, there are other issues — but these are some of the most important ones.
Remember, what counts is not which issues you put into your answer, but how you discuss them.

'Information Rich' and **'Information Poor'**

1) Computers aren't cheap, so not everyone can afford them.
2) Some people worry that this might create a two-tier society — those who are computer-literate (and 'information rich') and those unable to exploit the technology (and 'information poor').

The **Internet's** Changing How We **Interact**

1) The growth of e-mail and home shopping worries some people. They think that we will increasingly stay at home, becoming less physically fit, and communicating only via the Internet rather than through personal contact.
2) They also fear that Internet communication will cause people to lose personal skills and that communication will only be between people who have similar views, resulting in society becoming fragmented and depersonalised.

Over-Reliance on Technology

1) Fears about the Millennium Bug before the year 2000 showed how much people today rely on computers for the smooth running of society. We are dependent on computers in almost all aspects of our lives — banking, shopping, the media, industry, travel... the list is endless. If the computer systems around the world were to suddenly fail, it would cause widespread chaos.
2) Some people think parents who give their children mobile phones are making it harder for them to become independent and self-reliant.

Learn all the social issues on these two pages

It would be quite frightening if the world's computer systems all got wiped out. International stockmarkets would collapse. Cash machines wouldn't work. Let's hope it doesn't happen.

Social, Moral and Ethical Issues

Impact on Literacy

1) Some people worry that the increased use of computer games and multimedia CD-ROMs is resulting in people spending less time reading.
2) They say this will mean lower levels of literacy, especially among the young.
3) As a result, education standards will be lower and the quality of the workforce will suffer — making us all poorer.

Faster Pace of Life

1) It's argued that computers are increasing the pace of life (and stress levels).
2) Firstly, computer technology is rapidly changing — so people constantly have to adapt to new ways of working.
3) Secondly, computers can handle larger quantities of data, and process them much faster than manual methods — so humans have to work harder to keep up with the work generated.

But There's Some Good News...

1) The Internet and e-mail make it easier for people of different cultures and religions in different countries to communicate with each other. This could result in a more tolerant global society.
2) Computers are able to perform routine tasks, leaving humans to perform more complex ones. They also reduce the need for travel and paper and so are good for the environment.

That's the lot

There you go. This is the very last section of revision in the book. After these practice questions all you have left to do is a mock exam, and then you'll be on your way.

Warm-Up and Worked Exam Questions

Congratulations, you've reached the last section of questions in the book (before the exams...). I think it's one of the most interesting topics too. So, time for the final sprint...

Warm-up Questions

1) What is an ethical issue? Give one example relevant to the use of computers.
2) Why is the use of ICT causing unemployment in some areas? Give one example.
3) Give one reason why parents might think that computers have led to lower standards of literacy amongst children.
4) Give two reasons why the use of computers can cause stress.
5) What is meant by the term 'information rich'?

Worked Exam Questions

These questions are all about how ICT affects people. They can be quite tricky, so study them carefully. (You should have a try yourself before looking at the answers.)

1 Many people are worried that advances in Information Technology have led to greater restrictions on personal freedom. Give three examples.

1. *Government agencies could look at your e-mails, so you might not want to send private messages.*
2. *Technology which reads number plates for congestion charging can also be used to track an individual's movements round the country, even if they are not suspected of any crime.*
3. *It's possible to track which web sites you've visited, which you might think is an invasion of privacy.*

This one's quite tricky to think of good examples for. If you're struggling, it'd be well worth you learning these ones.

(6 marks)

2 Kelly believes that it is wrong to censor information on the Internet. She argues that the Internet is all about freedom of information and that censorship would destroy this. Suggest three points that could be made to Kelly in favour of censorship.

1. *Censorship is necessary to prevent children from accessing unsuitable material such as pornography.*
2. *Giving people free access to offensive material like racism and pornography may result in a lowering of morals in society.*
3. *Censorship is needed to prevent extreme groups from using the Internet to recruit impressionable people for terrorism.*

You don't have to necessarily agree with the points, but you need to be able to argue for both sides...

(3 marks)

Exam Question

The final question in the exam is often a short essay. Here's an example.
Plan your answer in rough using bullet points before you start writing.

There is no doubt that advances in ICT have changed society, but people would argue about whether computers have actually improved people's lives. Discuss five benefits and five disadvantages that the increased use of ICT has brought for society.

(10 marks)

Revision Summary for Section Ten

This was the last section of revision. Do all these questions, then you should be ready for your mock exam. If you get anything wrong, look it up, then have another go at the question.

But remember — this section's all about getting you to think about the overall impact of computers. So some of these questions won't have a right or wrong answer, just a good or bad answer.

1) What data is covered by the Data Protection Act?
2) Explain the eight principles covered in the Act (yes — all of them).
3) What three things are illegal under the Copyright, Design and Patents Act?
4) What three things are illegal under the Computer Misuse Act?
5) List and explain three jobs that have been replaced, and three jobs that have been created by increased computer use.
6) Explain the difference between teleworking and hot-desking.
7) Explain the benefits and problems of teleworking for employers and employees.
8) Explain the benefits and problems of hot-desking for employers and employees.
9) What do RSI and ULD stand for? List one cause of RSI/ULD.
10) Identify two other health problems from the overuse of computers, and explain their causes.
11) Identify and explain three ways that the risks associated with computer use can be reduced.
12) Explain three things that are covered by the Health and Safety (Display Screen Equipment) Regulations 1992.
13) Explain three moral or ethical issues resulting from increased computer use.
14) Explain three social issues resulting from increased computer use.
15) Explain three benefits to society of increased computer use.

The next questions are similar to what you might get asked in the exam. They include issues that have been covered elsewhere in the book. You need to cover the benefits and problems before making up your own mind whether the overall impact is good or bad.

16) Examine the effects on society of an increased reliance on computers.
17) Discuss the impact on society of the growth in home shopping.
18) Discuss the moral issues that result from an increase in computer use amongst children.
19) Examine the impact of the increased use of satellites to receive and transmit computer data.
20) Examine the impact on society of an increase in teleworking.
21) Discuss the impact of using robots instead of people to manufacture goods.
22) Discuss the relative advantages and disadvantages of an increase in the use of the World Wide Web and e-mail.

And finally, a few pearls of wisdom on the subject of modern technology:

"This 'telephone' has too many shortcomings to be seriously considered as a means of communication. The device is inherently of no value to us."
Western Union internal memo, 1876

"Computers in the future may weigh no more than 1.5 tons".
Popular Mechanics, 1949

By the year 2000, housewives will probably have a robot 'maid', shaped like a box with one large eye on the top, several arms and hands, and long narrow pads on the side for moving about."
New York Times, 1966

"There is no reason anyone would want a computer in their home."
Ken Olson, President, Chairman and founder of Digital Equipment Corp., 1977

"I think there is a world market for maybe five computers."
Thomas Watson, chairman of IBM, 1943

Practice Exam

Once you've been through all the questions in this book, you should feel pretty confident about the exam. As final preparation, here is a **practice exam** to really get you set for the real thing. It's split into **two papers** — which are in different formats. The papers are designed to give you the best possible preparation for the differing question styles of the actual exams, whichever syllabus you're following. If you're doing Foundation then you won't have learnt every bit — but it's still good practice. (Some exam boards have one long paper, rather than two short papers — if yours does this, you could do both papers together.)

General Certificate of Secondary Education

GCSE
Information and Communication Technology (ICT)

Centre name					
Centre number					
Candidate number					

Paper 1

Surname
Other names
Candidate signature

Time allowed: 1 hour 15 minutes

Instructions to candidates
- Write your name and other details in the spaces provided above.
- Answer **all** questions in the spaces provided.
- Do all rough work on the paper.
- In calculations show clearly how you work out your answers.

Information for candidates
- There are **8** questions in this paper. There are **no** blank pages.
- The marks available are given in brackets at the end of each question or part-question.
- Marks will not be deducted for incorrect answers.
- The total number of marks available for the paper is **60**.

Advice to candidates
- Work steadily through the paper.
- Don't spend too long on one question.
- If you have time at the end, go back and check your answers.

1 A mail order electronics company uses a computerised stock control system in its warehouse.

(a) In order to find an item, a six-digit item code number has to be entered into the computer. Give **two** validation checks which could be used on this number.

Check 1 Range check ....

....

Check 2 presence check. ....

....

(2 marks)

(b) Give **one** reason it is not suitable to store the database on a CD-ROM.

....

(1 mark)

OCR Specimen, 2003

2 A company has branches all over the world and uses electronic conferencing to communicate with its employees.

(a) Describe electronic conferencing.

....

....

....

....

(2 marks)

(b) Give **two** benefits to the company and its employees of using electronic conferencing.

Benefit 1 ....

....

Benefit 2 ....

....

(2 marks)

OCR Specimen, 2003

Lea bla

Leave blank

3 An expert system is to be created to help doctors diagnose illnesses. Describe the stages involved in creating this expert system.

....

....

....

....

....

....

....

....

....

....

....

....

....

....

....

(3 marks)

OCR Specimen, 2003

4 A library uses an extensive database system that was written to meet its specific needs. The system allows a variety of people to find out about the books the library owns. The database can be interrogated in many ways and can generate a wide variety of reports.

(a) Name **three** fields which you would expect the books database to contain.

Field 1 ....I.D number ....

Field 2 ....No of books ....

Field 3 ....book name ....

(3 marks)

(b) Give **three** ways in which a person wanting to borrow books might use the system.

Way 1 ....

....

Way 2 ....

....

Way 3 ....

....

(3 marks)

8/0

(c) Give **two** advantages to the library staff of having this system.

Advantage 1 ....

....

....

Advantage 2 ....

....

....

(2 marks)

AQA, 2003

Leave blank

5 Describe how the misuse of computers might give rise to legal and moral problems.

Data misuse act make it illegal to have anouthorized access to computer such as hacking and then deliting their file.

(4 marks)

OCR Specimen, 2002

6 Discuss the advantages and disadvantages of using information technology in shopping.

By using Ict it will help caushmer to buy 24/7.
they can compare different prices.
It is Cheap.
They can buy varity of things.

Disadvantages:-
(1) Need credit and debit card.
(2) Internet fraud.
(3) you cannot physically touch.

(4 marks)

OCR Specimen, 2002

7 An Asian restaurant uses a spreadsheet to record sales.
This is part of the spreadsheet.

	A	B	C	D
1	**Meal**	**Price**	**Quantity Sold**	**Takings**
2	Meat Bhuna	£4.50	2	£9.00
3	Chicken Tandoori	£5.00	5	£25.00
4	Lamb Balti	£6.50	3	£19.50
5	Vegetable Curry	£3.25	4	£13.00
6				
7			Total Takings =	£66.50

(a) (i) The cells in the spreadsheet contain different types of information.
Using words from the list, complete the sentences below.

text
a formula
a model
a menu
a number
a date

Cell A3 Contains......text......

Cell C4 Contains......Number......

Cell D3 Contains......formula......

(3 marks)

(ii) Tick **one** box to show the format of cell B2.

	Tick **one** box
currency	✓
number	
general	
percentage	
time	

(1 mark)

(b) (i) Write down the formula in cell D4.

(1 mark)

(ii) Write down the formula in cell D7.

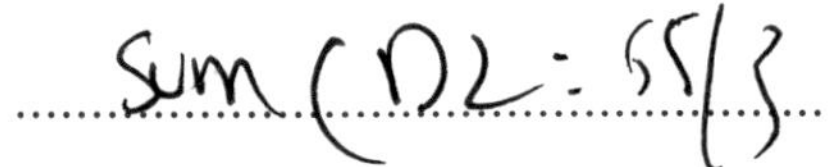

(2 marks)

Leave blank

(c) The price of Vegetable Curry is increased to £4.00.

(i) Describe how the spreadsheet must be edited.

the spreed sheet will atomaticly update new pric.

(2 marks)

(ii) When the spreadsheet has been edited, the values in some cells change automatically. Identify **two** cells which change automatically.

Cell 1: D5

Cell 2: D7

(2 marks)

(d) A spreadsheet can generate different types of graph. For each of the following, write down the type of graph shown.

(i)

Takings for meals

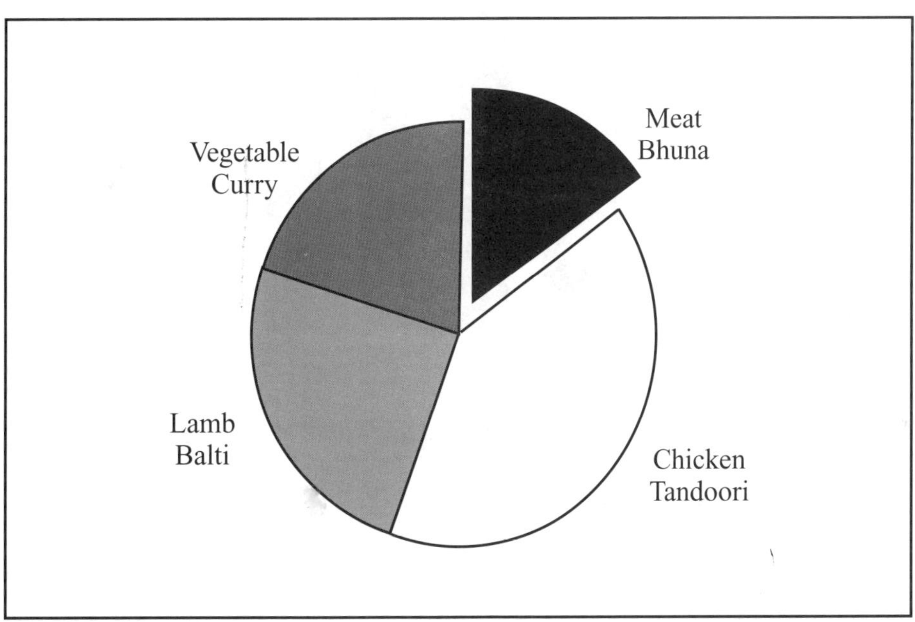

Type of graph Pic chat

QUESTION 7 CONTINUES ON THE NEXT PAGE

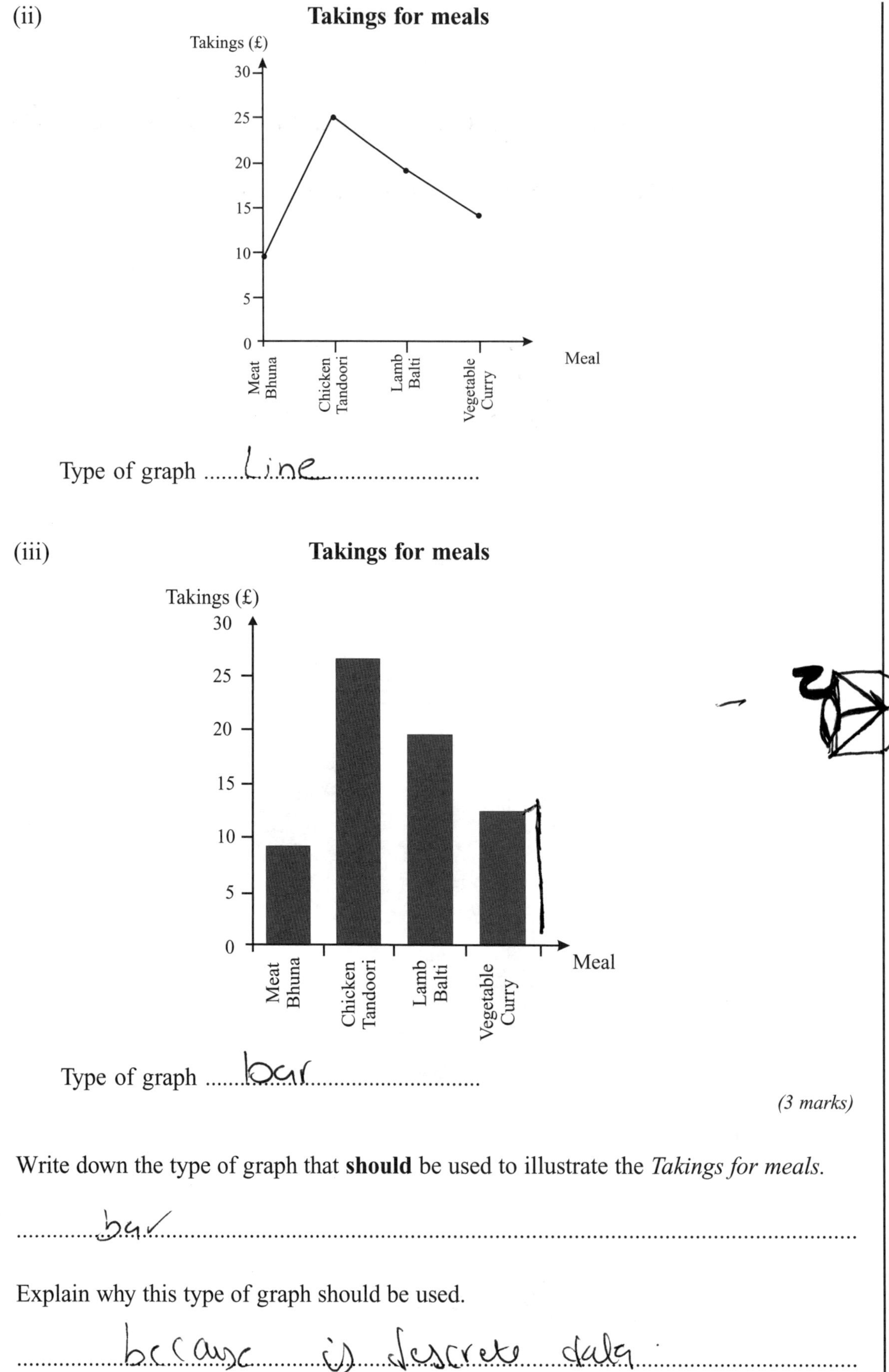

(3 marks)

(e) Write down the type of graph that **should** be used to illustrate the *Takings for meals*.

..........bar ✓..........

Explain why this type of graph should be used.

..........because is descrete data..........

....

(1 mark)

AQA, 2003

Leave blank

8 The residents in the village of Little Haven are worried about the large increase in traffic in their village. Traffic comes in and out of the village along any one of four roads.

There have been several accidents in the village and pollution levels are high. In addition there has been some damage to some very old properties on the roadside.

The residents want a by-pass to take traffic round their village.

The local authority want to collect data to see if a by-pass is necessary.

(a) Explain how a data logging system could be used to monitor the flow of traffic in and out of Little Haven throughout the day.

....

....

....

....

....

....

....

....

....

(3 marks)

(b) Explain why it is necessary to record the time when a vehicle is detected.

....

....

....

....

....

....

(2 marks)

(c) In most cases coaches and heavy lorries are longer than cars.

Explain how the data logging system could detect approximately how many lorries and coaches pass through Little Haven.

....

....

....

....

....

(3 marks)

QUESTION 8 CONTINUES ON THE NEXT PAGE

(d) Little Haven Council insist that data collection must take place for a full year before a decision about the by-pass can be made.

Explain why they insist on this.

....

....

....

(2 marks)

(e) The data that is collected is stored in a computer file called BYPASS.

The time a vehicle is detected is stored.

Give the names of **four** other fields that **must** be part of each record in BYPASS.

1 ....

2 ....

3 ....

4 ....

(4 marks)

(f) Name the **type** of software package that could be used to analyse the BYPASS file.

....

(1 mark)

(g) When the route for the by-pass was surveyed some old underground workings were found. The surveyor used a video camera connected to a robot to investigate the workings.

Explain **two** reasons why this equipment was necessary.

1 Robot are more accurate than human

....

....

2 It can be used in may dagrus places

....

....

(4 marks)

Edexcel, 2002

END OF QUESTIONS

General Certificate of Secondary Education

GCSE
Information and Communication Technology (ICT)

Centre name					
Centre number					
Candidate number					

Paper 2

Surname
Other names
Candidate signature

Time allowed: 1 hour 15 minutes

Instructions to candidates

- Write your name and other details in the spaces provided above.
- Answer **all** questions in the spaces provided.
- Do all rough work on the paper.
- In calculations show clearly how you work out your answers.

Information for candidates

- This paper has **two** sections.
  Section A consists of **20 multiple choice questions**.
  Section B consists of **3 structured questions**.
- The marks available are given in brackets at the end of each question or part-question.
- There are **20** marks available in total in section A.
  There are **40** marks available in total in section B.
- Marks will not be deducted for incorrect answers.
- There are **no** blank pages.

Advice to candidates

- Work steadily through the paper.
- Don't spend too long on one question.
- If you have time at the end, go back and check your answers.

SECTION A **Attempt all questions. Write your answers in the boxes.**

Lea
bla

A1 The central processing unit includes

a processor and main storage
b input devices and processor
c input devices, output devices and backing storage
d all of the above

Answer

(1 mark)

A2 The process of data capture involves

a input of data, process and output
b collection of data, validation, processing
c evaluating output
d collection of data, verification, input

Answer

(1 mark)

A3 A record structure is

a the number of files on a disk
b the length of the record
c the definition of each field in a record
d the number of records in a file

Answer

(1 mark)

A4 An example of sensible and economical coding for a date field is

a 23 March 2000
b 23/03/2000
c 23/Mch/2000
d 23032000

Answer

(1 mark)

A5 The data capture device in a computer controlled system might be

a a multiple choice form
b a thermometer
c a keyboard
d a sensor

Answer

(1 mark)

A6 The appropriate technique to produce an individualised mail shot is

a mail merge
b copy and paste
c search and replace
d a word processing macro

Answer

(1 mark)

A7 The evaluation of a computer-based solution to a problem involves

a designing the solution
b performing the technical testing of the working solution
c obtaining the user's reaction to the working solution
d documenting the history of how the solution was developed

Answer

(1 mark)

Leave blank

A8 A sales assistant records the sales of compact discs in a music shop in a spreadsheet. Part of the spreadsheet is shown below.

	A	B	C	D	E	F	G	H
1	SALES OF COMPACT DISCS							
2		MAR	APR	MAY	JUN	JUL	AUG	TOTAL
3	POP	189	245	255	198	176	188	**1251**
4	JAZZ	93	119	103	66	99	75	**555**
5	ROCK	56	45	59	39	58	72	**329**
6	CLASSICAL	127	155	172	135	115	92	**796**
7	TOTAL	**456**	**564**	**589**	**438**	**448**	**427**	**2931**

The assistant finds that she has made an error and changes the figure in cell E4 to 60. When the spreadsheet is recalculated

- a all the values in row 4 will change
- b there would be no change to the other values in row 4 or column E
- c the values in cells E7, H4 and H7 will change
- d all the values in column E will change

Answer 

(1 mark)

A9 A shop manager wants to use a spreadsheet to display a running total of sales. The essential feature of the spreadsheet software for this task is

- a formatting
- b fill down / replication
- c automatic recalculation
- d relative addressing

Answer 

(1 mark)

A10 A computer simulation is

- a the same as a computer model
- b a model NOT running real time
- c the design of a computer-controlled robot
- d the output of a computer program that represents a model

Answer d

(1 mark)

A11 An example of an operating systems utility is

- a a screen saver
- b a printer driver
- c database software
- d a spreadsheet

Answer 

(1 mark)

A12 A Health club is using a computer to enter details of new members. A data entry screen is to be created for the receptionist. The information needed before the screen can be designed is

- a a list of all current members of the club
- b a list of all staff at the club
- c a list of all data items for each member
- d a list of all facilities available at the club

Answer 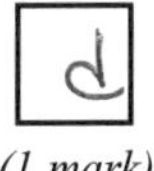

(1 mark)

A13 A hospital uses a computer system which contains a patient database. Access to the database is restricted for these possible reasons

1 to make sure the data is not misunderstood
2 to make sure the data is kept confidential
3 to comply with the law
4 for technical reasons

The TWO MAIN reasons are

a 1 and 2
b 2 and 3
c 3 and 4
d 4 and 1

Answer b

(1 mark)

A14 A doctor wants to send personalised standard letters to all children aged 13-16 who have not had a BCG injection. The data handling processes which will be used are

a sorting and searching
b searching and merging
c merging and updating
d updating and sorting

Answer b

(1 mark)

A15 The quickest way to access a particular Web Page is

a search the web using a single keyword
b leave a message with a relevant Newsgroup
c type in the full web page identifier
d search the web with a combination of keywords

Answer c

(1 mark)

A16 A macro is written to insert the current day's date in a letter. Which TWO of these are the purposes of the macro?

1 to date stamp all correspondence received
2 to improve security
3 to reduce input errors
4 to standardise procedures

a 1 and 2
b 2 and 3
c 3 and 4
d 4 and 1

a

Answer c

(1 mark)

Leave blank

A17 Which TWO tasks does an operating system carry out?

1 allows a user to load files
2 displays an error message if a device is not available
3 works out staff payroll
4 calculates formulae with accuracy

a 1 and 3
b 1 and 2
c 2 and 3
d 3 and 4

Answer [b]
(1 mark)

A18 Which TWO of the following computer applications can work in batch processing mode?

1 processing cheques
2 patient monitoring
3 producing gas bills
4 traffic light control

a 1 and 2
b 2 and 3
c 2 and 4
d 1 and 3

Answer [d]
(1 mark)

A19 When a new program has been developed it must be tested

a to make sure that all the formulae are correct
b to make sure all the output is guaranteed correct
c to make sure that it will always stop you inputting wrong data
d to make sure it will never crash

Answer [b]
(1 mark)

A20 Which of these is a use of macros which speed up the operator's work?

a replicating data
b replacing key stroke sequences
c reducing software code
d removing complex diagrams

Answer [b]
(1 mark)

Total marks for section A: 20 marks

Edexcel Specimen, 2003

SECTION B **Attempt all questions. Write your answers in the spaces provided.**

B1 From the list below, choose the **most** suitable type of application software to use for each task described.

Charts	Drawing
Communications	Mail-merging
Database	Spreadsheet
Data logging	Web design
Desk top publishing	Word processing

Task	**Application Software**
(a) storing a video club's membership records	....
(b) sending a personalised letter to all members of a club	....
(c) writing a book	....
(d) calculating the monthly cost of running a car	....
(e) automatically collecting temperatures at a weather station	....
(f) organising the layout of a school newspaper	....

(6 marks)

AQA, 2003

B2 At the Heaton Medical Centre there are five doctors. Each doctor has an office and there is a large office in reception.
Each doctor has a computer workstation in their office. These computer workstations are connected in a network. The computer network is controlled by a file server.

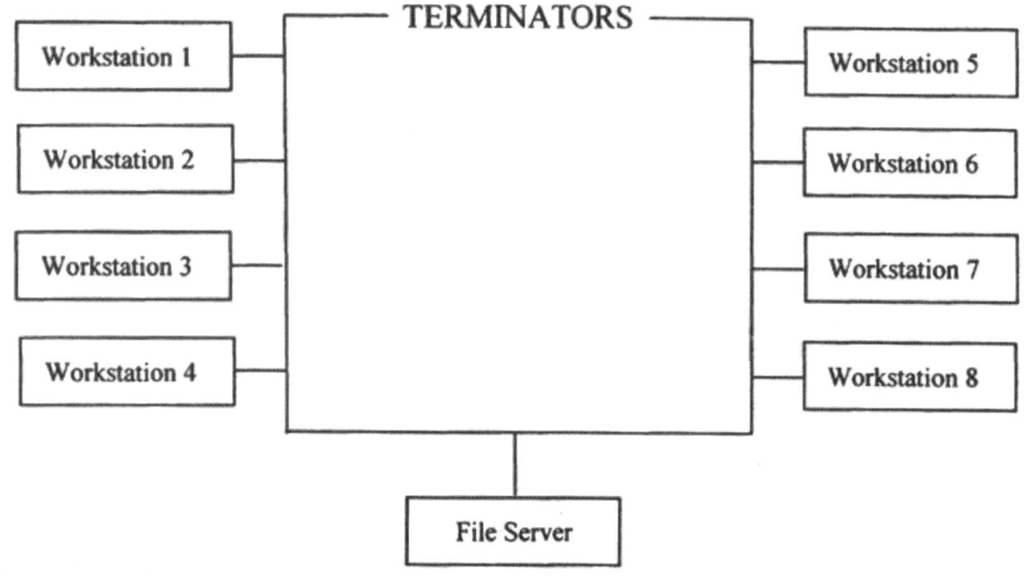

Leave blank

(a) (i) Give **two** advantages of using a computer network rather than a stand-alone computer for each doctor in the Heaton Medical Centre.

1 ....

....

2 ....

....

(2 marks)

(ii) Describe a situation where it would be a disadvantage to have a computer network rather than stand-alone computers for each doctor.

....

....

....

(2 marks)

(b) The doctors in the Heaton Medical Centre want to have their computer network connected to the Newtown Hospital Trust computer system.

The doctors are concerned about linking up to the hospital computer system because of security.

Give **two** security concerns the doctors might have.

1 ....

....

....

....

2 ....

....

....

....

(4 marks)

QUESTION B2 CONTINUES ON THE NEXT PAGE

(c) In the Heaton Medical Centre all doctors have a printer in their office.

In addition there is a printer connected to the network server.

(i) Give **one** reason why there is a printer in each consulting room.

....

....

....

(1 mark)

(ii) Give **one** use for the printer connected to the file server.

....

....

....

(1 mark)

(iii) Give **one** use for the file server in the network in the Heaton Medical Centre.

....

....

....

(1 mark)

(d) Computer systems are being developed to diagnose illnesses automatically.

(i) Give **two** advantages of such a system.

1 ....

....

....

....

2 ....

....

....

....

(4 marks)

Lea… bla…

Leave blank

(ii) Give **two** disadvantages of such a system.

1 ....

....

....

....

2 ....

....

....

....

(4 marks)

(Total 19 marks)

Edexcel, 2001

B3 (a) Discuss the advantages and disadvantages to a customer of Internet banking and on-line shopping.

Le
blc

(8 marks)

If D2<16.5, U, (If D2<=25 "A" If (E2>25, "O")))

Leave blank

(b) Internet banks and on-line shops collect personal information about their customers. They know where their customers live and what they buy. Sometimes they give this personal information to other companies.

Discuss the advantages and disadvantages to a customer because Internet banks, on-line shops and other companies know this personal information.

....

....

....

....

....

....

....

....

(4 marks)

(c) Describe **three** principles of data protection that protect customers from companies misusing their personal information.

Principle 1: ....

....

Principle 2: ....

....

Principle 3: ....

....

....

(3 marks)

AQA, 2003

END OF QUESTIONS

Section One — What is a Computer?

Page 10 (Warm-up Questions)

1

Workstation A
Workstation B
Workstation C
File Server
Workstation D

2 A LAN is a Local Area Network — a computer network on one site connected by cables or radio signals, e.g. at a school.

3 A WAN is a Wide Area Network — a computer network that is spread across a wide geographical area, e.g. a country, and is connected using telecommunications.

4 Answers include:
Keeping record of serial numbers, burglar alarms, locking doors and windows and using window blinds, fireproof doors and smoke alarms.

5 A back-up file is a file that contains a copy of the data for security purposes.

6 A read only file is one that can only be viewed and the data it contains cannot be changed in any way by the user.

Page 11 (Exam Questions)

1 a)

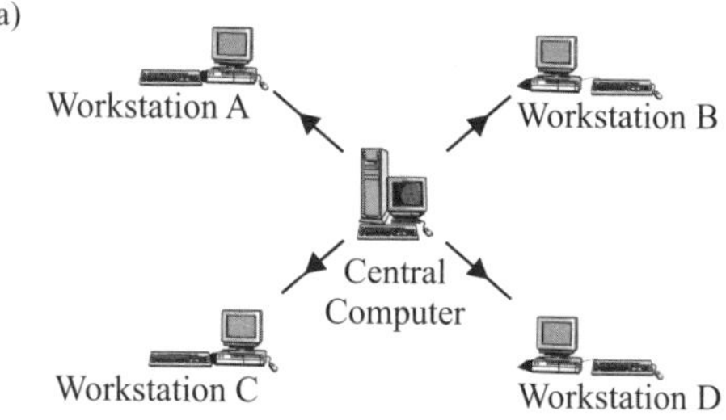

2 marks for the diagram — 1 mark for a correctly labelled central computer / server, 1 mark for correctly showing workstations connected as above.

Advantages include:
Cable failure can be more easily identified than on a line or ring network; if a cable fails, only that workstation is affected.
1 mark available for a correct answer.
Disadvantages include:
If the main computer fails then the whole network will fail; it uses more cabling so can be more expensive.
1 mark available for a correct answer.

b) Answers include: Record serial numbers; install burglar alarms; keep computer room doors locked; use fireproof doors; smoke alarms; keep computers out of view e.g. not on the ground floor of buildings, use window blinds to hide them.
Award 1 mark for each correct answer (maximum of 4 marks)

2 Answers include:
A LAN means that peripherals such as printers can be shared; software can be shared amongst users; users are able to communicate quickly across the network; terminals are cheaper than stand-alone PCs.
Award 1 mark for each correct advantage (maximum of 2 marks)

3 a) (i) A username is a name given to an authorised user of the network which determines what level of access they are allowed ***(1 mark)***.
(ii) A password enables the user to gain access to the network and prevents unauthorised access ***(1 mark)***.

Make sure you understand why you need a username and a password — the username identifies you and the password proves that it's actually you.

b) (i) A backup is a copy of the data that is on the computer ***(1 mark)***.
(ii) The backup files should be kept in a secure location, preferably off-site and in a locked fireproof safe / room ***(1 mark)***.

Section Two — The Parts of a Computer System

Page 19 (Warm-up Questions)

1 The first six letters on the top row of letters of the keyboard.

2 Optical Character Recognition.

3 Optical Mark Recognition.

4 Microphone.

5 Scanner.

6 Converts analogue video images e.g. from a videotape or video camera, into digital images which can be manipulated using imaging software.

Page 20 (Exam Questions)

1 a) A concept keyboard contains symbols or buttons — each symbol or button represents an item of data such as a meal on the menu ***(1 mark)***; when a symbol is pressed, the data is entered onto the computer system ***(1 mark)***.

b) Answers include: it's quicker than typing each character individually; fewer errors are likely to be made; more customers can be served.
Award 1 mark for a correct benefit.

2 Possible benefits include:
no need to print and scan a photographic print — the image can be uploaded straight onto the computer system; the image can be edited using photo-editing software; the image can be used straight away.
Possible drawbacks include: i) digital cameras are more expensive than film cameras; ii) high quality images take up a lot of computer memory; iii) digital cameras are expensive to operate as they consume a lot of battery power.
Award 1 mark for a correct benefit and 1 mark for a correct drawback.

3 a) Possible drawbacks:
a mouse needs to be moved across a flat surface, there may not be one where the laptop is being used; the mouse needs space in which it can be operated, this may be inconvenient if the laptop is being used in a confined space, such as a car.
Award 1 mark for 1 correct drawback.

b) The tracker ball is built into the surface of the laptop computer; the hand or finger is used to rotate the surface of the ball; the direction and speed of rotation causes the cursor to move on the computer screen.
Award 1 mark for each of two correct points.

c) Possible benefits of a tracker ball:
The tracker ball is located on the laptop; so less space is needed to operate it; there are no trailing wires, unlike a conventional mouse.
Possible drawbacks include:
Using a tracker ball can be fiddly; it can take time to learn how to use it properly; it is not as effective as a mouse for working with graphic images.
Award 1 mark for each correct point up to a maximum of four marks. If only benefits or drawbacks are described, award a maximum of 3 marks.

You don't need to memorise benefits and drawbacks of things like tracker balls. If you understand how a tracker ball works, it's really easy to work out them out for yourself.

Page 26 (Warm-up Questions)

1 Laser printers.

2 1200 dpi.

3 Visual Display Unit.

4 LCD (Liquid Crystal Display) and CRT (Cathode Ray Tubes). LCD monitors have flat screens and are used in laptops. CRT monitors use similar technology to TVs — the monitors are generally much larger and heavier. They can cause eye damage if used for long periods.

5 Computer Output on Microfilm.

6 Actuators.

Page 27 (Exam Questions)

1 a) Pages per minute ***(1 mark)***.

b) Possible advantages include: fast printing time; high quality printed document; laser printers are relatively cheap to use; relatively quiet printing.
Possible disadvantages include: likely to be expensive to buy; print quality may not be worth the extra expense; generally much larger than other (ink-jet) printers; expensive to repair.

Award 1 mark for each of four relevant points. Award a maximum of 3 marks if only advantages or disadvantages discussed.

2 (Flat-bed) graph-plotter ***(1 mark)***.

3 a) Possible devices include: lights; sirens/alarm bells; recording equipment; equipment to send telephone signal to a police/security guard station. ***Award 1 mark for each of 2 appropriate devices.***

b) Possible answers include: the output devices might not be able to communicate directly with the burglar alarm system; the output devices might operate at a different electrical voltage to the burglar alarm system; the output devices might operate at a different processing speed to the burglar alarm system.
Award 1 mark for a relevant reason.

Page 35 (Warm-up Questions)

1 Random Access Memory and Read Only Memory.

2 Hard disk (accept hard drive).

3 1.44 megabytes.

4 Compact Disk Read-Write.

5 DVD.

6 The operating system can appear to carry out more than one process or program at the same time.

Page 36 (Exam Questions)

1 a) RAM is where the data needed to operate computer programs and new data is stored. ***Award 1 mark for a partial answer and 2 marks for a detailed answer.***

b) Answers include:
The computer with 256 Mb of RAM will probably be able to run complex programs faster; it will be able to run more programs at the same time; it may also run some programs that the 64 Mb RAM computer cannot run at all. ***Award 1 mark each for up to 2 correct points.***

2 Accept CD, CD-RW, CD-R, (or DVD equivalents), ZIP drive.
Do not accept: floppy disk, CD-ROM, hard-disk, etc.
Reasons: These disks have a large storage capacity that will be big enough for the required files. ***Award 1 mark for a valid medium and 1 mark for a valid reason.***

3 a) Possible answers: a GUI combines a menu-driven interface with buttons/icons; a GUI is the means by which the user communicates with the operating system; it uses menus, icons, windows and pointers.
Award 1 mark for each of 2 relevant points.

b) Possible benefits:
the user doesn't need to learn lots of commands; the layout of the user-interface can make it easier to navigate; icons can reduce the number of commands that need to be given.
Possible drawbacks:
the layout of the menus can be confusing until they have been used a number of times; the GUI can require a lot of memory to operate; they can be time-consuming to use.
Award 1 mark for each of 4 relevant points, award a maximum of 3 marks if only benefits or drawbacks are discussed.

Remember: GUIs are known as WIMPs — Windows, Icons, Menus, Pointers. Look back to page 34 if you don't know what I'm talking about.

Section Three — Using a Computer System

Page 41 (Warm-up Questions)

1 Answers include data-capture forms; questionnaires.

2 Answers include faster than manual systems; more accurate; can capture data in dangerous conditions.

3 25/12/04.

4 Range check.

5 Check digit.

6 Answers include proof reading; double-entry.

Page 42 (Exam Questions)

1 a) Possible benefits: meter reading will be up-to-date; might be cheaper than an automatic system; providing employment.
Possible drawbacks: data only collected if the customer is at home; cost of the meter readers' wages; time consuming method; chance of human error.
Award 1 mark for a correct benefit and 1 mark for a correct drawback.

Questions like this are common sense really — just think about it and you should come up with some reasonable answers. Remember — <u>cost</u> and <u>time</u> come into almost every advantage/disadvantage question.

b) Possible answer:
the meter could record its own value; the meter could be connected to the telephone network; once a month, the meter could connect to the office computer via the telephone network; the meter could then transmit its reading directly to the office computer.
Other answers possible. Award 1 mark for each of 3 relevant points.

2 a) Possible data includes: name; address; date of birth; telephone number; favourite types of book (e.g. fiction, non-fiction).
Award 1 mark for each of 3 relevant items of data.

b) Answers include: keep the design simple: e.g. leave enough space to answer each question; make sure the document is useful — only ask for relevant and useful information; make sure the form is accurate: check it for errors and test it before using it.
Award up to 2 marks for each of 2 relevant pieces of advice (1 mark for identifying a point, 1 mark for explanation).

3 a) Possible answers include: range check; presence check; data type check.
Award 1 mark for each of 2 correct answers.

b) Answers include: data validation ensures that data is of the right type, not that the data is correct e.g. she might type 45 instead of 54; the original information may have been wrong e.g. incorrect test totals.
Award 2 marks for one well explained answer. Award 1 mark for one partially explained answer.

c) She could proofread the spreadsheet...and compare it with her original test results...and then change any incorrect entries on the spreadsheet.
Award 2 marks for a well explained answer. Award 1 mark for a partially explained answer.

Page 48 (Warm-up Questions)

1 Extension.

2 Field.

3 Real-time processing.

4 Serial (or sequential) access.

5 Direct access.

6 What You See Is What You Get.

Page 49 (Exam Questions)

1 a) A record is a complete unit of data that contains information about a particular object. The data will be divided into different fields.
Award 2 marks for a good definition (e.g. that includes a reference to fields or data object). Award 1 mark for a partial definition.

b) Serial access is used with storage mediums such as magnetic tape where records are stored one after the other. The computer has to go through all the data in the order it is stored to find the data it requires.
Award 2 marks for a good definition (e.g. that makes reference to the storage medium or explains how the data is arranged on the medium). Award 1 mark for a partial definition.

Remember — serial and sequential access aren't quite the same thing. It's all explained on page 44.

2 a) Real time processing ***(1 mark)***.

b) Possible benefits:
customers have up-to-date information; no double-bookings.
Possible drawbacks: system is expensive; system may be slower for customers as the system has to extract current data; tickets need to be purchased there and then, otherwise the information becomes out of date.
Award 1 mark each for 1 correct benefit and 1 correct drawback.

3 a) Screen display/monitor ***(1 mark)***.

b) Printed copy/hard copy ***(1 mark)***.

Page 50 (Exam Questions)

4 a) Batch processing ***(1 mark)***.

b) Records are stored one after the other but they are stored in a sensible (logical) order. This method is used for magnetic tape based systems. ***Award 2 marks for a good definition (e.g. that makes reference to the logical order or storage medium). Award 1 mark for a partial definition.***

c) The original master file contains the original data ***(1 mark)***; the transactions file contains the new and updated records ***(1 mark)***; the two files are merged one record at a time ***(1 mark)***; to create a new master file ***(1 mark)***.

5 a) Multimedia combines text, graphics and sound information. Each type of information complements the others. Examples include CD-ROM encyclopedias and websites. ***Award 2 marks for a good definition (e.g. including reference to complementary nature or giving examples). Award 1 mark for a partial definition.***

b) Possible benefits:
the Headteacher can study the content at length; the Headteacher can write notes onto the printed copy; the Headteacher can keep a copy of the webpages; a computer is not needed to view the webpages.
Possible drawbacks:
the multimedia elements will not be included; the website is not designed to be a static document, so it will not look as intended; sound and moving images will not be observed and so cannot be discussed; difficult to see how the website all fits together, i.e. how you navigate it, from separate sheets of paper.
Award 1 mark for each of 4 relevant points. Award a maximum of 3 marks if only the benefits or drawbacks are discussed.

6 Possible benefits:
information can be extracted from the website by partially sighted/blind people or anyone not looking directly at their screen; moods can be set more powerfully than just by colour or text; sound can communicate some information better than other media.
Possible drawbacks:
a sound card and speakers are needed to hear the sounds; sound takes up a lot of memory, so download time may be slow; sound can distract from other information and media contained in the website.
Award 1 mark for each of 4 relevant points. Award a maximum of 3 marks if only the benefits or drawbacks are discussed.

Sometimes exam questions aren't very clear about exactly what you have to do. "Evaluate the use of sounds" basically means they want you to give some good points and bad points about it. Since the question's worth 4 marks, 2 good and 2 bad points would be the thing to go for...

Section Four — Systems analysis

Page 55 (Warm-up Questions)

1

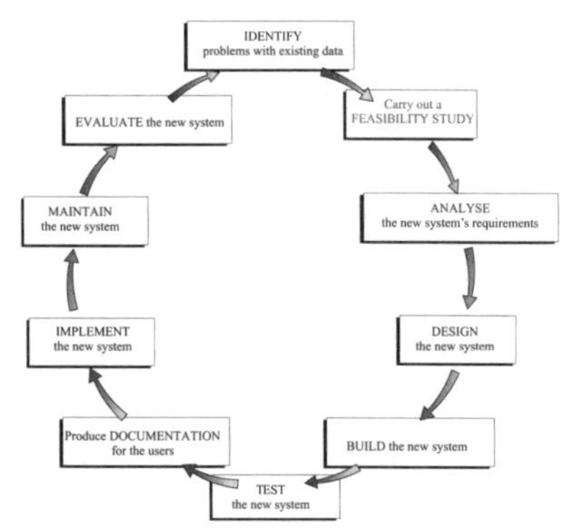

2 Answers include: i) interviewing users; ii) questionnaires; iii) observation; iv) studying documents.

3 The feasibility study analyses the requirements of the new system and helps to decide if the new system is worth creating.

4 Decide on the objectives of the new system, identify the hardware and software needed, carry out a cost-benefit study, make a recommendation.

5 Input, process, output.

6 Data that lies at the limit of acceptable data, e.g. months 1 and 12.

Page 56 (Exam Questions)

1 a) Possible answers: the system will replace a manual system; the existing computer system is working at full capacity; the existing computer system cannot perform all the tasks the bank wants it to perform.
Award 1 mark for each of 2 correct points.

b) Possible answers: i) decide where the data will come from; ii) design data capture forms; iii) decide how the data needs to be structured; iv) decide how data will be entered onto the system; v) design input screens; vi) decide how data will be validated.
Award 1 mark for each of 4 correct points.

2 a) Evaluation ***(1 mark)***

b) Analysis ***(1 mark)***

c) Design ***(1 mark)***

d) Analysis ***(1 mark)***

e) Testing ***(1 mark)***

f) Implementation ***(1 mark)***

3 Answers include:
a cost-benefit study helps decide if the new system is feasible; it identifies the potential benefits of the new system; for example the time savings; it identifies the potential costs of the new system; for example the costs of building the new system; the benefits are then compared with the costs; if the benefits outweigh the costs, the new system is recommended.
Award 1 mark for each of 4 correct points.

Remember to always look at the number of marks for the question — that tells you how much detail to go into — if there aren't 4 points in your answer, you won't get the 4 marks.

Page 62 (Warm-up Questions)

1

manual input

2 'System testing' and 'acceptance testing'.

3 Installation guide.

4 User guide.

5 When the new system is introduced all in one go, but the old system is kept running.

6 The system is checked to see if it still meets the objectives that were originally set for it.

Page 63 (Exam Questions)

1 a) Answers include:
technical documentation is written for computer engineers and programmers, so uses technical language; user documentation is written for general users, so uses less technical language; technical documentation explains how to maintain and manage the computer system, user documentation describes how to operate the system; technical documentation explains how to solve major problems with the system, user documentation explains how to solve simple software problems.
Award 1 mark for each of two correct answers.

b) Answers include:
when something goes wrong with the system and it needs to be repaired; when the system needs to be upgraded and new components installed; when the system needs to be closed down and reinstalled.
Award 1 mark for each of two correct answers.

2 a) Phased implementation is when different parts of the new system are introduced one at a time...whilst the old system is kept operating.
Award 2 marks for a good definition that refers to both the new and old systems. Award 1 mark for a partial answer (e.g. that only refers to the new system).

b) Benefits:
there is time to fully test the new system in operation; problems can be solved without affecting the operations of the old system.
Drawbacks:
it can take a long time to fully implement the new system; it will take a long time before the system as a whole can be tested.
Award 1 mark for a correct benefit and 1 mark for a correct drawback.

c) When the new system has been fully introduced and has passed all the tests set for it ***(1 mark)***.

3 Answers include:
to check if the system meets the objectives originally set for it; to establish whether or not the system has become obsolete; to establish if the computer system has the capacity to cope with the current needs of its users. ***Award 1 mark for each of two correct reasons.***

Section Five — Text and Image Processing Software

Page 71 (Warm-up Questions)

1 Spell check is a program used by the computer to check the words against a list in its dictionary. Proof reading is where the document is checked through, usually manually, for errors.

2 Words which are not the correct spelling for the context, but are still actual words, eg "beech" rather than "beach", or words where the order of the letters has been accidentally changed to make another word, eg "form" instead of "from". Spell-checkers won't pick up missing or extra words, unless they include a grammar-checker.

3 Answers include: Bold (emboldening), underlining, italics, font size, font style, font colour, capitals, spaced capitals.

4 The standard font size is generally 12 point (or could be 10 point).

5 Documents can become difficult to read if too many font styles are used. It can be confusing to the reader and nothing draws the attention.

6 Mail-merge lets you send personalised letters by combining a standard letter with information in a database.

7 A macro is a sequence of commands that have been recorded by the computer and saved, using a short code as a filename. You run the macro by keying in the code.

Page 72 (Exam Questions)

1 a) Answers include:
change the font style; change the font size; highlight or emphasise the text; changing the alignment.
Award 1 mark for each correct answer, up to a maximum of 3 marks.

b) Answers include: (i) cut/copy and paste – text is highlighted and then the cut or copy function is used; the cursor repositioned and the paste function used, (ii) search and replace – where some or all instances of a word or phrase can be replaced with an alternative, (iii) delete and retype – text is deleted using the delete or backspace key and the new text input, (iv) drag and drop – the text to be moved is highlighted and then dragged to its new location, (v) highlight and overtype – the text to be replaced is highlighted and the new text typed over the top of it.
Award 1 mark each for up to two correct methods and a further mark for an explanation of each method (max 4 marks).

2 a) Answers include:
tables neatly line up the information, making it easier to read than a list; tables can be formatted with borders and colour to make the information stand out better; they can make documents look more professional.
Award 1 mark each for up to 2 correct answers.

b) (i) portrait – where the paper is positioned with the shorter side at the top, making a tall and narrow page, (ii) landscape - where the paper is positioned with the longer side of paper at the top, making a short and wide page. ***Award 1 mark each for the two layout formats and 1 additional mark for correct explanation.***

3 Mail merge ***(1 mark)*** but also accept document template.

4 a) Word Count – this function counts the number of words in a document; if you have a required word limit, this can help you to quickly find out how much more you need to write.

b) Readability Score – this checks things like length of words and complexity of grammar to give the document a measure (score) of how easy it is to read. If your work is aimed at a particular audience, it can help you to find out how suitable it is.
Award 1 mark for correct description of each function and 1 mark for an explanation of how it can help users (max 4 marks).

Word processing is an easy topic — if you've learnt all the features mentioned on pages 65 - 70, you shouldn't have any problems at all.

Page 76 (Warm-up Questions)

1 pixel-based / bitmap-based / painting software AND object-based / vector-based / drawing software.

2 Clip Art on CD-ROM; Clip Art from the Internet; scanned-in existing images; photos (scanned or from a digital camera); images created using graphics software.

3 A JPEG file is compressed and has a smaller file size than a bitmap. Sometimes you can lose some picture quality when a bitmap is converted to a JPEG.

4 Computer Aided Design.

5 Cropping is where unwanted parts of the image are removed. Resizing is where the size of the whole image is changed.

Page 77 (Exam Questions)

1 a) Possible answers include: rotate; skew. ***(1 mark)***

b) Cropping ***(1 mark)***

c) Possible answers include: resize; use the handles to change size. ***(1 mark)***

2 a) Possible answers include:
CAD (Computer Aided Design); drawing software; object-based software; vector-based software. ***Award 1 mark for a correct answer.***
(NB Give no marks for trade names of software eg "2D-Design" etc.)

b) Possible answers include:
designs can be rotated to view from any angle; calculations about the item can be carried out; software can suggest materials and components; software can carry out simulations about how the product will perform under certain conditions; designs can be created quickly; designs can be changed quickly and easily; product simulations can be produced.
Award 1 mark for each correct answer, up to a maximum of 3 marks.

c) Possible answers include: powerful hardware required to run the software; software is expensive; software is hard to use / users require training.
Award 1 mark for a correct answer.

3 a) JPEG ***(1 mark)***

b) Accept answers similar to: it is compressed and so takes up much less file space therefore making it easier to send as an attachment.
Award 1 mark for statement and another mark for explanation.

Page 83 (Warm-up Questions)

1 Desk Top Publishing.

2 DTP software uses (text and graphics) frames, word processing software does not.

3 Newsletters, newspapers, leaflets, posters, etc.

4 A teacher, salesperson, etc.

5 A slide.

6 A commentary.

7 Text, images, animations, videos, sound effects, music.

Page 84 (Exam Questions)

1 a) Possible answers include:
frames can be resized / stretched / squashed / moved; frames can be layered, the text in different frames can be linked together (so that it flows from one frame to the other) or kept separate, giving more layout options.
Award 1 mark for a correct answer.

b) Possible answers include: text frames could be linked together to fit the overflow text in; the size and shape of the frames could be altered to fit the text in; frames could be moved to create more space on the page; size of text could be resized to make it fit.
Award 1 mark for each correct answer up to a maximum of 2 marks.

This frame business can all seem a bit puzzling unless you've "been there". If you have access to DTP software, have a go and it'll make a lot more sense.

2 a) A template (or style sheet) ***(1 mark)***

b) Possible answers:
the quality of the printer being used; the paper quality; the resolution of graphics. ***Award 1 mark for a correct answer.***

c) Possible answers:
send the newsletter to a professional printer company; buy a high quality printer; use high quality paper; make sure graphics are of sufficiently high resolution.
Award 1 mark for a correct answer.

3 a) Possible answers:
animations e.g. flying bullet points, images, video clips, sound clips.
Award 1 mark for a correct answer.

b) Possible answers include:
they could click the mouse button; they could use a remote control button; they could push a button on the keyboard; they could push a button on screen if they are using an interactive whiteboard.
Award 1 mark for a correct answer.

c) Possible answers include:
timings can be set for the show to run automatically; it could be set up for the reader to control — so intended reader would, e.g. click a mouse, to move between slides.
Award 1 mark for a correct answer.

Page 85 (Exam Questions)

4 a) (i) Possible advantages include: cheap to produce; easy to use; don't need expensive computer equipment.

Possible disadvantages include: easy to muddle up the order of the slides; have to cover up information you don't want the audience to see yet; can look unprofessional.
Award 1 mark for an advantage and 1 mark for a disadvantage.

(ii) Possible advantages include:
looks more professional; information can appear a bit at a time; animation can be used to liven up a presentation; animation can happen at set times; speaker can control speed of presentation; can keep audience interested; can be reused time after time; can edit presentations to adapt for different audiences.

Possible disadvantages include: special effects can be overused; equipment needed to run the show can be expensive; speaker may not know how to use the software or equipment.
Award 1 mark for an advantage and 1 mark for a disadvantage.

b) Hints for presentation designer could include:
research topic thoroughly; keep the design of the slides simple; keep text on each slide to a minimum; test animation effects to make sure they work.
Award 1 mark for each piece of advice, up to a maximum of 3 marks.

c) Hints for presentation speaker could include:
know answers to any possible questions; rehearse the presentation thoroughly.
Award 1 mark for each piece of advice, up to a maximum of 2 marks.

All the answers to this question are on pages 80-82. But a lot of this you should be able to work out for yourself. My advice is to learn it, then you won't even need to think...

Section Six — Spreadsheets and Databases

Page 93 (Warm-up Questions)

1 Numbers, text and formulas.

2 Comma-separated variable.

3 Taking data from one application (like a database) into another (like a spreadsheet).

4 An instruction for the computer to process the data held in specific cells (using functions you can type or select from a list.)

5 Line graph.

6 A relative cell reference refers to the cell in a certain position relative to the formula cell (e.g. 2 cells left). If the formula cell is copied to another location, the reference cell moves relative to it. An absolute cell reference is one that is fixed, so if the formula cell is copied to somewhere else, it still refers to the same cell.

Page 94 (Exam Questions)

1 a) (i) When the formula is copied from cell C5 and pasted into cell C6, the rows in the formula are increased by one giving a formula of B6 × B3. B3 is empty and so the formula gives a value of zero. This is because relative addressing is used.
Award 1 mark for answer.

(ii) In order to stop B2 changing, a dollar sign is used before the row and the column, so the formula should be B5 × B2.
This is using absolute addressing for cell B2.
Award 1 mark for answer.

b) A bar chart is most suitable as each category is discrete (separate) and a bar chart can show them in chronological order more clearly than, e.g. a pie chart.
Award 1 mark for bar chart and 1 for reason.

2 a) If the mark (in cell B4) is more than 50, the message "pass" is put in cell C4; if it is less than or equal to 50, the message "fail" is put in cell C4.
Award 2 marks, 1 for each part.

b) The formula should be IF(B4>B2, "pass", "fail").
Award 1 mark for use of cell B2 and 1 mark for the use of the $ sign for absolute addressing.

If you found this question a bit perplexing, go back to p90 and make sure you understand absolute / relative cell references and logic functions...

3 **(Bonus question)**
Answers include: using italics to emphasise column headings; colour (e.g. red) to indicate temperatures below freezing; bold text to indicate the cities; different colours for each column.
Award 1 mark for each correct answer (up to 3 marks).

Page 99 (Warm-up Questions)

1 An organised collection of data.

2 Any two from text, integer, real numbers, dates.

3 A field that contains data that is unique to each record.

4 It takes up less memory (also easier to search, less errors likely).

5 A search where only part of the search item is known and asterisks (or similar) are used to represent the unknown part.

6 A flat-file has only one table whilst a relational database has several tables that are linked together.

Page 100 (Exam Questions)

1 a) Customer ID / membership number ***(1 mark)***, not customer name as this may not be unique.

b) Answers include:
video title, video ID, video genre, certificate, date borrowed, customer ID, loan cost.
Award 1 mark each for up to 3 correct fields.

c) This is a relational database ***(1 mark)*** because there is more than one table and the two tables are linked ***(1 mark)***.

2 a) i) 5 fields ***(1 mark)***; ii) 9 records ***(1 mark)***.

b) mileage field ***(1 mark)***, ascending order ***(1 mark)***.

c) (i) 4 cars ***(1 mark)***

(ii) 2 cars ***(1 mark)***

(iii) 4 cars ***(1 mark)***

3 Advantages include:
the data can be stored and accessed quickly and efficiently; less space is needed to store the data; data is less likely to get lost; using a search, it is faster to find details about a particular painting.
Award 1 mark for each correct advantage (up to 3 marks).

Disadvantages include:
she would need to buy computer hardware and software which is expensive; Jane would need to be trained to use it properly.
Award 1 mark for a correct disadvantage.

Question 3 here is about as "standard bookwork" as they come. All you need to do is learn it. There's a very good chance you'll get asked it, so it's lots of easy marks in the tin...

Section Seven — Measurement, Control and Simulation

Page 109 (Warm-up Questions)

1 Capturing and storing information using sensors.

2 Any three from light, temperature (heat), sound, pressure, infra-red, air pressure or radioactivity (e.g. Geiger counter).

3 An analogue signal can take any value in a certain range, a digital signal can only take certain values.

4 The time between one measurement and the next.

5 Analogue to digital converter.

6 A feedback loop is when a sensor monitors the output of a system and sends back (inputs) information to control the output. E.g on a heater, a temperature sensor monitors the output (temperature) of the heater and feeds back information to control when to switch the heater off.

Page 110 (Exam Questions)

1 a) Temperature sensor ***(1 mark)***. It is analogue ***(1 mark)*** because the temperature recorded can be any value within a certain range ***(1 mark)***.

b) The sensor records the temperature and sends a signal to the computer. If the temperature is below a certain value, the heater is switched on, otherwise it is switched off. This cycle occurs continuously and when the temperature is high enough the heater is switched off.
1 mark for recording, 1 mark for comparison and 1 mark for output.

c) Humidity sensor ***(1 mark)***.

2 a) Answers include:
heat (temperature) sensor; ADC converter; computer/processor.
Award 1 mark for each item (up to 3 marks).

b) Answers include:
data logging can be collected regularly over a long period of time; it is more accurate than humans taking the readings; data loggers don't need breaks, they can work continuously.
Award 1 mark for each item (up to 2 marks).

c) Data can be imported into a spreadsheet package and then graphs could be drawn. ***(1 mark for this or other sensible answer.)***

3

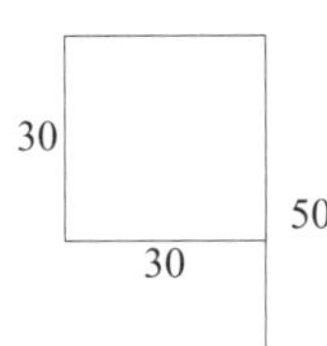

Award 3 marks for correct shape and dimensions (lose a mark for each mistake made when following the procedure).

Page 114 (Warm-up Questions)

1 A model is an artificial re-creation of an object or situation which should behave in the same way as the real thing, a simulation is when a model is used to imitate a real-life situation (e.g. flight simulation).

2 Computer-aided design (CAD), spreadsheet, virtual reality (VR) and expert system.

3 Any three of these: it is much safer than using a real plane; it is cheaper than using a real aircraft; different conditions and airports can be simulated; it can be used when the weather is too bad to fly.

4 The user experiences all-round sound, views and movement (using a special visor and headphones) which simulate the real experience.

5 The user changes input values to see the effect on the output of the model.

6 A "knowledge bank" about a particular subject and a set of instructions (or rules) for processing the knowledge.

Page 115 (Exam Questions)

1 a) Cell C3 contains the formula = B3 * (A10 – A9)
Award 2 marks for the complete formula, or 1 mark if correct apart from 1 fairly minor mistake.

b) When the price of T-shirts goes up, the number sold may go down. It cannot be assumed that sales will stay the same. ***(1 mark)***

c) Use a bar chart to show the sales figures. ***(1 mark)***

Spreadsheet modelling is covered on page 112. Look back if you're struggling. Part b) is an example of using a spreadsheet for "what-if analysis".

2 The four main features are: i) real-time images, which mean that the program reacts immediately to the actions of the pilot; ii) hydraulic arms, which hold up the cockpit and move it according to the actions of the pilot and to simulated weather conditions; iii) a closed environment, so that the cabin can be pressurised and lighting set to simulate reality; iv) feedback loops, so that when the pilot alters the controls, signals are sent to the computer which then changes the output of the simulation (e.g. image, position of the arms).
Award 1 mark for up to 3 correct answers and 1 mark for each explanation.

Section Eight — The Internet

Page 121 (Warm-up Questions)

1 A hyperlink is a link to another website or web page. It can take the form of a piece of text or a graphic which the user clicks on.

2 Internet Service Provider.

3 A search engine is a website that allows the user to search for other websites using a keyword search. A portal is a website offering access to various services such as e-mail, on-line shopping and searching.

4 A modem converts digital signals to analogue (and vice-versa), allowing transmission of data between computers using the telephone network.

5 To store Internet pages temporarily on the user's hard disk so they can be quickly accessed if needed again.

6 Uniform Resource Locator.

Page 122 (Exam Questions)

1 http — "hypertext transfer protocol" — the language of the web;
www — "world wide web", showing it is a web site;
softsell — the domain name identifying the company;
co — the domain type, showing it is a company;
uk — the country where the web site is held — in this case, the UK;
home — the page being accessed on the website.
Award 1 mark for each correct answer (up to 4 marks).

Make sure you've learnt all the different bits that make up a URL from page 119. It's handy to know them anyway if you use the Internet a lot. You can tell a surprising amount about a website from its URL.

2 a) Answers include:
The favourites folder — this contains the web address (URLs) of sites that have been stored (bookmarked) because they are accessed often.
The history — this contains the web addresses of sites that the user has accessed recently.
Award 1 mark for each of 2 correct features and 1 mark for each explanation.

b) Music files can be compressed (e.g. MP3 files) so they take up less space and can be downloaded faster.
Award 1 mark for this or another sensible answer.

3 Back — goes back to the previously viewed web page ***(1 mark)***.
Stop — aborts download of a particular web page ***(1 mark)***.
History — opens the history folder which contains links to recently viewed webpages ***(1 mark)***.
Home — goes to the web browser's home page (this page can usually be set by the user) ***(1 mark)***.

Page 126 (Warm-up Questions)

1 A cookie is a text file placed on the user's hard disk when some web pages are accessed.

2 HTML (hypertext mark-up language).

3 Care should be taken in case the attachment contains a virus.

4 Hacking means the accessing of a computer system and its files without permission.

5 Using a computer (PC), a mobile phone or a digital television.

6 Data is coded so that it cannot be read (except by the intended receiver) even if it is intercepted.

Page 127 (Exam Questions)

1 a) Steps are: i) Becky creates the e-mail using the e-mail package ***(1 mark)***; ii) she connects to the Internet ***(1 mark)***; iii) she presses the 'send' button ***(1 mark)***; iv) the message is sent from Becky's ISP to Brad's ISP ***(1 mark)***; v) Brad logs onto his e-mail account and reads the message ***(1 mark)***.

Other answers are possible, e.g. if web-based e-mail is described instead. The key thing here (as always) is making sure you do have 5 steps. And that you include what's happening at both ends...

b) Advantages include:
i) e-mail is much quicker than sending a letter; ii) e-mails are cheaper than paying the postage to Canada; iii) e-mails are more reliable, unlike letters which may get lost in the post.
Award 1 mark for each answer (up to 2 marks).

Disadvantages include:
i) both Becky and Brad need to have access to the Internet and e-mail accounts; ii) the hardware and software needed is expensive;
iii) Brad will not know he has an e-mail until he looks at his e-mail account; iv) e-mails don't feel as special / personal as receiving a hand-written letter.
Award 1 mark for each answer (up to 2 marks).

2 a) A virus is a computer program that copies itself. It can corrupt (damage) or wipe files on the hard disk.
Award 2 marks for correct definition (one for program and one for 'copies itself') and 1 mark for the effect.

b) Answers include:
i) by opening an e-mail attachment that is infected;
ii) by using a floppy disk that has a virus on it.
Award 1 mark for a correct answer.

c) Answers include:
i) using anti-virus software; ii) by never opening an e-mail attachment unless she can trust the source; iii) setting her web-browser and e-mail programs to a high security setting so that they will warn before downloading high-risk pages / messages.
Award 1 mark for each correct answer (up to 2 marks).

3 a) An intranet is a private network that uses internet technology ***(1 mark)***.

b) The intranet could be protected so that students would need a user-name and password to access it ***(1 mark)***.

c) A web counter could be used to record how many visits have been made to the site ***(1 mark)***.

Page 128 (Exam Questions)

4 a) Answers include:
Log onto Shoprite's web-site; choose items and put them in the electronic shopping basket; pay for the goods using a credit card; give / confirm customer details (including delivery address).
Award 1 mark for each answer (up to 3 marks).

b) Personal details such as credit card numbers can be encrypted ***(1 mark)*** into a code which cannot be read without a special password or key ***(1 mark)***.

5 a) Answers include:
to buy tickets on-line; to order merchandise on-line; to give contact details for a mailing list; to give payment details.
Award 1 mark for a correct answer.

b) Answers include:
a search engine to find information from other web-sites on the Internet; a counter to keep track of the number of visits (hits) that the site has received.
Award 1 mark for the program and 1 mark for explanation.

c) http://www.brfc.co.fr
Award 1 mark for http://www (accept just www), 1 mark for brfc, 1 mark for co and 1 mark for fr.

6 a) No ***(1 mark)*** — Modems convert between analogue and digital signals. ISDN lines are digital, so the signal does not need converting ***(1 mark)***.

b) It will transfer data at a speed of 56 kilobytes per second ***(1 mark)***.

c) A plug-in is a program that will enable a piece of software such as a web-browser to perform an extra function ***(1 mark)***, e.g. plug-ins can be downloaded to enable web-browsers to play video-clips ***(1 mark)***.

If you use the Internet a lot, you've probably come across plug-ins. You often need a plug-in to play a certain file type, e.g Quicktime or MP3. Web browsers tell you if you're missing one and often try to download them automatically.

Section Nine — Computers in the Real World

Page 134 (Warm-up Questions)

1 MICR: Magnetic Ink Character Recognition;
CAL: Computer-Aided Learning;
EFTPOS: Electronic Funds Transfer at the Point of Sale.

2 Automatic Telling Machine. It is a cash machine.

3 The check digit is used for validation. The barcode reader sends the number to the computer system, which re-calculates the check digit to ensure the number is valid.

4 Advantages:
Customers can access their accounts when the bank is closed; customers can carry out transactions, such as paying bills, without having to go into the bank; it's quicker for customers to access their accounts because they don't have to go out to the bank; it's more convenient for disabled or elderly customers who might not find it easy to get to the bank; banks can save costs by employing fewer staff or having fewer branches.

Disadvantages:
Hackers might break into the system and steal funds; security isn't 100% watertight; a cashier can see you aren't Mrs Smith if you're a large man with a beard. You can't tell that over the Internet; some customers prefer face-to-face contact and find home banking too impersonal; it's not as easy for banks to advertise their other services, which they can do when you go to the bank; not all transactions can be done over the Internet, e.g. paying in cheques.

5 Communication is done electronically, rather than on paper; e-mails replace written memos or letters, documents and other resources are shared on a network, rather than being printed and distributed manually or by post.

Page 135 (Exam questions)

1 a) Advantages for the company of installing a teleconferencing system:
There are no travel or accommodation costs; the set up costs are small and are quickly recouped by future cost savings; meetings won't be cancelled when bad weather would make travel very difficult; staff are more productive because they don't waste time travelling and are not tired after a journey; meetings can be set up very quickly; meetings can be held more often; other staff can be involved in a meeting at short notice.
Award 1 mark for each of 3 correct answers.

b) Disadvantages of the company using teleconferencing:
Meetings are more impersonal; meetings are more difficult to chair — it's not as easy to organise who speaks when; it's not as easy to guarantee the confidentiality of a meeting; equipment failure in one office would ruin a meeting or cause it to be cancelled; some materials for discussion, e.g. large models, cannot be sent electronically.
Award 1 mark for each of 2 correct answers.

2 a) Answers include:
He has access to much more information; he can copy text from a web site rather than retyping it from a book; he can put pictures into his work without having to scan them in; he can find multimedia resources such as sound files and video clips for his project; it's quicker to use a search engine than to look through a pile of books; he can work at home on his project when the library is closed; he can get very up-to-date information.
Award 1 mark for each of 3 correct reasons.

b) Answers include:
Information overload — there is so much information, it's hard to know what to select and he may waste time; poor quality information — there is no quality control on most web sites — some web site authors have biased viewpoints; information on a web site is more likely to be incorrect; web site material may be too advanced; the school librarian can guide him to the best resources; the library books are pitched at a suitable level for school pupils; he may just copy material from the web without editing it.
Award 1 mark for each of 2 correct reasons.

3 Benefits include:
The supermarket has a profile of what each customer buys; the supermarket can increases sales by sending targeted mailshots advertising products or offers which the customer is likely to be interested in; the supermarket can offer in-store promotions to card holders to increase sales of certain products; the supermarket can use the data collected to plan future purchasing strategies; the supermarket can use the data collected to plan future marketing campaigns.
Award 1 mark for each of 3 correct benefits.

Teleconferencing... loyalty cards... Internet research... the strategy is always the same — learn the pros and cons, the advantages and disadvantages, the benefits and drawbacks, the good and the ugly, the peas and beans, ...

Page 139 (Warm-up Questions)

1 Geographical Information System — a computer application that combines information in a database with mapping software. An example of their use is to assist drivers in planning routes.

2 An embedded computer is one where input, process and output devices are all contained inside the machine they are meant to control.

3 A sensor is a device that detects a change in the environmental conditions and as a result of that change sends a signal to a processing device.

4 The DVLA stores data such as the registration number of the car, year of first registration, the colour, make, model, engine capacity and the registered keeper.

5 Answers include microwave, washing machine, video recorder, burglar alarm and satellite television.

Page 140 (Exam questions)

1 a) A virtual tour is created using digital cameras and interactive software. It allows potential holiday makers to see interactive images of the holiday accommodation without actually being there. This type of software may have interactive features which simulate being there e.g. where you can look around in any direction you choose.
Award 1 mark for a correct answer.

b) Benefits include:
They can see their accommodation before they book their holiday, so they will not be disappointed when they arrive; they can check that the accommodation will meet their needs, e.g. if they have young children or a disabled person travelling with them.
Award 1 mark for each of two correct benefits.

2 a) Geographical Information System — a computer application that combines information in a database with mapping software that can be used to assist drivers in planning routes.
Award 1 mark for correct answer. (You won't get the mark for just saying what GIS stands for.)

b) Answers include:
calculating the quickest routes between places, meaning that they will be able to do more jobs in one day; calculating the shortest routes between places, so they use the minimum amount of fuel; working out the most effective route between all the places on the delivery route.
Award 1 mark for each of 2 correct answers.

The question doesn't just ask for general uses of GIS. Remember to answer in the context of the questions.

3 Answers include:
Meteorological data such as rainfall or air pressure is collected from an automated data-logging system using sensors; the data is sent to a central computer; the data is processed by a Geographical Information System (GIS) and used to produce weather maps;
Images created with GIS systems can be put together to create moving images of weather systems;
Data is also collected from weather satellites; these are usually photographic images which have been converted into digital data;
Collected data can be fed into computer models of the way that weather patterns change and interact; this enables detailed weather forecasts to be made.
Award 1 mark for each of 5 correct points.

Questions like this are a bit like eat-as-much-as-you-can buffets. You're not given much guidance, you just have to write down as much as you know about the topic until you've written 5 good points. Try to cover as many different features as you can — don't try to make 2 points into 5 by waffling...

Section Ten — Computers and Society

Page 147 (Warm-up Questions)

1 It's illegal to copy a file without permission from the owner or copyright holder. Examples:
Downloading text or graphics files from the Internet and using them without indicating where you got them or obtaining the copyright holder's permission; not having the proper licence for the software you use. This normally happens when software is installed on more computers than the licence permits or software is borrowed from someone else and installed; copying software from school or a business onto a home computer without the copyright holder's permission.

2 A data subject is someone who has data stored about them on a computer system. Your bank keeps details such as your name, address, employer and salary. The bank is the data controller and you are the data subject.

3 The Computer Misuse Act 1990. Unauthorised changing of computer files is an infringement of the Act and could lead to a fine or prison sentence.

4 Hot-desking is a system where office staff don't have their own individual office, but use whatever desk is free in an open-plan layout. ICT makes this possible because the employees can log on to their files, save, edit and print them at any computer terminal on the company network.

5 ULD stands for Upper Limb Disorder. It's also called Repetitive Strain Injury and is caused by overusing a keyboard or a mouse.

Page 148 (Exam Questions)

1 Correct statements are c, d, f, g.
a) is wrong because data may be transferred to EU countries, b) is wrong because compensation is paid only if you suffer through personal data being inaccurate, e) is wrong because data can be kept for as long as it is reasonably needed.

Award 1 mark for each correct tick (up to max 4).
If 5 boxes are ticked, lose 2 marks.
If more than 5 boxes are ticked, award 0 marks.

2 a) Advantages for the company:
Cost savings: needs less office space, pays less for heating, lighting, rates; less need to provide fringe benefits such as staff canteens or leisure facilities; more flexibility in employing staff — can employ more staff on a part-time or short-term basis as required.

Disadvantages for the company:
Workers may be less productive at home because of possible distractions; work could be of lower quality: more difficult to supervise and encourage workers; less employee involvement in and loyalty to the company; no meetings to spark good ideas; more difficult to ensure data is secure and confidential.

1 mark for a correct advantage and 1 mark for a correct disadvantage.

b) Advantages for Rebecca:
No transport costs; no time wasted commuting; ideal if Rebecca is disabled and finds travelling difficult; flexibility of work schedule: she can choose how many hours to work a day and which days to work; she can look after a small child or elderly relative and still work.

Disadvantages for Rebecca:
May become less motivated because the workplace is more impersonal; less likely to have a clear career structure with regular promotion; may become lonely because there is much less human contact; increased heating and lighting costs.
1 mark for a correct advantage and 1 mark for a correct disadvantage.

c) Advantages for society:
Environmental benefits: less pollution from cars. Less road congestion and fewer road accidents; less unemployment and a wider range of people able to find work; better for society if people can work and still look after small children and elderly relatives at home as these people will be happier.

Disadvantages for society:
Jobs may be lost in other areas, e.g. car manufacturers; it could reduce the sense of community as workers would have less human contact / meet less people.
1 mark for a correct advantage and 1 mark for a correct disadvantage.

The last part of the question might be stepping into sociology, but ICT's impact on society is an important concept that comes up in many different situations. There's no right and wrong answers here, so any sensible ideas that you can come up with should get the marks.

Page 152 (Warm-Up Questions)

1 An ethical issue is whether something is morally right or wrong.
E.g. Should there be censorship of web sites which contain politically extreme material or information on making bombs?

2 Answers include:
Jobs where information is retrieved manually are disappearing, e.g. databases replace filing clerks and wordprocessors replace typists;
ICT has meant that fewer workers are needed, e.g. if more people book their holidays on-line, fewer jobs are needed in travel agencies;
ICT has globalised the work place, e.g. an airline company can set up a bookings centre in a country where labour is cheaper, so workers in countries where salaries are higher lose their jobs.

3 It has been argued that children are playing games on computers and mobile phones rather than reading books. They are also copying, but not reading, chunks of text from websites or using CD-ROMs rather than researching material using library books. Spell checkers and grammar checkers automatically correct mistakes, so children don't learn where they have gone wrong.

4 Answers include:
Using laptops connected to the office via a mobile phone means that executives are never really out of the office even when travelling on a train

or at home at the weekend; the increasing use of e-mail means that some staff spend so much time ploughing through electronic messages that they don't have time to do their job; computers can process data much more quickly than humans could in the past, but this has led to workers being expected to be more productive rather than giving them more leisure time; stress can also be caused by people having to keep up with software packages and their constant upgrades as well as doing their normal job, especially for those who don't find ICT easy.

5 People who are computer-literate and therefore have access to the increased information available by means of ICT, such as the Internet.

Page 153 (Exam Question)

Exam Essay

You could look at five topics and discuss a benefit and disadvantage for each one, or you could look at five examples of the ways ICT has benefited society and five unrelated disadvantages. For each one, all you have to is clearly state the benefit or disadvantage and then use an example to make it clear.
Pages 150 and 151 contain lots of possible answers for this question.
Here are some more examples not already given earlier in the section:

Electronic communication:
The use of e-mail has made it quicker and cheaper for people to communicate with relatives in a foreign country and send family photos; but it has also meant that criminal groups and terrorist organisations can co-ordinate their activities more effectively.

Internet shopping:
People have access to a wider variety of goods than they might find in the high street, especially if they live in a remote area; however this has led to increased credit card fraud with thieves setting up phoney websites and taking people's money for goods they don't deliver.

Education:
Interactive whiteboards and projectors mean teachers can use more exciting materials in their lessons; however, schools have to spend a lot of money on ICT equipment which constantly needs updating and therefore might not have enough resources to buy games equipment or materials for Art and Design, for example.

Internet resources:
People have access to a lot more information through the Internet and can take part in interactive surveys and games organised by television programmes; however, it is very easy to download pirated software and music, making a lot more people into criminals and causing prices to rise for legitimate purchasers.

Health:
Computer simulations can be used to make cancer diagnosis more accurate and to predict whether new drugs will be successful; surgeons can perform operations in other countries using a robotic arm and an Internet connection; however, computerisation of medical records could mean that people's medical histories could be obtained more easily; computerised records of people's DNA could be used by insurance companies to charge higher premiums to people more at risk of dying from genetically related illnesses.

Award 1 mark for each of 5 correct benefits and 1 mark for each of 5 correct disadvantages.

You don't have to restrict yourself to these answers — it's a very open question, so anything sensible and well-explained should be OK.
As always, remember that filling all the space won't get you the marks — you've got to have 5 benefits and 5 disadvantages which are all backed up with examples.

Please note: The answers to the past exam questions have not been provided by or approved by the examining bodies (AQA, OCR and London Qualifications Ltd - Edexcel). As such, AQA, OCR and London Qualifications Ltd do not accept any responsibility for the accuracy or method of the working in the answers given. CGP has provided suggested solutions — other possible solutions may be equally correct.

Practice Exam Paper 1

1 a) Answers include (other answers possible):
Range check, existency check, check digit, check if all the characters are digits, check if there are less than six characters entered.
Award 1 mark for each of 2 correct answers.

b) No new items could be added. CD-ROM may not have sufficient capacity.
(1 mark for this or other suitable answer.)

2 a) Employees are connected to an on-line system at the same time; Each member contributes to the conversation by typing their text which appears on everyone else's screen; Real time images of the people in the conference may appear on the screen like a TV picture; Can use a point to point telephone connection instead of the internet; Hardware: Video / microphone / speaker.
Award 1 mark for each of 2 points above (or similar).

b) Answers include (other answers possible):
Companies do not have to transport their employees to a common meeting place; instant communication with all employees; each employee can contribute equally to the conference; cost of travel eliminated; time saved because of travelling; can work from home.
Award 1 mark for each of 2 correct points.

3 Explanation should include at least 3 of the following:
Gathering data from experts (either books or people); designing the structure of the database; creating a data base of knowledge; creating a structure to relate each item in the database; verifying the data which is input; creating an interrogation technique to get at the data; designing a method of displaying the results; testing the system; evaluating the system. Any other suitable step.
1 mark for each explanation of a point above, up to max of 3 marks.

4 a) Answers include: subject, quantity, borrowed/lent, location, author, title etc. ***1 mark for each relevant field, up to max of 3 marks.***

b) Answers include: search for books about a certain topic; search for specific title to see if it's present or when it will be returned; search for the location of a certain book.
1 mark for each explanation of a use, up to max of 3 marks.

c) Answers include: locating books quickly; being able to check when books are due back; easy to check whether the library owns a book.
1 mark for each advantage, up to max of 2 marks.

5 Problems include:
Selling lists of names to other companies e.g. junk mail; hacking to deliberately change data; receiving data signals over the air; tapping into network cables; plagiarism; illegal access to personal records (Data Protection Act); storage of personal data; fraud; changing / deleting data; pornography; viruses can be spread.
Award 1 mark each for a good explanation of up to 4 problems.

6 Four points from:
Information retrieval system; speeding stock taking; credit cards; debit cards; security systems in shops; automatic money machines; records of who buys what products; running up large bills on credit cards; Employees need training; dependence on systems – vulnerable to power/systems failures; point of sale machines; automated vending machines; unemployment; automatic doors.***Award 1 mark each for an advantage or disadvantage on a topic above or other suitable topic (max 4 marks). Max of 2 marks on each topic. Award a max of 3 marks if only disadvantages or advantages are given.***

7 a) i) A3: text; C4: a number; D3: a formula.
Award 1 mark for each correct answer up to max of 3 marks.

ii) Currency
Award 1 mark for the correct answer.

b) i) =B4*C4
Award 1 mark for the correct answer.

ii) =D2+D3+D4+D5 or SUM(D2:D5)
Award 2 marks for the correct answer (or 1 mark if syntax is wrong).

c) i) Change the currency entry in B5 from £3.25 to £4.00.
Award 1 mark for the correct answer.

ii) The correct answers are:
D2, D3, D4, D5, D7.
Award 1 mark for any 2 of the correct answers.

d) i) pie chart ii) line graph iii) bar graph or bar chart
Award 1 mark for each of the 3 correct answers.

e) Pie chart: provides a very visual representation of the contribution each dish makes to the total takings.
Award 1 mark for the correct answer.

8 a) Answer might include the following points:
Sensors linked to computer; on each of the four roads; will monitor entry and exits to the roads; ADC used to convert analogue data from sensors into digital data; input data will be stored / recorded for later analysis.
Award 1 mark each for good explanation of up to 3 points.
Note: answers must be about monitoring, not controlling the traffic.

b) Answers include:
Traffic flow / volume is likely to vary between different times of day / week / year; traffic volume / flow is likely to be affected by the "rush hour"; by school times / busy times of day; by holidays, etc.
Award 1 mark for any sensible answer up to max 2 marks.

c) Answer may include:
Appropriate sensor e.g. light, pressure, infra-red; what it measures e.g. time, weight; how / why it works; different totals being kept for cars and lorries. ***Award 1 mark for any sensible idea and 1 mark for up to 2 points that explain the idea.***

d) Answers include:
Don't want to waste resources / money; decision might be made on insufficient data; traffic flow is seasonal, must get whole picture.
Award 1 mark for each point up to maximum of 2 marks.

e) Possible answers:
Date; speed; weight (allow size if neither length nor weight); length; which road; which direction (IN / OUT); type of vehicle – car / lorry; amount of pollution. ***Award 1 mark for each field up to a maximum of 4.***

f) Spreadsheet OR database ***(1 mark)***.

g) Data recorded on video camera to give a permanent record; danger in underground workings; e.g. gases, chemicals, danger of collapsing; robots can operate in smaller places than humans.
For each reason, award 2 marks for a good explanation or 1 mark for a partial explanation. Max 4 marks for 2 reasons.

Practice Exam Paper 2

Section A

A1 a	A2 d	A3 c	A4 d	A5 d	A6 a	A7 c
A8 c	A9 c	A10 d	A11 b	A12 c	A13 b	A14 b
A15 c	A16 c	A17 b	A18 d	A19 a	A20 b	

1 mark for each correct answer.

Section B

B1 a) Database ***(1 mark)***

b) Mail-merging ***(1 mark)***

c) Word processing ***(1 mark)***

d) Spreadsheet ***(1 mark)***

e) Data logging ***(1 mark)***

f) Desk top publishing ***(1 mark)***

B2 a) i) Advantages include:
Can share peripherals; can communicate for second opinion etc., can access key patient records from any office.
1 mark each to a maximum of 2 marks.

ii) Answers include:
Network problems can affect all, e.g. if one computer became infected with a virus, all computers on the network could be easily infected; or sharing network hardware like printers can be a problem when hardware breaks down; doctors may have confidential files on their computer that could be viewed by others over a network.
2 marks for a well explained situation, 1 mark for partial answer.

b) Answers include:
More people have access to the data — meaning data might be seen by the wrong person, confidentiality of files could be compromised; the chance of interception / hacking increased; doctors may have less control over the information they keep as it could be accessed and changed (accidentally or deliberately) by others.
2 marks available for each of 2 well explained concerns. Award 1 mark for partial explanations.

c) i) Specific use, e.g. to print prescriptions / letters to consultants etc; Doctor does not need to leave the room to get printouts.
1 mark for a correct answer.

ii) Answers include:
Management of the system – logging usage, etc; may be a shared printer for use by all those on the network, e.g. for printing higher quality documents than the individual printers are capable of.
1 mark for a correct answer.

iii) Answers include:
Handling user files; passwords / security; controlling the hard disc; managing access to shared resources; monitoring use of the network; holding central data such as patient records and drugs information.
1 mark for a correct answer.

d) i) Advantages include:
Doctors would have time to see more patients; specialist knowledge available, perhaps more than the doctor has; some patients like / trust a computer rather than a doctor.
2 marks available for each of 2 correct advantages. Award 2 marks for a well explained advantage, 1 mark for a partial explanation.

ii) Disadvantages include:
Lacks personal touch; program cannot replace the doctor, doctors may rely on them too much; program does not have the experience of a real doctor and could miss things that a doctor would pick up; program will never be 100% reliable; people may find it difficult to trust a program's diagnosis over that of a real doctor; some people may not be able use the computer, or use it incorrectly.
2 marks available for each of two correct disadvantages. 2 marks for a well explained advantage, 1 mark for a partial explanation.

B3 a) Answers include:
Able to do everything from home — convenient; no transport costs for the customer; home delivery useful for those who don't have transport; open 24 hours so purchases and transactions can be made out of office hours; immediate money transfers; less temptation to buy unnecessary things when shopping; can set up 'favourites' lists to speed up shopping and banking; BUT, difficult to check quality; easy to miss items and forget things; risk of credit card details being intercepted and misused.
Award 1 mark for each correct point. Max of 8 marks available in total for the question.

b) Answers include:
Receiving information about new products and offers; targeted marketing, BUT junk mail and phone calls; illegal access to personal information leading to fraud and invasion of privacy; deleting/changing data, loss of freedom of choice.
Award 1 mark for each correct answer (up to max of 4 marks).

c) Answers include:
Data must not be processed unless there is a specific lawful reason to do so; data must only be obtained and then used for specific purposes; data should be adequate, relevant, and not excessive for the specified use; data must be accurate and, where relevant, kept up to date; data should not be kept longer than is necessary for the specified purpose; data processing should meet the legal rights of the data subjects; data holders should protect the data against loss, theft or corruption; data should not be transferred to others without permission; data should not be transferred abroad, unless data security can be guarenteed to UK data protection levels.
Award 1 mark for each correct answer (up to max of 3 marks).

Working out your Grade

- *Find your average percentage for the whole exam.*
- *Look it up in this table to see what grade you got. If you're borderline, don't push yourself up a grade — the real examiners won't.*

Average %	85+	74 – 84	61 – 73	47 – 60	37 – 46	29 – 36	22 – 28	15 – 21	under 15
Grade	A*	A	B	C	D	E	F	G	U

Important
- *This is a Higher paper — if you're doing Foundation, you'll need more marks in the real exam. E.g. you'll generally need 26 marks or more to get a G grade.*
- *Obviously these grades are only a guide, and the more practice you do the better...*

Index

Index

Make sure you're not missing out on another superb CGP revision book that might just save your life...

Dot per inch.

...order your **free** catalogue today.

CGP customer service is second to none

We work very hard to despatch all orders the **same day** we receive them, and our success rate is currently 99.7%. We send all orders by **overnight courier** or **First Class** post.
If you ring us today you should get your catalogue or book tomorrow. Irresistible, surely?

- Phone: 0870 750 1252 (Mon-Fri, 8.30am to 5.30pm)
- Fax: 0870 750 1292
- e-mail: orders@cgpbooks.co.uk
- Post: CGP, Kirkby in Furness, Cumbria, LA17 7WZ
- Website: www.cgpbooks.co.uk

...or you can ask at any good bookshop.

IHS41